TWELVE SERMONS

ON

PEACE

BY

C. H. SPURGEON

BAKER BOOK HOUSE
Grand Rapids, Michigan

Reprinted 1979 by
Baker Book House
from the edition issued by
Fleming H. Revell Company

ISBN: 0-8010-8163-7

Second printing, December 1981

PHOTOLITHOPRINTED BY CUSHING - MALLOY, INC.
ANN ARBOR, MICHIGAN, UNITED STATES OF AMERICA

Contents

1. The God of Peace 5
2. Spiritual Peace 13
3. Peace by Believing 21
4. The Jewel of Peace 33
5. The Peace of God 45
6. The Reason Why Many Cannot Find Peace 57
7. Peace: A Fact and a Feeling 69
8. Rare Fruit 81
9. The Song of a City, and the Pearl of Peace 93
10. The Lover of God's Law Filled with Peace 105
11. Peace: How Gained, How Broken 117
12. A Gracious Dismissal 129

1 The God of Peace

"Now the God of peace be with you all. Amen."—Rom. xv. 33.

PAUL once advised the Romans to strive. Three verses before our text he actually gives them an exhortation to strive, and yet he here utters a prayer that the God of peace might be with them all. Lest you should think him to be a man of strife, you must read the verse. He says: "Now I beseech you, brethren, for the Lord Jesus Christ's sake, and for the love of the spirit, that ye strive together with me in *your* prayers to God for me." That is a holy strife, and such a strife as that we wish always to see in the church, a strife in prayer, a surrounding the throne together, besieging God's mercy seat, a crying out before God, until it actually amounts to a striving together in our prayers. There is also another kind of striving which is allowed in the church, and that is striving earnestly after the best gifts: a sweet contention which of us shall excel all others in love, in duty, and in faith. May God send us more strife of that kind in our churches, a strife in prayer, a strife in duty. And when we have mentioned these strifes we find them of so peaceable a kind that we come back to the benediction of our text: "Now the God of peace be with you all. Amen." Without any preface, we shall consider, first, *the title*—"the God of peace;" and secondly, *the benediction*—"the God of peace be with you all. Amen."

I. First of all, *the title*. Mars amongst the heathens was called the god of war; Janus was worshipped in periods of strife and bloodshed; but our God Jehovah styles himself not the God of war, but the God of peace. Although he permits wars in this world, sometimes for necessary and useful purposes; although he superintends them, and has even styled himself the Lord, mighty in battle, yet his holy mind abhors bloodshed and strife; his gracious spirit loves not to see men slaughtering one another; he is emphatically, solely, and entirely, and without reserve, "the God of peace." Peace is his delight; "peace on earth and goodwill towards men." Peace in heaven (for that purpose he expelled the angels): peace throughout his entire universe, is his highest wish and his greatest delight.

If you consider God in the trinity of his persons for a few moments, you will see that in each—Father, Son, and Holy Ghost—the title is apt and correct, "the God of peace." There is *God the everlasting Father*; he is the God of peace, for he from all eternity planned the great covenant of peace, whereby he might bring rebels nigh unto him, and make strangers and foreigners fellow-heirs with the saints, and joint-heirs with his Son Christ Jesus. He is the God of peace, for he justifies, and thereby implants peace in the soul; he accepted Christ, and, as the God of peace, he brought him again from the dead; and he ordained peace, peace eternal with his children, through the blood of the everlasting covenant; he is the God of peace. So is *Jesus Christ*, the second person, the God of peace; for "he is our peace who hath made both one, and hath broken down the middle wall of partition between us." He makes peace between God and man. His blood sprinkled on the fiery wrath of God turned it to love; or rather that which must have broken forth in wrath, though it was love for ever, was allowed to display itself in loving-kindness through the wondrous mediatorship of Jesus Christ. And he is the God of peace because he makes peace in the conscience and in the heart. When he says, "Come unto me all ye that are heavy laden," he gives "rest," and with that rest he gives "the peace of God which passeth all understanding," which keeps our heart and mind. He is moreover the God of peace in the Church, for wherever Jesus Christ dwells, he creates a holy peace. As in the case of Aaron of old, the ointment poured upon the head of Christ trickles down to the very skirts of his garments, and thereby he gives peace,—peace by the fruit of the lips, and peace by the fruit of the heart, unto all them that love Jesus Christ in sincerity. So is *the Holy Ghost* the God of peace. He of old brought peace, when chaotic matter was in confusion, by the brooding of his wings: he caused order to appear where once there was nothing but darkness and chaos. So in dark chaotic souls he is the God of peace. When winds from the mountains of Sinai, and gusts from the pit of hell sweep across the distressed soul; when, wandering about for rest, our soul fainteth within us, he speaks peace to our troubles, and gives rest to our spirits. When by earthly cares we are tossed about, like the sea-bird, up and down, up and down, from the base of the wave to the billows' crown, he says, "Peace be still." He it is who on the Sabbath-day brings his people into a state of serenity, and bids them enjoy

"That holy calm, that sweet repose,
Which none but he that feels it knows."

And he shall be the God of peace when at life's latest hour he shall still the current of Jordan, shall hush all the howlings of the fiends, shall give us peace with God through Jesus Christ, and land us safe in heaven. Blessed Trinity! however we consider thee, whether as Father, Son, or Holy Ghost, still is thy name thrice well deserved, the God of peace, and the God of love.

Let us now enter into the subject, and see wherein God is a God of peace. We remark that he is the God of peace, for he created peace originally. He is the God of peace, for he is the restorer of it; though wars have broken out through sin. He is the God of peace, because he preserves peace when it is made; and he is the God of peace because he shall ultimately perfect and consummate peace between all his creatures and himself. Thus he is the God of peace.

First of all, he is the God of peace *because he created nothing but peace.* Go back in your imagination to the time when the majestic Father stepped from his solitude and commenced the work of creation. Picture to yourself the moment when he speaks the word and the first matter is formed. Before that time there had been neither space, nor time, nor aught existing, save himself. He speaks and it is done; he commands and it stands fast. Behold him scattering from his mighty hands, stars, as numerous as the sparks from an anvil. Witness how by his word worlds are fashioned, and ponderous orbs roll through that immensity which first of all he had decreed to be their dwelling place. Lift up now your eyes and behold these great things which he has created already, let the wings of your fancy carry you through the immensity of space and the vast profound, and see if you can discover anywhere the least sign or trace of war. Go through it from the north even to the south, from the east even unto the west, and mark well if ye can discover one sign of discord; whether there is not one universal harmony, whether everything is not lovely, pure, and of good report. See if in the great harp of nature, there is one string which when touched by its Maker's finger giveth forth discord; see if the pipes of this great organ God has made do not all play harmoniously; mark ye well, and note it. Are there bulwarks formed for war? Are there spears and swords? Are there clarions and trumpets? Hath God created any material with which to destroy his creatures and desolate his realms? No; everything is peaceable above, beneath, and all around; all is peace, there is nothing else but calm and quietness. Mark when he makes the angels. He speaks—winged seraphs fly abroad, and cherubs flash through the air on wings of fire. He speaks, and multitudes of angels in their various hierarchies are brought forth, while Jesus Christ as a mighty Prince of angels is decreed to be their head. Is there now in any one of those angels one sign of sorrow? When God made them did he make one of them to be his enemy? Did he fashion one of them with the least implacability or ill-will within his bosom? Ask the shining cohorts, and they tell you, "We were not made for war, but for peace. He has not fashioned us spirits of battle, but spirits of love, and joy, and quietness." And if they sinned, he made them not to sin. They did so; they brought woe into the world of their own accord. God created no war. The evil angel brought it first.—Left to his free will, he fell. The elect angels being confirmed by grace, stood fast and firm. But God was not the author of any war, or any strife. Satan of himself conceived the rebellion, but God was not the author of it. He may from all eternity have foreseen it, and it may even be said in some sense that he ordained it to manifest his justice and his glory, and to show his mercy and sovereignty in redeeming man; but God had no hand in it whatsoever. The Eternal abjures war; he was not the author of it. Satan led the van, that morning star who sang together with the rest, fell of himself; God was not the author of his confusion, but the author of eternal and blessed order. Look, too, at God in the creation of this world. Go into the garden of Eden: walk up and down its bowers; recline under its trees, and partake of its fruits. Roam through the entire world. Sit down by the sea-shore, or stretch yourself upon the mountain. Do you see the least sign of war? Nothing like it. There is nothing of tumult and of noise, no preparation of destruction. See Adam and Eve: their days are perpetual sunshine, their nights are balmy evenings of sweet repose. God has put nothing in their hearts which can disturb them; he has no ill will towards them, but on the contrary, he walks with them in the evening under the trees in the cool of the day. He condescends to talk with his creatures, and hold fellowship with them. He is in no sense whatever the author of the present confusion in this world; that was brought about by our first parents through the temptation of the evil one. God did not create this world for strife. When he first fashioned it, peace, peace, peace, was the universal order of the day. May there come a time when peace once more shall be restored to this great earth, and tranquility to this world! Do you not observe that God is the God of peace because he created it originally? When he pronounced his creation "very good," it was entirely without the slightest exception, a peaceful creation. God is the God of peace.

But, secondly, he is the God of peace *because he restores it.* Nothing shows a man to be much fonder of peace than when he seeks to make peace between others; or, when others have offended him, he endeavours to make peace between himself and them. If I should be able at all times to maintain peace with myself, and should never provoke a quarrel, I should of course be considered a peaceful spirit; but if other persons choose to quarrel and disagree with me, and I desire and purposely set to work to bring about a reconciliation, then everyone says I am a man of peace. "Blessed are the peacemakers, for they are the children of God." God is the great Peacemaker; and thus he is indeed the God of peace. When Satan fell, there was war in heaven. God made peace there, for he smote Satan and cast him and all his rebel hosts into eternal fire. He made peace by his might and power and majesty, for he drove him out of heaven, and expelled him by his flaming brand, never again to pollute the sacred floor of bliss, and never more to endanger Paradise by misleading his peers in heaven. So he made peace in heaven by his power. But when man fell, God made peace not by his power, but by his mercy. Man transgresses. Poor man! Mark how God goes after him to make peace with him! "Adam! where art thou?" Adam never said "God, where art thou?" But God came after Adam, and he seemed to say with a voice of affection and pity, "Adam, poor Adam, where art thou? Hast thou become a God? The evil spirit said thou wouldst be a God; art thou so? Where art thou now, poor Adam? Thou wast once in holiness and perfection, where art thou now?" And he saw the truant Adam running away from his Master, running away from the great Peacemaker, to hide himself beneath the trees of the garden. Again God calls, "Adam, where art thou?" But he says, "I heard thy voice in the midst of the garden, and I was afraid, because I was naked, and I hid myself." And God says, "Who told thee that thou wast naked?" How kind it is. You can see he is a Peacemaker even then. But when, after having cursed the serpent, and sent the cursed obliquely on the ground, he comes to talk to Adam, you see him as the Peacemaker still more. "I will," said he, "put enmity between thee and the woman, between thy seed and her seed. It shall bruise thy head, and thou shalt bruise his heel." There he was making peace through the blood of the cross. Do not conceive, however, that that was the first preparation of peace God ever made. That was the first display of it, but he had been making peace from all eternity. Through the covenant he made with Jesus Christ from all eternity, God's people were at peace with God. Although God saw that man should fall; though he foresaw that his elect would with the rest depart from rectitude, and become his enemies, yet he did long before the, fall draw up a covenant with Jesus, wherein Jesus stipulated that he would pay the debts of all his people, and the Father on their behalf did actually and positively forgive their sins, and justify their persons, take away their guilt, acquit them, accept and receive them unto peace with him. Though that was never developed until the fall, and though to each of us it is not known until we believe, yet there was always peace between God and the elect. I must tell you a tale of a poor bricklayer who met with an accident, and every one thought he was going to die, and he did die. A clergyman said to him, "My poor fellow, I am afraid you will die. Try to make your peace with God." With tears in his eyes, he looked the clergyman in the face, and said, "Make my peace with God, sir? I thank God that was made for me in the eternal covenant by Jesus Christ, long before I was born." So beloved, it was. There was a peace, a perfect peace which God made with his Son. Jesus was not our ambassador merely, but he *was* our peace; not the maker of peace merely, but *our peace*; and since there was a Christ before all worlds, there was peace before all worlds. Since there always will be a Christ, so there always will be peace between God and all those interested in the covenant. Oh, if we can but feel we are in the covenant, if we know we are numbered with the chosen race, and purchased with redeeming blood, then we can rejoice, because God has been to us the Restorer of breaches, the Builder of cities to dwell in, and hath given us peace which once we lost; he is the Restorer of peace.

Thirdly, *he is the preserver of peace.* Whenever I see peace *in the world*, I ascribe it to God, and if it is continued, I shall always believe it is because God interferes to prevent war. So combustible are the materials of which this great world is made, that I am ever apprehensive of war. I do not account it wonderful that one nation should strive against another; I account it far more wonderful that they are not all at arms. Whence come wars and fightings? Come they not from your lusts? Considering how much lust there is in the world, we might well conceive that there would be more war than we see. Sin is the mother of wars; and remembering how plentiful sin is, we need not marvel if it brings forth multitudes of them. We may look for them. If the coming of Christ be indeed drawing nigh, then we must expect wars and rumours of wars through all the nations of the earth. But when peace is preserved, we consider it to be through the immediate interposition of God. If, then, we desire peace between nations, let us seek it of God, who is the great Pacificator. But there is an *inward peace* which God alone can keep. Am I at peace with myself, with the world, and with my Maker? Oh! if I want to retain that peace, God alone can preserve it. I know there are some people who once enjoyed peace, who do not possess it now. Some of you once had confidence in God, but may have lost it; you once thought yourselves to be in a glorious state from which you now seem to have somewhat departed. Beloved, no one can maintain peace in the heart but God, as he is the only one who can put it there. Some people talk about doubts and fears, and seem to think they are very allowable. I have heard some say, "Well, a sailor in the sunshine knows his reckoning, and can tell where he is; he has no doubt; but if the sun withdraws, he cannot tell his longitude and latitude, and he knows not where he is." That is not however a fair description of faith. Always wanting the sun is wanting to live by sight; but living by faith is to say, "I cannot tell my longitude and my latitude, but I know the Captain is at the helm, and I will trust him everywhere." But still you cannot keep in that peaceful state of mind unless you have God in the vessel to help you to smile at the storm. We can be peaceful at times, but if God goes away, how we begin quarrelling with ourselves! God alone can preserve peace. Backslider! hast thou lost it? Go and seek it again of God. Christian! is thy peace marred? Go to God, and he can say to every doubt, "Lie down doubt," and to every fear, "Begone." He can speak to every wind that can blow across thy soul, and can say, "Peace, be still;" for he is the God of peace, since he preserves it. Trust in him.

Fourthly, God is the God of peace *because he shall perfect and consummate it at last.* There is war in the world now; there is an evil spirit walking to and fro, a restless being, eager, like a lion to devour; walking through dry places, seeking rest and finding none; and there are men bewitched by that evil spirit who are at war with God, and at war with one another. But there is a time coming—let us wait a little longer—when there shall be peace on earth and peace throughout all God's do minions. In a few more years we do look for a lasting and perpetual peace on earth. Perhaps, to-morrow, Jesus Christ, the Son of God will come again, without a sin-offering unto salvation. We know not either the day or the hour wherein the Son of man shall come; but by-and-bye he shall descend from heaven with a shout, and with the noise of a trumpet; he shall come, but not as once he came, a lowly and humble man, but a glorious and exalted monarch. Then he will cause wars to cease. From that day forth and for ever they will hang the useless helm on high, and study war no more; the lion shall lie down with the kid and eat straw like the ox; the cockatrice and the serpent shall lose their hurtful powers; the weaned child shall lead the lion and the leopard, each one by his beard with his little hands. The day is coming, and that speedily, when there shall not be found on earth a single man who hates his brother, but when each one shall find in every other a brother and a friend; and we shall be able to say, as the old poet did, but in a larger sense, "I know not that there is one Englishman alive with whom I am one jot at odds more than the infant that is born to-night." We shall all be united; nationalities will be levelled, because made into one, and the Lord Jesus Christ shall be king of the entire earth. After that time shall come the consummation of peace, when the last great day shall have passed away, and the righteous have been severed from the wicked, when the monster battle of Armageddon shall have been fought and won, when all the righteous shall have been gathered into heaven, and the lost sent down to hell. Where will be the room for the battle then? Look at the foemen, bruised and mangled in the pit, perpetually howling, the victims of God's vengence; there is no fear of war from them. There is Satan himself, crest-fallen, bruised, battered, slain; his head is broken; there he lies despoiled, a king without his crown; there can be no fear of war from him. And mark the angels, who were once under his supremacy, can they arise? No; they writhe in tortures, and bite their iron bands in misery; they have no power to lift a lance against the God of heaven. And look on sinful man, condemned for his sin to dwell with those fallen beings; can he again provoke his Maker? Will he again blaspheme? Can he oppose the gospel? No; immured in dungeons of hot iron there he is, an abject, ruined spirit; ten thousand times ten thousand lost and perished sinners are there; but could all unite in solemn league and covenant to break the bands of death and sever the laws of justice, he that sitteth in the heavens would laugh at them; the Lord would have them in derision. Peace is consummated because the enemy is crushed. Then look up yonder; there is no fear of war from those bright spirits; the angels cannot fall now; their period of probation is passed for ever, a second Satan shall never drag with him a third part of the stars of heaven; no angel will totter any more, and the ransomed spirits, blood-bought, and washed in the fountain of Jesu's blood, will never fall again. Universal peace is come; the olive branch hath outlived the laurel, the sword is sheathed, the banners are furled, the stains of blood are washed out of the world; again it moves in its orb, and sings like its sister stars; but the one song is peace; for the God who made it is the God of peace.

II. Now we come to the *benediction.* "The God of peace be with you all." I am not about to address you concerning that inward peace which roots in the heart. I am sure I wish above all things that you may always enjoy a peace with your conscience, and be at peace with God. May you always know that you have the blood of Jesus to plead, that you have his righteousness to cover you, that you have his atonement to satisfy for you, and that there is nothing which can hurt you. But I wish to addres you as a church, and exhort you to peace.

First, I will remind you that there is great need to pray this prayer for you all, because *there are enemies to peace always lurking in all societies.* Petrarch says there are five great enemies to peace—avarice, ambition, envy, anger, and pride. I shall alter them a little, but use the same number. Instead of avarice I shall commence with *error.* One of the greatest means of destroying peace is error. Error in doctrine leads to the most lamentable consequences with regard to the peace of the church. I have noticed that the greatest fallings out have been among those who are most erroneous in doctrine. Though I admit that some called Calvinists are the most quarrelsome set breathing, this is the reason—while they have the main part of the truth, many of them are leaving out something important, and therefore God chastises them because they are some of his best children. It may be a sign of life that they are so eager after truth, that they kill one another in order to get it; but

I wish they would leave off their quarrelling for it is a disgrace to our religion. If they had more peace I might hope better for the progress of truth. Every one says to me—"Look there at your brethren! I never saw such a set of cut-throats in my life. I never saw a church, where they have the gospel. where they are not always falling out." Well, that is nearly the truth, and I am ashamed to confess it. I pray God, however, to send a little more peace where he has sent the gospel. There are, however, strifes among our opponents which we do not see. The bishop uses his strong hand, and the people dare not disagree; the pastor has such power and authority, that the crush of his mailed hand is sufficient to put down everything, because there is no freedom. Now, I would rather have a row in the church than have the members all asleep. I would rather have them falling to ears than sitting down in indifference. You never expect dead churches to have strife, but where there is a little life, if there is error, it always begets strife. What is the most litigious denomination now existing? No one would have a difficulty in pointing to our excellent friends the Wesleyans, for just at this moment they are quarrelling and finding fault with one another, splitting up into numberless sections, and making reformed churches, and so on. What is the cause of it? Because they are in the wrong track altogether with regard to church government, and with regard to some other things. John Wesley was a good man at making churches, I dare say; but he did not understand what the church ought to be in these days. He might do for a hundred years ago, but he bound his poor followers too tightly, and now they are trying to break out into freedom and liberty. If they had been right at first they might have gone on, and a thousand years would not have spoiled their system. It would have done now as well as then. Error is the root of bitterness in the church. Give us sound doctrine, sound practice, sound church government, and you will find that the God of peace will be with us. My brethren, seek to uproot error out of your own hearts. If one of you do not really believe the great cardinal doctrines of the gospel, I beseech you, then, for the good of the church to leave it, for we want those who love the truth.

The next enemy to peace is *ambition*. "Diotrephes loveth to have the pre-eminence," and that fellow has spoiled many a happy church. A man does not want, perhaps, to be pre-eminent, but then he is afraid that another should be, and so he would have him put down. Thus brethren are finding fault; they are afraid that such an one will go too fast, and that such another will go too fast. The best way is to try to go as fast as *he* does. It is of no use finding fault because some may have a little pre-eminence. After all, what is the pre-eminence. It is the pre-eminence of one little animalcule over another. Look in a drop of water. One of these little fellows is five times as big as another, but we never think of that. I dare say he is very large, and thinks, "I have the pre-eminence inside my drop." But he does not think the people of Park Street ever talk about him. So we live in this little drop of the world, not much bigger in God's esteem than a drop of the bucket; and one of us seems a little larger than the other, a worm a little above his fellow worm. But, O how big we get! and we want to get a little bigger, to get a little more prominent, but what is the use of it? for when we get ever so big we shall then be so small that an angel would not find us out if God did not tell him where we were. Whoever heard up in heaven anything about emperors and kings? Small tiny insects: God can see the animalculæ, therefore he can see us; but if he had not an eye to see the most minute he would never discover us. O may we never get ambition in this church. The best ambition is, who shall be the servant of all. The strangers seek to have dominion, but children seek to let the father have dominion, and the father only.

The next enemy to peace is *anger*. There are some individuals in the world that cannot help getting angry very quickly. They grow on a sudden very wrathful; while others who are not passionate, who take a longer time to be angry, are fearful enough when they do speak. Others who dare not speak at all, are worse still, for they get brewing their anger.

"Nursing their wrath to keep it warm."

They go into a sulky fit, disagreeing with everybody, eternally grumbling; they are like dogs in the flock—only barking, and yielding no fleece. O that nasty anger! If it gets into the church it will split it to pieces. Somehow or other we cannot help getting angry sometimes. O that we could come into the church and leave ourselves behind us! There is nobody I should like to run away from half so much as from myself. Try, beloved, to curb your tempers; and when you do not exactly see with another brother, do not think it necessary to knock him in the eyes to make him see; that is the worst thing in all the world to do, he will not see any the better for it, for

" The man convinced against his will,
Is of the same opinion still."

Then *envy* is another fearful evil. One minister, perhaps, is envious of another, because one church is full and the other not. How can teachers agree in the Sunday-school if there is any envy there? How can church members agree if envy creeps in? One member thinks another is thought more highly of than he deserves. Why, beloved, you are all too much thought of. But, after all, it does not matter what you are thought of by man, it only matters what God thinks of you—and God thinks as much of Little-faith as of Great-heart; he thinks as much of Mrs. Despondency as of Christiana herself. Drive, then, that "green-eyed monster" away, and keep him at a distance.

Again, there is *pride*, which gives rise to ill-feeling and bad blood. Instead of being affable to one another, and "condescending to men of low estate," we want that every punctilio of respect should be given to us, that we should be made lords and masters. That I am sure can never exist in a peaceable church.

Here, then, are our five great enemies. I would I could see the execution of them all. Banish them, transport them for ever, send them away amongst lions and tigers; we do not want any of them amongst us. But though I thus speak, it is not because I conceive that any of these have thoroughly crept in amongst you, but because I would have kept them away. I am most jealous in this matter. I am always afraid of the slightest contention, and I desire the God of peace to be ever with us.

Now let me briefly show you the appropriateness of this prayer. We indeed ought to have peace amongst ourselves. Joseph said to his brethren when they were going home to his father's house, "See that ye fall not out by the way." There was something extremely beautiful in that exhortation. "See that *ye* fall not out by the way." Ye have all one father, ye are of one family. Let men of two nations disagree; but you are of the seed of Israel; you are of one tribe and nation; your home is in one heaven. "See that ye fall not out *by the way.*" The way is rough; there are enemies to stop you. See that if ye fall out when ye get home, ye do not fall out by the way. Keep together; stand by one another; defend each other's character; manifest continual affection, for recollect you will want it all. The world hateth you because you are not of the world. Oh! you must take care that you love one another. You are all going to the same house. You may disagree here, and not speak to one another, and be almost ashamed to sit at the same table even at the sacrament; but you will all have to sit together in heaven. Therefore do not fall out by the way. Consider, again, the great mercies you have all shared together. You are all pardoned, you are all accepted, elected, justified, sanctified, and adopted. See that *ye* fall not out when ye have so many mercies, when God has given you so much. Joseph has filled your sacks, but if he has put some extra thing into Benjamin's sack, do not quarrel with Benjamin about that, but rather rejoice because your sacks are full. You have all got enough, you are all secure, you have all been dismissed with a blessing, and, therefore, I say once more, "See that ye fall not out by the way."

Now, dear brethren, is there anything I can plead with you this morning, in order that you may always dwell in peace and love? God has happily commenced a blessed revival amongst us, and under our means, by the help of God, that revival will spread through the entire kingdom. We have seen that "the word of the Lord is quick and powerful;" we know that there is nothing that can stop the progress of his kingdom, and there is nothing that can impede your success as a church except this. If the unhappy day should arrive—let the day be accursed when it does come— when you amongst yourselves should disagree, there would be a stop to the building of the Lord's house at once; when those that carry the trowel and bear the spears do not stand side by side, then the work of God must tarry. It is sad to think how much our glorious cause has been impeded by the different fallings out amongst the disciples of the Lamb. We have loved one another, brethren, up till now, with a true heart and fervently, and I am not afraid but that we shall always do so. At the same time, I am jealous over you, lest there should come in by any possibility any root of bitterness to trouble you. Let us this morning throw around you the bands of a man, let us unite you together with a three-fold cord that cannot be broken; let us entreat you to love one another; let us entreat you by your one Lord, one faith, one baptism, to continue one; let us beg of you, by our great success, to let our unity be commensurate therewith. Remember "how good and how pleasant it is for brethren to dwell together in unity!" The devil wants you to disagree, and nothing will please him better than for you to fall at ears among yourselves. The Moabites and Ammonites cut down one another. Do not let us do that.

"Those should in strictest concord dwell,
Who the same God obey."

It is continual bickering and jealousy that has brought disgrace upon the holy name of Christ. He has been wounded in the house of his friends. The arrows we have shot at one another have hurt us more than all that ever came from the bow of the devil. We have done more injury to the escutcheon of Christ by our contentions, than Satan has ever been able to do. I beseech you, brethren, love one another. I know not how I could endure anything like discord among *you*. I can bear the scoff of the world, and the laughter of the infidel; methinks I could bear martyrdom; but I could not bear to see you divided. I beseech my God and Master to suffer me first to wear my shroud, before I ever wear a garment of heaviness on account of your divisions. While I feel that I have your love and affection, and that you are bound to one another, I care not for the devils in hell, nor for men on earth. We have been, and we shall be omnipotent, through God; and by faith we will stand firm to one another and to his truth. Let each one resolve within himself—"if there is strife, I will have nothing to do with it." "The beginning of strife is like the letting out of water," and I will not turn the tap. If you will take care not to let the first drop in, I will be surety about the second. Brethren, again I say, for the gospel's sake, for the truth's sake, that we may laugh at our enemies, and rejoice with joy unspeakable, let us love one another.

Though I may not have preached to the worldly this morning, I have been asking you to preach to them, for when you love one another, that is a beautiful sermon to them. There is no sermon like what you can see with your own eyes. I went to the Orphan-house, last Wednesday, on Ashley Down, near Bristol, and saw that wonder of faith—I had some conversation with that heavenly-minded man Mr. Müller. I never heard such a sermon in my life as I saw there. They asked me to speak to the girls, but I said, "I could not speak a word for the life of me." I had been crying all the while to think how God had heard this dear man's prayer, and how all those three hundred children had been fed by my Father through the prayer of faith. Whatever is wanted, comes without annual subscriptions, without asking anything, simply from the hand of God. When I found that it was all correct that I had heard, I was like the queen of Sheba, and I had no heart left in me. I could only stand and look at those children, and think, did my heavenly Father feed them, and would he not feed me and all his family? Speak to them? They had spoken to me quite enough, though they had not said a word—Speak to them? I thought myself ten thousand fools that I did not believe God better. Here am I, I cannot trust him day by day; but this good man can trust him for three hundred children. When he has not a sixpence in hand he never fears. "I know God," he might say, "too well to doubt him. I tell my God, thou knowest what I want to-day to keep these children, and I have not anything. My faith never wavers, and my supply always comes." Simply by asking of God in this way, he has raised (I believe) £17,000 towards the erection of a new orphan-house. When I consider that, I sometimes think we will try the power of faith here, and see if we should not get sufficient funds whereby to erect a place to hold the people that crowd to hear the Word of God. Then we may have a tabernacle of faith as well as an orphan-house of faith. God send us that, and to Him shall be all the glory.

2 Spiritual Peace

"Peace I leave with you, my peace I give unto you."—John xiv. 27.

Our Lord was now about to die, to depart from this world, and to ascend to his Father; he therefore makes his will; and this is the blessed legacy which he leaves to the faithful—"Peace I leave with you, my peace I give unto you."

We may rest well assured that this testament of our Lord Jesus Christ is valid. You have here his own signature; it is signed, sealed, and delivered in the presence of the eleven apostles, who are faithful and true witnesses. 'Tis true a testament is not in force while the testator liveth, but Jesus Christ has died once for all; and now none can dispute his legacy. The will is in force, because the testator has died. It may, however, sometimes happen that a testator's wishes in a will may be disregarded; and *he*, powerless beneath the sod, is quite unable to rise and demand that his last will should be carried out. But our Lord Jesus Christ who died, and therefore made his will valid, rose again, and now he lives to see every stipulation of it carried out; and this blessed codicil, "Peace I leave with you, my peace I give unto you," is sure to all the blood-bought seed. Peace is theirs, and must be theirs, because he died and put the will in force, and lives to see the will fulfilled.

The donation, the blessed legacy which our Lord has here left, is *his peace*. This might be considered as being peace with all the creatures. God has made a league of peace between his people and the whole universe. "For thou shalt be in league with the stones of the field: and the beasts of the field shall be at peace with thee." "All things work together for good to them that love God." Providence that was once estranged, and seemed to work counter to our welfare, has now become at peace with us. The wheels revolve in happy order, and bear us blessings as often as they turn. The words of our Lord may also refer to the peace which exists among the people of God toward one another. There is a peace of God which reigns in our hearts through Jesus Christ, by which we are bound in closest ties of unity and concord to every other child of God whom we may meet with in our pilgrimage here below. Leaving, however, these two sorts of peace, which I believe to be comprehended in the legacy, let us proceed to consider two kinds of peace, which in our experience resolve themselves into one, and which are surely the richest part of this benediction. Our Saviour here means peace *with God*, and peace *with our own conscience*. There is first, peace with God, for he "hath reconciled us to himself by Jesus Christ;" he hath put away the wall which separated us from Jehovah, and now there is "peace on earth" and "goodwill toward men." When sin is put away, God has no cause of warfare against his creature: Christ has put *our* sins away, and therefore there is a virtual substantial peace established between God and our souls. This, however, might exist without our clearly understanding and rejoicing in it. Christ has therefore left us peace in the conscience. Peace with God is the treaty; peace in the conscience is

the publication of it. Peace with God is the fountain, and peace with conscience is the crystal stream which issues from it. There is a peace decreed in the court of divine justice in heaven; and then there follows as a necessary consequence, as soon as the news is known, a peace in the minor court of human judgment, wherein conscience sits upon the throne to judge us according to our works.

The legacy, then, of Christ is a twofold peace: a peace of friendship, of agreement, of love, of everlasting union between the elect and God. It is next a peace of sweet enjoyment, of quiet rest of the understanding and the conscience. When there are no winds above, there will be no tempests below. When heaven is serene, earth is quiet. Conscience reflects the complacency of God. "Therefore being justified by faith, we have peace with God, through Jesus Christ our Lord, by whom also we have received the atonement."

I propose this morning, if God the Holy Spirit shall graciously assist, to speak of this peace thus:—first, its *secret ground-work;* then its *noble nature;* thirdly, its *blessed effects;* fourthly, its *interruptions and means of maintenance;* and then I shall close by some words of *solemn warning* to those of you who have never enjoyed peace with God, and consequently never have had true peace with yourselves.

I. First, then, THE PEACE WHICH A TRUE CHRISTIAN ENJOYS WITH GOD AND HIS CONSCIENCE HAS A SOLID GROUNDWORK TO REST UPON. It is not built upon a pleasing fiction of his imagination, a delusive dream of his ignorance; but it is built on facts, on positive truths, on essential verities; it is founded upon a rock, and though the rains descend, and the winds blow, and the floods beat upon that house, it shall not fall, because its foundation is secure. When a man hath *faith in the blood of Christ* there is but little wonder that he hath peace, for indeed he is fully warranted in enjoying the most profound calm which mortal heart can know. For thus he reasons with himself:—God hath said, "He that believeth is justified from all things;" and, moreover, that " he that believeth on the Lord Jesus Christ *shall* be saved." Now, my faith is unfeignedly fixed in the great substitutionary sacrifice of Christ, therefore I am now justified from all things, and stand accepted in Christ as a believer. The necessary consequence of that is, that he possesses peace of mind. If God has punished Christ in my stead, he will not punish me again. " Being once purged I have no more conscience of sin." Under the Jewish ceremonial, mention was made of sin every year; the atoning lamb must be slaughtered a thousand times, but "this man, having made one atonement for sins, for ever sat down at the right hand of the majesty in the heavens." How, I ask, can that man tremble who believes himself forgiven? It were strange indeed if his faith did not breathe a holy calm into his bosom.

Again, the child of God receives his peace from another golden pipe, for *a sense of pardon has been shed abroad in his soul.* He not only believes his forgiveness from the testimony of God, but he has a sense of pardon. Do any of you know what this is? It is something more than a belief in Christ; it is the cream of faith, the full ripe fruit of believing, it is a high and special privilege which God gives after faith. If I have not that sense of pardon I am still bound to believe, and then, believing, I shall by and by advance to the seeing of that which I believed and hoped for. The Holy Spirit sometimes sheds abroad in the believer a consciousness that he is forgiven. By mysterious agency he fills the soul with the light of glory. If all the false witnesses on earth should rise up and tell the man at that time that God is not reconciled to him, and that his sins remain unforgiven, he would be able to laugh them to scorn; for, saith he, "the love of God is shed abroad in my heart by the Holy Spirit." He *feels* that he is reconciled to God. He has come from faith up to enjoyment, and every power of his soul feels the divine dew as it gently distils from heaven. The understanding feels it, it is enlightened; the will feels it, it is subjected to the will of God; the heart feels it, it is fired with holy love; the hope feels it, for it looks forward to the day when the whole man shall be made like its covenant head Jesus Christ. Every flower in the garden of humanity feels the sweet south wind of the Spirit, as it blows upon it, and causes the sweet spices to send forth their perfume. What wonder, then, that man has peace with God when the Holy Ghost becomes a royal tenant of the heart, with all his glorious train of blessings ? Ah! poor tried soul, what peace and joy unspeakable would reign in your soul if you did but believe on Christ? "Yes," say you, " but I want God to manifest to me that I am forgiven." Poor soul, he will not do that at once; he bids you believe Christ *first,* and *then* he will make manifest to you the pardon of your sin. It is by faith we are saved, not by enjoyment; but when I believe Christ, and take him at his word, even when my feelings seem to contradict my faith, then, as a gracious reward, he will honour my faith by giving me to *feel* that which I once believed when I did not feel it.

The believer also enjoys, in favoured seasons, such *an intimacy with the Lord Jesus Christ,* that he cannot but be at peace. Oh! there are sweet words which Christ whispers in the ears of his people, and there are love-visits which he pays to them, which a man would not believe even though it should be told unto him. Ye must know for yourselves what it is to have fellowship with the Father and with his Son Jesus Christ. There is such a thing as Christ manifesting himself to us as he does not unto the world. All black and frightful thoughts are banished. "I am my Beloved's, and my Beloved is mine." This is the one all-absorbing feeling of the spirit. And what wonder is it, that the believer has peace when Christ thus dwells in his heart, and reigns there without a rival, so that he knows no man, save Jesus only. It were a miracle of miracles if we did not have peace; and the strangest thing in Christian experience is that our peace is not more continued, and the only explanation of our misery is, that our communion is broken, that our fellowship is marred, else would our peace be like a river, and our righteousness like the waves of the sea.

That venerable man of God, Joseph Irons, who but a little while ago ascended to our Father in heaven, says, "What wonder that a Christian man has peace when *he carries the title-deeds of heaven in his bosom!*" This is another solid groundwork of confidence. We know that heaven is a prepared place for a prepared people, and the Christian can sometimes cry with the apostles, "Thanks be unto the Father, who hath made us meet to be partakers of the inheritance of the saints in light." Feeling that God has given him the meetness, he discovers that this preparation is a warrant for the hope that he shall enter into the dwelling-place of the glorified. He can lift his eye above, and say, "Yon bright world is mine, my entailed inheritance; life keeps me from it, but death shall bring me to it; my sins cannot destroy the heaven-written indentures; heaven is mine; Satan himself cannot shut me out of it. I must, I shall be where Jesus is, for after him my spirit longs, and to him my soul is knit." Oh, brethren, it is not a marvel when all is blest within, and all is calm above, that justified men possess "a peace with God which passeth all understanding."

You will perhaps be saying, well, but the Christian has troubles like other men— losses in business, deaths in his family, and sickness of body! Yes, but he has another groundwork for his peace—*an assurance of the faithfulness* and covenant fidelity of his God and Father. He believes that God is a faithful God—that whom he hath loved he will not cast away. All the dark providences to him are but blessings in disguise. When his cup is bitter, he believes it is mixed by love, and it must all end well, for God secures the ultimate result. Therefore, come foul, come fair, come all weathers, his soul shelters itself beneath the twin wings of the faithfulness and power of his Covenant God. The sanctified spirit is so resigned to his Father's will that he will not murmur. To him, as Madame Guyon was wont to say,—"It is equal whether love ordain his life or death, appoint him weal or woe." He is content to take just what his Father sends him, knowing that his Father understands him better than he understands himself. He gives up the helm of his ship to the hand of a gracious God; and he, himself, is enabled to fall asleep softly in the cabin; he believes that his Captain hath power over winds and waves; and when he sometimes feels his ship rocking in the storm, he cries with Herbert—

> "Though winds and waves assault my keel,
> He doth preserve it; he doth steer,
> Even when the bark seems most to reel.
> Storms are the triumph of his art;
> Sure he may hide his face, but not his heart."

No wonder, then, that he has peace, when he can feel this, and knows that he who hath begun the good work, has both the will and the power to perfect it, unto the day of Christ.

II. Having hurriedly unveiled the secret groundwork of the Christian's peace, we must dwell for a few minutes upon ITS NOBLE CHARACTER.

The peace of other men is ignoble and base. Their peace is born in the purlieus of sin. Self-conceit and ignorance are its parents. The man knows not what he is, and therefore thinks himself to be something—when he is nothing. He says—"I am rich and increased in goods," while he is naked, and poor, and miserable. Not such is the birth of the Christian's peace. *That* is born of the Spirit. It is a peace which God the Father gives, for he is the God of all peace; it is a peace which Jesus Christ bought, for he has made peace with his blood, and he is our peace; and it is a peace which the Holy Spirit works—he is its author and its founder in the soul.

Our peace then, is God's own child, and God-like is its character. His Spirit is its sire, and it is like its Father. It is *"my peace,"* saith Christ! not man's peace; but the unruffled, calm, the profound peace of the Eternal Son of God. Oh, if we had but this one thing within our bosoms, this divine peace, a Christian were a glorious thing indeed; and even now kings and mighty men of this world are as nothing when once compared with the Christian; for he wears a jewel in his bosom which all the world could not buy, a jewel fashioned from old eternity and ordained by sovereign grace to be the high boon, the right royal inheritance of the chosen sons of God.

This peace, then, is divine in its origin; and it is also *divine in its nourishment.* It is a peace which the world cannot give; and it cannot contribute towards its maintenance. The daintiest morsels that ever carnal sense fed upon, would be bitter to the mouth of this sweet peace. Ye may bring your much fine corn, your sweet wine, and your flowing oil, your dainties tempt us not, for this peace feeds upon angels' food, and it cannot relish any food that grows on earth. If you should give a Christian ten times as much riches as he has, you would not cause him ten times as much peace; but probably, ten times more distress; you might magnify him in honour, or strengthen him with health; yet, neither would his honour or his health contribute to his peace; for that peace flows from a divine source; and there are no tributary streams from the hills of earth to feed that divine current; the stream flows from the throne of God, and by God alone is it sustained.

It is, then, a peace divinely born and divinely nourished. And let me again remark, it is *a peace that lives above circumstances.* The world has tried hard to put an end to the Christian's peace, and it has never been able to accomplish it. I remember, in my early childhood, having heard an old man utter in prayer, a saying which stuck by me—" O Lord, give unto thy servants that peace which the world can neither give nor take away." Ah! the whole might of our enemies cannot take it away. Poverty cannot destroy it; the Christian in his rags can have peace with God. Sickness cannot mar it; lying on his bed, the saint is joyful in the midst of the fires. Persecution cannot ruin it, for persecution cannot separate the believer from Christ, and while he is one with Christ his soul is full of peace. "Put your hand here," said the martyr to his executioner, when he was led to the stake, " put your hand here, and now put your hand on your own heart, and feel which beats the hardest, and which is the most troubled." Strangely was the executioner struck with awe, when he found the Christian man as calm as though he were going to a wedding feast, while he himself was all agitation at having to perform so desperate a deed. Oh, world! we defy thee to rob us of our peace. We did not get it of thee, and thou canst not rend it from us. It is set as a seal upon our arm; it is strong as death and invincible as the grave. Thy stream, O Jordan, cannot drown it, black and deep though thy depths may be; in the midst of thy tremendous billows our soul is confident, and resteth still on him that loved us, and gave himself for us. Frequently have I had to remark, that Christians placed in the most unfavourable circumstances are, as a rule, better Christians than those who are placed in propitious positions. In the midst of a very large church of persons in all ranks, with the condition of most of whom I am as thoroughly conversant as man can well be, I have observed that the women who come from houses where they have ungodly husbands, and trying children—that the young people who come from workshops where they are opposed and laughed at—that the people who come from the depths of poverty, from the dens and kens of our city, are the brightest jewels that are set in the crown of the church. It seems as if God would defeat nature—not only make the hyssop grow on the wall, but make the cedar grow there too—he finds his brightest pearls in the darkest waters, and bring up his most precious jewels from the filthiest dung hills.

"Wonders of grace to God belong,
Repeat his mercies in your song."

And this I have found too, that often the more disturbed a Christian man is, the purer is his peace; the heavier the rolling swell of his griefs and sorrows, the more still, and calm, and profound is the peace that reigns within his heart. So then, it is peace divinely born, divinely nourished, and one which is quite above the influence of this poor whirling world.

Further, I must remark briefly upon the nature of this peace, that it is *profound and real*. "The peace of God," saith an apostle, "that passeth all understanding." This peace not only fills all the senses to the brim, till every power is satiated with delight, but the understanding which can take in the whole world, and understand many things which are not within the range of vision, even the understanding cannot take in the length and the breadth of this peace. And not only will *the* understanding fail to compass it, but *all* understanding is outdone. When our judgment hath exerted itself to the utmost, it cannot comprehend the heights and depths of this profound peace. Have you ever imagined what must be the stillness of the caverns in the depth of the seas, a thousand fathoms beneath the bosom of the floods, where the mariners' bones lie undisturbed, where pearls are born, and corals that never see the light, where the long lost gold and silver of the merchants lie sprinkled on the sandy floor—down in the rock caves, and the silent palaces of darkness where waves dash not, and the intruding foot of the diver hath never trodden? So clear, so calm is the peace of God, the placid rest of the assured believer. Or lift up your eyes to the stars. Have you never dreamed a sweet dream of the quietude of those noiseless orbs? Let us mount beyond the realm of noise and riot, let us tread the noiseless highway of the silent orbs. The thunders are far below us, the confused tumult of the crowd defiles not the sanctity of this wondrous quiet. See how the stars sleep on their golden couches, or only open their bright eyes to keep watch upon that stormless sea of ether, and guard the solemn boundaries of the reign of peace. Such is the peace and calm that reigns in the Christian's bosom. "Sweet calm," one calls it; "perfect peace," David styles it; another one calls it "great peace." "Great peace have all they that love thy law, and nothing shall offend them." Last year—I tell you now a secret of my own heart—I had one text which thrust itself upon my recollection many times a day. I dreamed of it when I slept; when I awoke it went with me, and I verified it, and rejoiced in it: "His soul shall dwell at ease." It is my promise now. There is such an *ease*—quite consistent with labour, with agony for the souls of men, with an earnest desire for yet greater attainments in divine life; there is such an ease—it is not to be gained by all the appliances of luxury, by all the aggrandisement of wealth—an ease in which "not a wave of trouble rolls across the peaceful breast," but all is calm, and all is clear, and all is joy and love. May we evermore dwell in that serene atmosphere, and never lose our hold of this peace.

Lest there should be any of you who do not understand what I have said, I will try and say it over again briefly in an example. Do you see that man? He has been taken up before a cruel tribunal; he is condemned to die. The hour draws nigh: he is taken to prison, and placed there with two soldiers to guard him, and four quarternions of soldiers outside the door. The night comes on: he lies down, but in how uncomfortable a position! Chained between two soldiers! He lies down and he falls asleep—not the sleep of the guilty criminal, whose very sense of dread makes his eyelids heavy; but a calm sleep which is given by God, and which ends in an angelic vision, by which he is delivered. Peter sleeps, when the death sentence is above his head, and the sword is ready to penetrate his soul. See you another picture? There are Paul and Silas yonder: they have been preaching, and their feet are thrust in the stocks for it. They will die on the morrow; but in the midnight they sing praises unto God, and the prisoners hear them. One would have thought in such a loathsome dungeon as that, they would have groaned and moaned all night long, or that at best they might have slept; but no, they sang praises to God, and the prisoners heard them. There is the peace—the calm, the quietude of the heir of heaven I might give you another picture—of our ancient Nonconformists, in the days of that most persecuting Queen Elizabeth. She cast into prison among very many others, two of our forefathers, of the name of Greenwood and Barrow. They were caused to lie in that loathsome stinking dungeon—the Clink Prison—shut in one huge room with maniacs, murderers, felons, and the like, compelled to listen to their frightful conversation. One day there came a warrant, that they must die. The two men were led out, and tied to the cart, and were about to be taken away to death; but they were no sooner outside the gate than a messenger rode up. The Queen had sent a reprieve. They were taken back;

calmly and quietly they returned to their prison; and the next day they were taken to Newgate, and, just as suddenly, there came a second messenger, to say they must be taken away to Tyburn to die. They were again tied to the cart; they ascended the scaffold; the ropes were put round their necks, and they were allowed to stand in that position and address the assembled multitude, and bear witness to the liberty of Christ's church, and to the right of private judgment among men. They concluded their speech, and a second time that wretched Queen sent them a reprieve, and they were taken back a second time to the dungeon, and there they lay in Newgate, but only for few days more, and then a third time they were taken out, and this time they were hanged in reality; but they went as cheerfully to the scaffold on each occasion as men go to their beds, and seemed as joyous, as though they were going to a crown, rather than to a halter. Such specimens all the churches of Christ can show. Wherever there has been a true Christian, the world has tried its best to put out his peace; but it is a peace that never can be quenched —it *will* live on, what halter about its neck, with the hot pincers tearing away its flesh, with the sword in its very bones; it will live, till, mounting from the burning bush of earth, this bird of paradise shall wear its glittering plumage in the midst of the garden of paradise.

III. Having detained you longer on this point than I thought I should do, I hasten to the third point, THE EFFECTS OF THIS DIVINE PEACE.

The blessed effects of this divine peace are, first of all, *joy*. You will notice that the words "joy," and " peace " are continually put together; for joy without peace were an unhallowed and an unhappy joy—the crackling of thorns under a pot, unsound, mere flames of joy, but not the red glowing coals of bliss. Now, divine peace gives joy to the Christian; and *such* joy! Have you ever seen the first gleam of joy when it has come into the eye of the penitent? It has been my happy lot to pray with many a convinced sinner, to witness the deep agony of spirit, and deeply to sympathise with the poor creature in his trouble for sin. I have prayed and have exhorted to faith, and I have seen that flash of joy, when at last the hopeful word was spoken, " I do believe on the Lord Jesus Christ with all my heart." Oh! that look of joy! It is as if the gates of heaven had been opened for a moment, and some flash of glory had blazed upon the eye and had been reflected therefrom. I remember my own joy, when I first had peace with God. I thought I could dance all the way home. I could understand what John Bunyan said, when he declared he wanted to tell the crows on the ploughed land all about it. He was too full to hold, he felt he must tell some one. Oh! there was joy in the household that day, when all heard that the eldest son had found a Saviour and knew himself to be forgiven—bliss compared with which all earth's joys are less than nothing and vanity. As the counterfeit to the real coin, so are the base joys of earth to the real joy which springs from peace with God. Young man! Young woman! if you could have a bliss such as you never knew before, you must be reconciled to God through the blood of Christ; for till then, real joy and lasting pleasure you can never know.

The first effect of this peace, then, is joy. Then follows another—*love*. He that is at peace with God through the blood of Christ is constrained to love him that died for him. " Precious Jesus!" he cries, " help me to serve thee! Take me as I am, and make me fit for something. Use me in thy cause; send me to the farthest part of the green earth, if thou wilt, to tell to sinners the way of salvation; I will cheerfully go, for my peace fans the flame of love, that all that I am and all I have shall be, *must be*, for ever thine."

Then next, there comes an anxiety after *holiness*. He that is at peace with God does not wish to go into sin; for he is careful lest he should lose that peace. He is like a woman that has escaped from a burning house; he is afraid of every candle afterwards, lest he should come again into the like danger. He walks humbly with his God. Constrained by grace, this sweet fruit of the Spirit, peace, leads him to endeavour to keep all the commandments of God, and to serve his Lord with all his might.

Then again, this peace will *help us to bear affliction*. Paul describes it as a shoe. As he says, " Your feet shod with the preparation of the gospel of *peace*." It enables us to tread on the sharpest flints of sorrow, yea, on adders, and on serpents also; it gives us power to walk over the briars of this world, and our feet are not wounded; we tread the fires, and we are not burned. This divine shoe of peace makes us walk without weariness, and run without fainting. I can do all things when my soul is at peace with God. There are no sufferings that shall move my soul to pain, no terrors that shall blanch my cheek, there are no wounds that shall compel me to an ignominious fear when my spirit is at peace with God. It makes a man a giant—swells the dwarf to a Goliath size. He becomes mightiest of the mighty; and while the weaklings creep about this little earth, bowed down to the very dust, he strides it like a Colossus. God has made him great and mighty, because he has filled his soul with peace, and with overflowing joy.

More might I tell you of the blessed effects of this peace; but I shall be content, after I have simply noticed that this peace gives *boldness at the throne*, and access to a Father's mercy-seat. We feel we are reconciled, and therefore we stand no longer at a distance, but we come up to him, even to his knees; we spread our wants before him, plead our cause, and rest satisfied of success, because there is no enmity in our Father's heart to us, and none in ours to him. We are one with God, and he is one with us, through Jesus Christ our Lord.

IV. And now I have a practical duty to perform, and with this I shall close, after having said a few words to those who know nothing of this peace. The practical remarks I have to make are upon the subject of INTERRUPTIONS OF PEACE.

All Christians have a right to perfect peace, but they have not all the possession of it. There are times when gloomy doubts prevail, and we fear to say that God is ours. We lose a consciousness of pardon, and we grope in the noonday as in the night. How is this? I think these interruptions may be owing to one of four causes.

Sometimes they are due to *the ferocious temptations of Satan*. There are periods when with unexampled cruelty Satan assaults the children of God. It is not to be expected that they will maintain perfect peace while they are fighting with Apollyon. When poor Christian was wounded in his head, and in his hands, and in his feet, no wonder that he did groan exceedingly, and as Bunyan hath it, "I never saw him all the while give so much as one pleasant look, till he perceived he had wounded Apollyon with his two-edged sword; then, indeed, he did smile, and look upward; but it was the dreadfullest fight that ever I saw." Mark, there is no such thing as a disturbance of the reality of the peace between God and the soul; for God is always at peace with those who are reconciled to him by Christ; but there is a disturbance of the enjoyment of that peace, and that is often effected by the howlings of that great dog of hell. He comes against us with all his might, with his mouth open ready to swallow us up quick, and were it not for divine mercy he would do so. It is but little marvel that sometimes our peace is affected, when Satan is fierce in his temptations.

At another time a want of peace may arise from *ignorance*. I do not wonder that a man who believes Arminian doctrine, for instance, has little peace. There is nothing in the doctrine to give him any. It is a bone without marrow; it is a religion that seems to me to be cold, sapless, marrowless, fruitless—bitter and not sweet. There is nothing about it but the whip of the law; there are no grand certainties—no glorious facts of covenant love, of discriminating grace, of Almighty faithfulness, and suretyship engagements. I will never quarrel with the man that can live on such stones and scorpions as conditional election, haphazard redemption, questionable perseverance, and unavailing regeneration. There may be some, I suppose, who can live on this dry meat. If they can live on it, be it so; but I believe many of our doubts and fears arise from doctrinal ignorance. You have not, perhaps, a clear view of that covenant made between the Father and his glorious Son, Jesus Christ; you do not know how to spell the word "gospel" without mixing up the word "law" in it. Perhaps you have not learned fully to look out of self to Christ for everything. You do not know how to distinguish between sanctification, which varies, and justification, which is permanent. Many believers have not come to discern between the work of the Spirit and the work of the Son; and what marvel, if ye are ignorant, that ye sometimes lack peace? Learn more of that precious Book, and your peace shall be more continual.

Then again, this peace is usually marred by *sin*. God hides his face behind the clouds of dust which his own flock make as they travel along the road of this world. We sin, and then we sorrow for it. God still loves his child, even when he sins; but he will not let the child know it. That child's name is in the family register; but the Father clasps up the book, and will not let him read it till he thoroughly repents again, and comes back once more to Jesus Christ. If you can have peace, and yet live in sin, mark this, you are unrenewed. If you can live in iniquity, and yet have peace in your conscience, your conscience is seared and dead. But the

Christian man, when he sins, begins to smart; if not the very moment he falls, it is not long before his Father's rod is on his back, and he begins to cry,

> "Where is the blessedness I knew,
> When first I saw the Lord?
> Where is the soul-refreshing view
> Of Jesus and his Word?"

Once more: our peace may be interrupted also by *unbelief.* Indeed, this is the sharpest knife of the four, and will most readily cut the golden thread of our enjoyments.

And now, if ye would maintain unbroken peace, take advice from God's minister this morning, young though he be in years. Take advice, which he can warrant to be good, for it is Scriptural. If ye would keep your peace continual and unbroken, look always to the sacrifice of Christ; never permit your eye to turn to anything but Jesus. When thou repentest, my hearer, still keep thine eye on the cross; when thou labourest, labour in the strength of the Crucified One. Everything thou doest, whether it be self-examination, fasting, meditation, or prayer, do all under the shadow of Jesus' cross; or otherwise, live as thou wilt, thy peace will be but a sorry thing; thou shalt be full of disquiet and of sore trouble. Live near the cross and your peace shall be continual.

Another piece of advice. Walk humbly with your God. Peace is a jewel; God puts it on your finger; be proud of it, and he will take it off again, Peace is a noble garment; boast of your dress, and God will take it away from you. Remember the hole of the pit whence you were digged, and the quarry of nature whence you were hewn; and when you have the bright crown of peace on your head, remember your black feet; nay, even when that crown is there, cover it and your face still with those two wings, the blood and righteousness of Jesus Christ. In this way shall your peace be maintained.

And again, walk in holiness, avoid every appearance of evil. "Be not conformed to this world." Stand up for truth and rectitude. Suffer not the maxims of men to sway your judgment. Seek the Holy Spirit that you may live like Christ, and live near to Christ, and your peace shall not be interrupted.

As for those of you who have never had peace with God, I can entertain but one sentiment towards you, namely, that of pity. Poor souls! poor souls! poor souls! that never knew the peace which Jesus Christ gives to his people. And my pity is all the more needed, because you do not pity yourselves. Ah! souls, the day is coming when that God to whom you are now an enemy, shall stare you in the face. You *must* see him; and he is "a consuming fire." You must look into that blazing furnace, and sink, and despair, and die. Die, did I say? Worse than that. You must be cast into the pit of damnation, where dying were a boon that can never be granted. Oh! may God give you peace through his Son! If you are now convinced of sin, the exhortation is, "Believe on the Lord Jesus Christ." Just as thou art, thou art bidden to put thy trust in him that did die upon the tree; and if thou doest this, thy sins shall all be forgiven now, and thou shalt have peace with God; and, ere long, thou shalt know it in thine own conscience and rejoice. Oh! seek this peace and pursue it; and above all, seek the Peace-maker, Christ Jesus, and you shall be saved. God bless you for Jesus' sake. Amen.

3 Peace by Believing

"Therefore being justified by faith, we have peace with God through our Lord Jesus Christ."—Romans v. 1.

A MOMENT'S contemplation would suffice to arouse any man to the terror of the position involved in being at war with God. For a subject to be in a state of sedition against a powerful monarch is to commit treason and to incur the forfeiture of his life. But for a creature to be in arms against its Creator; for a thing that dependeth for its existence upon the will of God to be at enmity with the God in whose hand its breath is; for a soul to know that God who is terrible in his power, and Almighty to protect or to destroy, is his foe; that he whose anger endureth for ever, and his wrath burneth even unto the lowest hell, is his chief and grand enemy—this is an appalling thing indeed. Could any man but understand and realize this, smitten through with terrors as great as those which surprised Belshazzar when he saw the handwriting on the wall, he would cry out in anguish—he would make a thrilling appeal for mercy. God is against thee, O sinful man! God is against thee, O thou who hast never submitted thyself unto his word! God is against thee; and woe unto thee when he shall rend thee in pieces, for none can deliver thee out of his hand! Happy! happy beyond all description is the man who can say with our apostle, "We have peace with God;" but wretched! wretched, again, beyond all description wretched must that man be who is at war with his own Maker, and sees heaven itself in arms against him!

Chiefly now we shall endeavour to talk of *the peace which the believer enjoys;* and then, I shall have *a few words of counsel, warning, and encouragement for those who have not this peace with God, or who may have had it, and for a time have lost the enjoyment of it.*

I. In speaking of THE PEACE OF GOD WHICH THE CHRISTIAN ENJOYS; we will commence with some remarks upon its basis.

There is the widest possible difference between a man being just in his own eyes, and his being *justified* in the sight of God. Yet, perhaps no fallacy is more common than to mistake the one for the other. Then, as a natural consequence of building on a weak foundation, the structure however fair to look upon, is insecure. The *peace* in which multitudes of professors delight themselves is merely peace with their own conscience, and not in any sense peace with God. I know of no greater contrast than there is between that peace which is a mere stagnation of thought, a lull of anxiety, or a blindness to danger, and that soul-satisfying peace which passes all understanding. The true peace of God flows like a river in unceasing activity; it preserves a tranquil frame amidst storm, tempest, and tribulation, by all of which it is frequently assaulted. It is a part of the panoply of God with which a Christian is clothed, to withstand principalities and powers and spiritual wickedness in the evil day. Or, to change the figure, Christ gave his disciples this peace as an amulet, when as he was about himself to depart and go to the Father, he sent them forth to be buffeted about in the world. Just so in the text, if you pursue the subject in the next few verses, you will find that this peace with God is given first, and afterwards cometh experience of tribulations everywhere else. We ourselves, brethren, have proved it. There is a natural disposition of sin to defile, but the blood of Christ speaks peace in the conscience; there is a constant tendency of the world to destroy our hope, but the peaceful word of Jesus comforts us; "Be of good cheer, I have overcome the world;" there is a painful proneness of human strength to fail, but the promise supports us—"This man shall be the peace when the Assyrian cometh into our land." And this true peace gives to the believer an inward sense of God's acceptance, like as Moses never lost sight of the goodwill of the Dweller in the bush; so, too, there is a more blessed assurance of goodwill in the faith that always realises "God in Christ reconciling the world to himself."

And now as to the experimental basis of that peace which the believer has with his God. It must have some solid rational ground; it must have some basis which judgment may estimate. I know some who have an apprehension of peace with God that has no foundation whatever. Let me describe the person. "Are you living in peace with God, my friend?" "Yes," says he, "thank God, I have enjoyed a sense of peace for twenty years." "How did you get it?" "Well, as I was walking one day, in great distress of mind, in such-and-such a road, a feeling of comfort came over me, and it has remained with me ever since." "Yes, but, friend, what is the reason of your hope? What is the ground of your confidence that you have peace with God?" "Well, you see, I felt comfortable, and I believe that I have felt comfortable ever since." "No, no—that's not the matter at which I aim. What is the ground; what is the doctrinal proof; what is the matter of fact that gives you comfort?" "Well, do not press me," says he, "for I do not know. Only this I know—I did feel happy, and I have felt happy ever since, and I have not had any doubt." That man, mark you, if I be not mistaken, is under a delusion. If I err not, it is very possible that that man has received a draught of the opium of hell. Satan has said to him, "Peace, peace," where there is no peace, and he is going undisturbed and quiet down to the place where he shall lift up his eyes and discover too late his error. The peace of a Christian is not such a lull of stupefaction as that. It has a reason; it has some ground-work; and when you come to pull it to pieces, it is as completely a logical inference from certain facts as any deduction that could be drawn by mathematical precision. Let me, however, bring up a few more who think they have peace, but they build their supposition on wrong grounds. Here is a man who very flippantly and joyously says, "Peace with God, sir! Yes— peace with God; I enjoy the unbroken satisfaction that I have made my peace with him." "Well, how?" "Why, you see, some years ago I never went to a place of worship on Sunday at all, and I felt one day that I was doing wrong. Here was I going to the theatre most nights, and I was doing my trade in a very bad way, and now and then I took too much drink, and I was doing a great many things that were wrong, and I thought it was time for me to turn over a new leaf, and I have done so. Now I generally go to a place of worship twice on the Sabbath-day. I may now and then indulge myself—well, who is there that never does anything wrong?—but still there is very great amendment in me. If you ask my wife, she sees a wonderful change; and if you ask my work-people, they will say I am a different man from what I used to be. Now, I think I am not like the man you brought up just now, with no ground for his peace. I think I have a very good ground for mine, for I am deserving very well of my Maker now. I feel now, if I go to a place of amusement where I ought not, I cannot pray that night; but the next night I try over again, and manage to get through my form of prayer, and on the whole I am doing so well that I think I may say I have a good bottom and ground for saying that I am at peace with God." Now, let this man be reminded that it is written, "By the works of the law there shall no flesh be justified in his sight." All these moral things of which he has spoken are good enough in themselves. They will be very excellent in the temple of Christianity if they be placed at the top; but, if they be used as foundations, a builder might as well use tiles, and slates, and chimney-pots for foundations and corner-stones, as use these reformatory actions as a ground of dependence. Man! do you not perceive that your foundation is not an even and secure one? For what about the past? What is to become of the sins already committed? How are you to get rid of these? Do you suppose that the payment of future debts will discharge old liabilities? Go to your tradesman, and tell him that you owe him a very great sum of money, and you cannot pay him a farthing of it, but you do not expect he will sue you in the court, for you never intend to get into his debt any more. I think he will tell you that is not a method of business he understands. Certainly this is not the way in which God will deal with you. Your old sins! your old sins! your old sins! What about those? Those debts unpaid! those crimes as yet unburied! Let your conscience give them a resurrection in your memory to-night. What about these? Surely you can have no peace with God while these remain unforgiven! Besides, you have an inward conviction that you have not peace with God, but only peace with yourself. You do feel a little better some-times, but it is a very poor sort of confidence that you have, for a little sickness shakes it. How would you do to die now? Would you wrap yourself up in these miserable rags of yours, and say, "Lord, thou knowest I have sinned, but then I have done my best to make up for it." You know and feel that this bed is shorter than a man can stretch himself on it, and this coverlet too narrow that a man should be able to wrap himself up in it. Renounce this confidence, for it is one that will never stand before God. To instance yet another case, in which I tread on more delicate ground. Beloved, there are some who have peace which they explain to you in such a way, that while I trust they have a peace with God, I fear they misunderstand the ground of it. Some true Christians will talk to you on this wise—"I hope I am at peace with God now, for my faith is in active exercise; my love is fervent; I have delightful seasons in prayer; the eyes of my hope are no longer dim; my patience can endure many things for Christ; my courage did not fail me yesterday in the midst of Christ's enemies; my graces are vigorous; the Spirit of God has been blowing across my soul as over a garden, and all the graces, like flowers, have yielded their best perfume, therefore I feel that I have peace with God." Oh, believer, believer! art thou so foolish as, having begun in the Spirit by faith, to be made perfect in the flesh by your own doing? Remember, if thou hast peace, if thou puttest thy peace here upon thy graces, then there will come another day—perhaps it may come to-morrow—when all those graces will droop like withered flowers, yielding no perfume; when, instead of beauty there shall be baldness, instead of ornament there shall be decay; when thou shalt see thyself in thy true natural colours, and discover thyself, like Job, and cry out as he did, "Lord, I am vile!" What wilt thou do then with thy peace? Why, if thou hast begun to look to thy graces in any way for peace, then thou art looking to a fickle source; thou art going to the cistern instead of living by the fountain; thou art using Hagar's bottle, instead of sitting like Isaac at the well to drink from never-ceasing streams. Yet this is an evil into which we are so apt to fall after having done well for the Master and being helped to serve him. It is true we do not trust in these things. I hope God has delivered us from self-righteousness; yet there is just that "Now *must* I be a child of God—now *must* I truly be an heir of heaven, for see how I have been sanctified; mark how I have been edified and built up in the faith." Ah, brother! there is the cloven foot there! Be thou on thy guard, it is an unclean thing; it will bring thee into pain and bondage; it will make thee sick, and put thy feet in the stocks, and thrust thee into the inner dungeon ere long. Flee from it as thou wouldest from a serpent. Stand thou ever under the dear cross of Christ, looking up to his wounds, rejoicing in his all-sufficiency, and building your peace there and there alone.

I fear me, too, that there are not a few who I trust have genuine peace, but who, nevertheless, are tempted to found their confidence upon their enjoyments. We have our enjoyments—God be thanked for this. Oh, there are times when our communion is with the Father and with his Son Jesus Christ. We have not been into heaven, but we have heard some of the songs of the angels on the other side the pearly gates, or, if not the songs, we have heard the echo of them in our hearts. When we have been in prayer, our soul has been like the chariots of Amminadib, swift and strong. We have had our seasons, as it were, of witnessing the transfiguration; we can remember Tabor's mount; well can we remember the hill Mizar and the Hermonites, for there he spake with us; we have had our experience of Jacob's dream, as well as our fellowship with Jacob's wrestling; we have seen the Lord, and by faith have put our finger into the print of the nails, and thrust our hand into his side. He has kissed us with the kisses of his love, and his love is better than wine. But the tendency is to say, "Now I *have* peace with God; now *must* I be reconciled to him; now will I press out the wine of comfort from these grapes." If we do this, let us remember that perhaps tomorrow we may be in Gethsemane; we may have our times of agonizing and fruitless prayer; we may be in the valley of despondency, or in the blacker valley of the shadow of death—no present joys, no promises applied with power, no whispers of Christ's love, no sweets of his covenant, no delighting ourselves in the Lord—all may be dark and dreary; well, what then? Ah, my brethren, we shall find ourselves weak, because we have taken our comforts to be the basis of our peace, instead of continuing still to look solely and only to Christ. Let me warn you, beloved, though this may not seem a case as dangerous as some others, yet let me warn you that it is essential to our comfort, that we should stand to this and to this only—being justified by faith we have peace with God. Our peace is solely the result of a justification achieved through faith, and not the result of enjoyments, nor of graces much less of good works, or of any foolish irrational impression which we may think we have been favoured with.

Where then does lie the Christian's conviction of his peace with God? Well it lies in this—that he is justified by faith. The process is plain. It is as clear, I say, as a proposition in Euclid. Christ stood in my stead before God. I was a sinner doomed to die; Christ took my place; he died for me. Well, then, how can I perish? How can I be punished for offences which have been punished already in the person of my substitute? God demands of me perfectly to keep his law. I cannot do it. Christ has done it for me—kept the law, magnified it, made it honourable. What more can God demand of me? I, a sinner, am washed in Jesu's blood. I, guilty, am clothed in Jesu's righteousness. You say "How? I cannot see it is so." True, it is so by faith. God says that he who believes in Christ shall be saved—I believe in Christ; therefore I am saved. He says, "He that believeth on him is not condemned." I believe on him; therefore I am not condemned. This is clear reasoning enough. Very well then, the man who has believed in Christ has his sins forgiven, and the righteousness of Christ imputed to him, and therefore he is at peace with God. Now this is reasoning which no logic can gainsay. There is a rebel—first he is pardoned, next merit is imputed to him, and he is at peace with his King, and a rebel no longer. There is a child; he has offended; his father takes him, accepts him for his elder brother's sake, and he is at peace with his father. The thing is clear enough. Here is a reason for the hope that is within us, which we may give with meekness and fear, it is true, never with diffidence and timidity. We may venture to give it in the presence of the old dragon and defy him to break its force. We might give it even in the midst of a congregation of assembled demons, and defy them, if they can, to break its power. We may give it in the presence of the Eternal God, for he will never gainsay the word on which he has caused us to hope. "Who is he that condemneth? It is Christ that died, yea rather, that is risen again, who is even at the right hand of God, who also maketh intercession for us." It stands for ever. Stand here, and you stand so fast that no howling tempest of temptation can sweep you down. Stand to this, that Christ has finished your salvation for you, that he has done everything that omnipotent justice can ask; he has endured all the penalty, drained the cup of wrath, obeyed the law completely, given to divine equity all it can demand, and therefore, believing in his name, standing in his righteousness, accepted in his suretyship, you must have peace with God. This is the basis of the Christian's peace—one on which he may sleep or wake, live or die, and live eternally, without condemnation or separation from the love of God which is in Christ Jesus the Lord.

Continuing our remarks on this subject, we shall now turn your attention to the channel of this peace. "Therefore being justified by faith, we have peace with God *through our Lord Jesus Christ.*"

Take it for a certain fact, then, that we are justified as the result of what Christ has done for us, seeing that he "was delivered for our offences, and raised again for our justification;" and the experience thereof, in so far as we have assurance of our being personally justified is the result of our trusting Christ. What then? How are we to enjoy the comfort of it? for there are times when we begin to doubt whether we are justified. Brethren, we must not come to our faith to get comfort, but to the primary cause of our justification. The channel through which the comfort comes is Jesus Christ. So then, though justification by faith is in itself a well of comfort, yet, even from that well we cannot get it, except we use Christ, who digged the well, to be the bucket to draw the water up from its depths. It must come through Christ. I will suppose, then, that I am in doubt and fear to-night, and want to get my peace restored—how shall I seek it? Through Jesus Christ, the surety and substitute himself, must I get it. How? First, by believing in Christ over again, just as I did at the first. Christ tells me that he came to save sinners, I am a sinner, therefore he came to save me. He says he can save me. This looks reasonable. He is very God; he is perfect man; he has suffered and offered a complete atonement. He tells me he is willing to save me. This also appears reasonable, for why else should he die, if he did not wish to save? Then he tells me if I will trust him, he will save me. I trust him, and I have not the shadow of a shade of a suspicion of doubt that he will be as good as his word. If he be faithful and just—of which, who dare to breathe a suspicion?—this soul of mine in heaven must be; it is committed to the Redeemer's charge with every pledge that God can give, with more security than we could ever ask, in him, I trust—in Jesus, and in Jesus only. Brother, this is how you must get your peace with God to-night—through Jesus Christ, by going to him, by a simple faith, just as you went at the first. Some silly people who have got high doctrine in their heads, so high that it smells offensive in the nostrils of those who read the scriptures—they say we teach that man is saved by mere believing. We do—by mere believing. There is a poor, starving man over there. I give him bread—his life is spared. Why do not these people say this man was saved by mere eating—by mere eating! And here is another person whose tongue cleaves to the roof of his mouth by thirst and is ready to die, and I give him water and he drinks, and his eyes sparkle, and the man is saved by mere drinking. And look at ourselves—why do not we drop down dead in our pews? Just stop your breath a little while and see. Surely we all live by mere breathing. All these operations of nature that touch the vital mysteries may be sneered at as merely this or merely that; and in like manner to speak with disparagement of "mere believing" is stupid nonsense. And yet, let me say it in my sense of the term—we are saved, we are reconciled to God through Jesus Christ by mere believing, by the simple act of trusting in the Lord Jesus Christ. And if I would get my peace made more full and perfect, having come to Christ by faith, I must continue to get peace from him by meditation upon him, for the more I go to Christ believingly, the deeper will my peace be. If I believe in Christ, and do not know much of him, my faith will necessarily be somewhat slender, but if I continue "to comprehend with all saints what are the heights and depths, and lengths and breadths, and to know the love of Christ which passeth knowledge," then my little faith will become strong faith; the bruised reed shall become a cedar, and the smoking flax shall become a beacon flaming to the very skies. I must take care above all that I cultivate communion with Christ, for though that can never be the basis of my peace—mark that—yet it will be the channel of it. If I live near to Christ, I shall not know fear. What sheep is afraid of the wolf when it is close to the shepherd's hand? What child fears when it hangs upon its mother's breast? Who should know fear when he is covered with the eternal wings, and underneath him are the everlasting arms? "While his left-hand is under my head, and his right-hand doth embrace me." I cannot but be at peace, and that peace, if my communion is continued, will be like a river, deep and broad, my righteousness being like the waves of the sea. It is Christ, the substance of my salvation; Christ, the sum of all my hope; Christ who performeth all things for me, and Christ made of God all things to me. As Christ was the first means of giving us peace, so he must still be the golden conduit through which all peace with God must flow to our believing hearts, and that through the act of merely believing, or merely trusting in him. By looking to him I drew all the faith which inspired me with confidence in his grace. And the word that first drew my soul —"Look unto me"—still rings its clarion note in my ears. There I once found conversion, and there I shall often find refreshing and renewal.

Having thus glanced at the basis of our peace, and the channel through which it flows, let us pass on to notice its certainty. I like to read these rolling sentences of Paul, without an "if" or a but" in them—"Therefore, being justified, we have peace with God." He talks as logically as if he were a mathematician, and as positively as though he could see the thing written before his eyes. Oh, how different is this from the way in which some talk—"I hope," "I trust," "I sometimes hope my poor soul may have peace with God." Now where this language is genuine it deserves sympathy, but I believe in many cases it is cant. There is a certain class of professors who think strong faith is pride, and doubts and fears are humility; therefore they look upon these base-born thorns as though they were choice flowers, and they will cull them together like a bouquet of nettles and noxious weeds—a fool's nosegay. Have you never seen it in the Magazine? I have observed it not unfrequently. Or they will dig up a nasty ugly thorn, put it in a flower-pot, place it in an ornamental situation, display it outside the window, and call you all to admire it, as being a special, a wonderful piece of Christian experience. Well, one likes to see a thorn when it is developed to the highest degree, but as soon as seen, one likes to see it burnt; and so with these doubts and fears; it is very well for us to know how far doubting and fearing may go, but we think we would like to have them plucked up by the roots and destroyed as soon as possible. Let those who are the subjects of these doubts be sympathized and cheered, but let their doubts and fears be rooted out utterly. O Christian man, it is not impudence, it is not presumption to believe what God tells you. If he says "You *are* justified," do not say "I *hope* I am." If I should say to some poor man —one terribly poor—" I will pay your rent for you to-morrow," and he should say, "Well, well, I hope you will," I should not feel best pleased with him. If you should say to your child to-morrow morning, " Well, William, I shall buy you a new suit of clothes to-day," and he should say, "Well, father, I sometimes hope you will, I humbly trust, I hope I may say, though I sometimes doubt and fear, yet I hope I may say I believe you," you would not encourage such a child as that in his uncomely suspicions. Why should we talk thus to our dear Father who is in heaven? He says to us, "I give unto you eternal life and ye shall never perish, neither shall any pluck you out of my hand." Is it humility for us to reply, "Father, I do not believe you, I cannot think it is possible?" Oh, no; that is true humility which sits at the feet of the Promiser because it is humble; looks up into the face of the Promiser because it is trustful, and doats on the word of the promise, because it is sincere. He *will* perform it. Avaunt, ye fiends that make me doubt! His honour is engaged to the carrying out of his covenant; he *will* perform it. He says by faith in Christ I am justified; therefore I say, I am justified and have peace with God, nor shall anyone stop me of this glory—I have peace with God through Jesus Christ. I should like to hear you all talking in this way and getting rid of that old Babylonish jargon of "ifs" and "buts," and doubts and fears, fully persuaded that what he hath promised he will fulfil, as those who *do* believe what God has said, just because he has said it. Here is the certainty of justification by faith.

And now, as to the effect produced. When a man can say he has peace with God—what then? Why, the first effect is joy. Who can be at peace with God and have him for a Father, and yet be miserable? I think I told you one night that, years ago I was waited upon by a woman who wished to convert me to a novel sect that had come up with a false prophet at its head. She talked much and talked long, and talked all to no purpose; but at last I told her I thought it best that she should tell me her way in which she wished to be saved, on condition that she would let me tell her mine. I need not tell you what she said, but I said, "This is how I hope to be saved: it is said in God's Word, 'This is a faithful saying, and worthy of all acceptation, that Christ Jesus came into the world to save sinners;' and it is also written, 'he that believeth on him shall be saved.' Now, I do trust in him, and I believe that therefore I shall be saved; nay, more, I *am* saved; my sins are all forgiven. A perfect righteousness, namely, that of Christ, is cast about me, and I am so saved to-day, that nothing by any possibility shall ever destroy me. I am saved for ever." The woman said, "If I believed that that were true, I would very gladly give up my faith for anything so bright as that. But you," she said, "you ought to be the happiest man in the world." And I said, "I thank you for that word, and so will I be, God helping me, for I ought to be; I have the utmost cause." And so should every believer feel he ought to be, because this great salvation, this solid hope, this rocky foundation for our everlasting peace should give us quiet, and calm, and security, till our joy should overflow and become an anticipation and an antepast of the joy of heaven. This peace should give the believer, beyond and in addition to his joy, a calm resignation, nay, a delightful acquiescence in his Father's will. Now smite me if thou wilt, my Father, for I am thy friend and thou art mine; now send the flame, for it shall only chasten, but cannot kill; now take away my goods, for thou art my all and I cannot lose thee; now let the floods of trouble come, for thou art my ark, and though the floods come around me higher and higher, still I shall abide in thee, secure from reach of harm, whilst thou dost shut me in! Thus with calm composure the believer walks along over life's hills and dales, and when he comes to the valley of the shadow of death he fears no evil, for his God is with him, his rod and his staff do comfort him. What fear is there to the man that is at peace with God? Life?—God provides for it. Death?—Christ hath destroyed it. The Grave?—Christ hath rolled away the stone and broken the seal. Affliction, tribulation, famine, peril, or the sword? "Nay, in all these things we are more than conquerors through him that hath loved us." To have peace with God, beloved, I cannot tell you what innumerable streams of good shall flow to you from this ocean of pleasure, and these rivers of delight. I have but skimmed over one of these placid streams; there are hundreds of blessed practical results that are sure to follow from a certain conviction of our peace with God through Jesus Christ.

II. In drawing to a close, I want to address myself to THREE CHARACTERS THAT I HAVE NO DOUBT ARE REPRESENTED HERE IN THIS LARGE CONGREGATION.

There is a man here to-night—I know he is here, though I do not know his name—a man who many years ago was a professor of religion. He has never been easy in his conscience since he forsook the ways of God. There has been some trembling hope sometimes in him that there was a little life not quite extinct, and since he has come in hither, he feels quite like a stranger in the House of Prayer where once faces were so familiar, and there is perhaps a groaning in his spirit as he says, "O that I knew the way of peace, and the sense of peace for which in happier days I once enquired. I have lost my roll, if I ever had it; I have lost my character, and with my character my faith, and with my faith my hope. Can I ever be at peace with God?" Backslider, if thou ever hast been called by grace, let me ask thee this question. Dost thou remember the time when thou hadst a hope? Say, does not memory revive before thee that time, when on thy knees in agony thou didst cry unto him that heareth prayer, and the mercy came, and thy spirit rejoiced in pardon bought with blood? Man, thou dost remember it. The tear is on thy cheek now. Thou wast not a hypocrite—let us hope that it was not all hypocrisy—not all a lie and a delusion. You did feel then that Christ could save, and you did trust yourself with him. Now then, man, do the same to-night, and the dew of thy youth is restored unto thee. Thy leprosy is white upon thy brow, but wash thee in Jordan seven times, and thy flesh shall come again unto thee, even as a little child. Jehovah seeks thee. He cries unto thee to-night, and by the lips of his ambassador says, "Return, O backsliding children, return unto me for I am married unto you saith the Lord. Ye have wearied me with your sins, ye have made me to serve with your iniquities, but I, even I, am he that blotteth out thy transgressions for my name's sake, and will not remember thy sins."

> "To thy Father's bosom press'd,
> Once again a child confess'd,
> From his house no more to roam;
> Come and welcome, sinner come."

"Oh! but I have forsaken him." Lay aside thy "buts" and "ifs." He bids thee come. Avaunt, ye doubts and fears, and black despairing thoughts. The sinner comes, and Jesus meets him. There is the kiss of his love. "Take off his rags, clothe him, put shoes upon his feet, bring forth the fatted calf and kill it, and let us eat and be merry, for this my son which was dead is alive again, he was lost and is found. O, I would I could persuade thee—though thou art growing old now—I wish I could persuade thee to fling thyself at the foot of his dear cross again! His hands are still nailed—he has not moved them yet; his feet are still fast—he has not stirred from the place where he waits for thee; his arms still open wide. O believe him! He is love still, and the blood is mighty still, and the plea in heaven is all-prevailing still. "Believe in the Lord Jesus and thou shalt be saved." Then I wanted to have said a word to some here who are not backsliders exactly, but they have lost their peace for a little time. Many young Christians are subject to these little fits, in which their evidence gets dark and they lose their peace. I have no need to say more to you, brother and sister, while you are walking in darkness and see no light. "Let him trust," is a prophetic admonition—it shall be mine to-night. When you cannot see a single reason why you should be saved, except that God says you shall, let that be enough for you. When you have nothing here or there, and nothing anywhere to look to; when there is no hope for you except in that Man whose wounds are bleeding, always think that enough, and come to Christ just as you came at first. I find it very convenient to come every day to Christ as a sinner—as I came at first. "You are no saint," says the devil. Well, if I am not, I am a sinner, and Jesus Christ came into the world to save sinners. Sink or swim, there I go—other hope I have none.

> "And when thine eye of faith is dim,
> Still trust in Jesus, sink or swim;
> And at his footstool bow thy knee,
> For Israel's God thy peace shall be."

On Christ with all my weight I lean; and, as I throw myself upon my bed to sleep, so on Christ will I stretch myself full length to rest, for he is able and he is willing; and if he can fail, then he fails me and fails all his Church; but if he cannot, then I shall see his face in glory everlasting.

By your leave, I must have two or three words with those who never had peace. They shall be brief. I have no doubt I address many here who never had faith, and you are wanting to get it. I ask you, first of all, not to seek peace at all as the first object; for, if you want peace before you get grace, you want the flower before you get the root, and you will be apt to be like little children who, when they have a piece of garden given them, will go and pluck up the flowers out of their father's bed, and put the flowers into their own ground, and then say, "What a nice garden I have got!" But to their dismay, on the morrow all is withered. Better put the roots in and wait a week or two till they sprout, and then the flowers will be living ones, not borrowed ones. Do not seek after peace first. Seek after Christ first. Peace will come next. Still, I pray you, do not think that peace is a qualification for grace. If you fancy this, you will be in error indeed. You are to come to Christ as Nicodemus did, by night, that is, in the night of your ignorance, in the night of your fear and trouble; you must come just as you are, bringing nothing to Christ, but coming empty-handed. No money, no price, no fee, "nothing to pay." He asks of you but that you would take all gratis from his liberal hand. And will you please to remember, that if you put your eye on anything but Christ, or anything with Christ, so as to disturb your whole thought and attention from being directed exclusively to him, then peace will be an impossibility to you. If thine eye be single, thy whole body shall be full of light; but if ye mix another trust, and so your eye be evil, your whole body will be full of darkness. Do not trust your repentance, do not trust your faith, do not rely upon your feelings, do not depend upon your knowledge; above all, do not depend upon your sense of need, do not come to Christ as a sensible sinner, do not come trusting Christ, feeling that you are a man who has a right to come, that you answer to a certain character that may come; but come because you are a sinner, because you have nothing to recommend you, because, if God should search you through and through, he could not find a point in you, a spot in you large enough to put the point of a pin upon that which was good. Come because you are vile, to be pardoned; come, because you are black, to be washed; come, because you are penniless, to be made rich; but look for nothing else save in Christ. Write this for thy motto—"None but Jesus." Oh, men and brethren, if those Israelites of old, who were inside their houses that night, had gone outside to the lintel of their door-post, and said, "Now here is this lintel made of very common wood; we will paint and grain it;" and if they had then gone inside, and trusted to the painting and graining of the lintel, the destroying angel would have found them out and destroyed them. If, again, they had said, "We will write up our name over the door—it is a respectable name; we will record the list of our charities and good works over the door," the plague-angel would have smitten through the whole, and there would have been a wailing through the house as through the houses of the Egyptians. But what did they do? They took the blood; they marked the lintel and the two side posts, and smeared them with a crimsoned stain. Then in they went, and sat contentedly down, or stood at least in peace, and ate the passover with joy; and, while the shrieks of Egypt went up in the cold midnight air, the sons of Israel went up also into heaven, for the angel of death, when he spread his wings on the blast, had seen the blood, and by that mark he knew that he must pass by that habitation, and smite none that were there. The word of the Lord was not "When I see your faith," but "when I see the blood, I will pass over you." Oh, soul, if thou trustest Christ the blood is on thy brow to-night, before the eye of God no condemnation. Why, then, needest thou to fear? Thou art safe, for the blood secures every soul that once is sheltered thereby. Believe in the Lord Jesus Christ and thou shalt be saved, and if thou believest not, trust where thou mayest, thou shalt be damned. God help thee to believe in Christ for his name's sake. Amen.

4 The Jewel of Peace

"Now the Lord of peace himself give you peace always by all means. The Lord be with you all."—2 Thessalonians iii. 16.

WHEN the heart is full of love it finds the hand too feeble for its desires. Hence it seeks relief in intercession and benediction; wishing, praying and blessing where it cannot actually effect its loving purpose. The apostle would have done for the Thessalonians all the good that was conceivable had it been in his power, but his wishes far outstripped his abilities, and therefore he betook himself to interceding for them, and to invoking upon them the blessing of the Lord and Master whom he served. Here is a lesson for us in the art of doing good; as we lengthen the eyesight with the telescope, as we send our words afar by the telegraph, so let us extend our ability to do good by the constant use of intercessory prayer. Parents, when you have done all you can for your children yourselves, be thankful that you may introduce them to a further and greater blessing, by commending them to the care of the great Father in heaven. Friends, do your friends the best possible deed of friendship by asking for them the friendship of God. You who love the souls of men, when you have poured out all your strength on their behalf, bless God that there is still something more which you can do, for by earnest entreaties and supplications you may bring down from on high the effectual energy of the Holy Spirit, who can work in their hearts that which it is not in your power to accomplish. The apostle saw that the Thessalonians were much troubled, and he wrote the most encouraging words to cheer them, but he knew that he could not take the burden from off their hearts, and therefore he turned to the God of all consolation, and prayed him to give them peace always by all means. The slenderness of our power to bless others will be no detriment to them if it lead us to lay hold upon the eternal strength, for that will bring into the field a superior power to bless, and our infirmity will only make space for the display of divine grace.

Let us look first at *the many-sided blessing* which the apostle invokes,—peace; and then let us note *the special desirableness of it.* Thirdly, let us observe *from whom alone it comes;* and fourthly, note *the wide sweep of the apostolic prayer.*

I. First, then, let us look at THE MANY-SIDED BLESSING,—" The Lord of peace himself give you peace." Some have thought to restrict the expression to peace within the church, since disorderly members were evidently increasing among the Thessalonians; but that is a very straitened and niggardly interpretation, and it is never wise to narrow the meaning of God's word. Indeed, such a contracted explanation cannot be borne, for it does not appear that the disorderly persons mentioned in the chapter had as yet created any special disturbance: they had been quietly fattening at the expense of their generous brethren and would not be very eager to quarrel with the rack from which they fed. Although no doubt church quiet is included as one variety of peace, yet it would be a sad dwarfing of the meaning of the Spirit to consider one phase of the blessing to the neglect of the rest. No, the peace here meant is " the deep tranquillity of a soul resting on God," the quiet restfulness of spirit which is the peculiar gift of God, and the choice privilege of the believer. " Great peace have all they that love thy law, and nothing shall offend them."

The peace of the text is a gem with many facets, but in considering its many-sidedness we must remember that its main bearing is *toward God.* The deepest, best, and most worthy peace of the soul is its rest towards the Lord God himself. I trust we know this, and are enjoying it at this moment. We are no longer afraid of God: the sin which divided us from him is blotted out, and the distance which it created has ceased to be. The atonement has wrought perfect reconciliation and established everlasting peace. The terrors of God's law are effectually removed from us, and instead thereof we feel the drawings of his love. We are brought nigh by the atoning sacrifice, and have peace with God through Jesus Christ our Lord. We know that all his thoughts to us are thoughts of love, and we bless his name that our thoughts toward him are no longer those of the slave towards a taskmaster, or of a criminal towards a judge, but those of a beloved child towards a kind and tender father. Fervent love reigns in our hearts, casting out all fear and causing us to joy in God by our Lord Jesus Christ. This is a great blessing. It is surely a choice delight for a man to know that whether he prospers or is afflicted, whether he lives or dies, there is nothing between God and him but perfect amity; for all that offends has been effectually put away.

Beloved, when the apostle wishes us peace in the words of our text, he no doubt means that our hearts should be at perfect peace, by being placed fully in accord with the will of God; for, alas, we have known some, who we hope are forgiven and are God's children, who nevertheless quarrel with God very sadly. They are not pleased with what he does, but even complain that he deals hardly with them: they are naughty children, and carry on a sort of sullen contention with their heavenly Father, because he does not indulge them in all their whims and fancies. Now may the Lord of peace put an end to all such grievous warfare of heart in his people. May you love the Lord so well and trust him so fully that you could not pick a quarrel with him, even if he smote you and bruised you and broke your bones. Whatever he does is not only to be accepted with submission, but to be rejoiced in. That which pleases him should please us. Then have we perfect peace when we can magnify and praise the Lord even for the sharp cuts of his rod, and the fierce fires of his furnace. May the Lord bring us into this state, for there is no joy like it; perfect peace with God is heaven below.

Yea, brethren, we reach a little further than reconciliation and submission, for we come into the enjoyment of conscious complacency. There are men who are at peace with God as to the forgiveness of sin, and in a measure are in accord with his will, but they are not walking carefully in the path of obedience, and so they are missing the sense of divine love. God is their Father, and he loves them, but he hides his face from them; they walk contrary to him, and so he walks contrary to them. We cannot consider such a condition to be one of the fullest peace. The truly restful state of mind is enjoyed when the heart and life are daily cleansed by grace, so that there is nothing to grieve the Spirit of God, and therefore the Lord feels it right to favour his child with the light of his countenance in full meridian splendour. O how blessed to bask in the sunlight of Jehovah's love, free from all doubt, and having no more conscience of sin ! In that sense of conscious favour lies the rest of heaven. May the Lord of peace himself give us this peace.

Peace because sin is forgiven, is the sweet fruit of justification— " therefore being justified by faith, we have peace with God." Peace because the heart is renewed and made to agree with the will of God is the blessed result of sanctification, for "to be spiritually minded is life and peace." Peace, because the soul is conscious of being the object of divine love, is a precious attendant upon the spirit of adoption, which is the very essence of peace. Brethren in Christ, may this threefold peace with God be with you always.

Now we look further and note that this peace spreads itself abroad and covers *all things* with its soft light. God is great, and filleth all things, and he who becomes at peace with him is at peace with all things else. Being reconciled to God, the believer says,—All things are mine, whether things present or things to come; all are mine, for I am Christ's and Christ is God's. Behold the Lord has made us to be in league with the stones of the field, and the beasts of the field are at peace with us. Providence is our pavilion, and angels are our attendants. All things work together for our good, now that we love God and are the called according to his purpose. No longer are we afraid for the terror by night, nor for the arrow that flieth by day, nor for the pestilence that walketh in darkness, nor for the destruction which wasteth at noonday. Behold the Lord God covereth us with his feathers, and under his wings do we trust ; his truth is our shield and buckler: because we have set our love upon him he doth deliver us, and he doth set us on high because we have known his name. At peace with the Lord of hosts we are at peace with all the armies of the universe, in alliance with all the forces which muster at Jehovah's bidding. Though we must be at war with Satan, yet even he is chained and made as a slave to accomplish purposes of good contrary to his own will. There is neither in heaven nor earth nor hell anything that we need fear when we are once right with God. Settle the centre, and the circumference is secure : peace with God is universal peace.

This practically shows itself in the Christian's inward peace with regard to *his present circumstances*, be they what they may. Being at peace with God he sees the Lord's hand in everything around him, and is content. Is he poor? The Lord makes him rich in faith, and he asks not for gold. Is he sick ? The Lord endows him with patience, and he glories in his afflictions. Is he laid aside from the holy service which he so much loves ? He feels that the Lord knows best. If he might be actively engaged in doing God's will he would be very thankful, and run with diligence the race set before him ; but if he must lie in the hospital, and suffer rather than serve, he does not wish to put his own wishes before the will of his Master, but he leaves himself in the Lord's hands, saying, " Lord, do as thou wilt with me. I am so at peace with thee that if thou use me I will bless thee, and if thou lay me aside I will bless thee : if thou spare my life I will bless thee, and if thou bring me down to the grave I will bless thee ; if thou honour me among men I will bless thee, and if thou make me to be trodden under foot like straw for the dunghill I will still bless thee : for thou art everything, and I am nothing, thou art all goodness and I am sin and emptiness." The soul which thus has perfect peace as to all its personal surroundings is indeed happy ; it is lying down in green pastures beside the still waters.

Blessed be God this peace is mainly to be found *in the soul itself* as to its own thoughts, believings, hopings, expectations, and desires. We have not only peace towards the outer world, but peace within. After all, happiness and peace lie more within the man than in anything about him. Heaven lies more in the heart than in golden streets, and hell's flame consists rather in man's tortured conscience than in the Tophet fire which the breath of God has kindled. So the peace which Jesus gives is within us ; " the good man is satisfied from himself." Some minds are strangers to peace. How can they have peace, for they have no faith? They are as a rolling thing before the whirlwind, having no fixed basis, no abiding foundation of belief. These are the darlings of the school of modern thought, whose disciples set themselves as industriously to breed doubt as if salvation came by it. Doubt and be saved is their gospel, and who does not see that this is not the gospel of peace? Forsooth they are receptive, and are peering about for fresh light, though long ago the Sun of Righteousness has arisen. Such uncertainty suits me not. I must *know* something or I cannot live : I must be sure of something or I have no motive from which to act. God never meant us to live in perpetual questioning. His revelation is not and cannot be that shapeless cloud which philosophical divines make it out to be. There must be something true, and Christ must have come into the world to teach us something saving and reliable ; he cannot mean that we should be always rushing through bogs and into morasses after the will-of-the-wisp of intellectual religion. There is assuredly some ascertainable, infallible, revealed truth for common people ; there must be something sure to rest upon. I know that it is so, and declare unto you what I have heard and seen. There are great truths which the Lord has engraven upon my very soul, concerning which all the men on earth and all the devils in hell cannot shake me. As to these vital doctrines, an immovable and unconquerable dogmatism has laid hold upon my soul, and therefore my mind has peace. A man's mind must come to a settlement upon eternal truths by the teaching of the Holy Ghost, or else he cannot know what peace is.

I would ask for every one of my brethren that they may find an anchorage of mind and heart and never leave it. We have been often spoken of as an old-fashioned church, and your minister is said to be *Ultimus Puritanorum*, the last of the Puritans, a man incapable of any thought beyond the limit of the old-fashioned theology. I bless the Lord that it is even so. I am indeed incapable of forsaking the gospel for these new-fangled theories. Down went my anchor years ago: it was a great relief to me when I first felt it grip, and it is a growing joy to me that I know whom I have believed, and am persuaded that he is able to keep that which I have committed to him. Pretensions to original thought I have never made. I invent nothing, I only tell the old, old story as God enables me. "Ah," said a certain divine to me one day, "it must be very easy to you to preach because you know what you are going to say; your views are fixed and stereotyped. As for me," he said, "I am always seeking after truth, and I do not know one week what I may preach the next." Thus speak the teachers—do you wonder if the disciples wander into scepticism? Has the Lord taught the man nothing of sure truth? Then let him wait till he has received his message. Till he knows the gospel in his own heart experimentally as the power of God unto salvation let him sit on the penitent form and ask to be prayed for, but never enter a pulpit. What are the churches at to tolerate these sowers of infidelity? Time was when the fathers in our Israel would have chased from their pulpits those who glory in the unbelief which is their shame. May the Lord of peace himself give you peace as to your personal beliefs and convictions, and then when you get into deep waters of trial and sorrow you will say, "Ah, I did believe the right doctrine after all. I can feel the grip of my anchor on the things unseen. I have not been deceived. I have not followed cunningly devised fables, for the promise is true and I feel the power of it, it sustains and cheers and comforts me under all my trials, and I know that it will do so even to my dying hour." May every troubled thinker find the peace of faith and never lose it.

Many minds are for ever restless as to their fears. It is a great thing to know what you tremble at, for when you know what you fear your fear is half gone. The indefinable shape, the mysterious hand which has no arm, but writes upon the wall in strange characters,—the cloudiness of all things dreaded makes the mind more restless. But blessed is the man to whom the Lord has taught his fear, so that he knows what he fears, and does not permit his hopes to be in perpetual eclipse.

Of this many-sided peace we must say something more. The Thessalonian church had been troubled three ways. They had been *persecuted from without*. That is not a pleasant thing, but the apostle says, "You that are troubled rest with us." Now, when the Lord Jesus Christ says to a persecuted saint, "I am with you: all the evil which is done unto you is done unto me, and you are bearing it for my name's sake," then, beloved, no persecution can break the peace of the soul, but rather the sufferer rejoices and is exceeding glad that he is counted worthy, not only to believe in Christ, but to suffer for his sake.

Next, the Thessalonian church was annoyed by certain *false teachers*. They did not absolutely teach novel doctrine, but upon a basis of truth they erected an edifice of error. They exaggerated one special truth, and carried its teaching to extravagance. They said, Christ is coming, therefore the day of the Lord is immediately at hand. They belonged to that order of fanatics who are always raving about " the signs of the times," and pretending to know what will happen within the next twenty years. There were impostors of that sort in Paul's day, and there are such impostors now. Believe them not, they can see no more of the future than blind horses. I put them all together as impostors, whether they are preachers or literary hacks, for no man knoweth the future, and no man can tell his fellow about it. I care no more for their explanations of prophecy than for the pretended winking of the eyes of the Madonna; yet will they continue the cheat, and will be saying, one this thing, and another that, that this and that wonder shall happen, and that terrible judgments shall overwhelm our nation. The apostle would not have the Thessalonians disturbed in their minds by fears about the future. Brethren in Christ, the most terrible fact of the future can be no just cause of alarm to a true believer. The Lord comforts his people, and there is nothing in his plans or purposes which is intended to disquiet them. You may rest assured that if any doctrine in the Bible prevents a godly man from enjoying peace it must be because he has not yet understood it fully, or else has mistaken its bearing towards himself. Truth must minister peace to true men. All truth, whether doctrinal or prophetic, is on the side of the children of God; how can it be otherwise? The apostle tells the Thessalonians not to be disturbed about the coming of Christ. "The Lord be with you all," saith he, and if the Lord be with us, what matters it to us whether he personally comes at once or chooses to delay? We should be looking for his coming, but not with alarm, for the fact that he has come already is a well-spring of delight. We glory in his first advent, and do not dread the second: since we are already raised up into the heavenly places to sit with him by faith, what matters it to us whether he is up there or down here, or whether we are in heaven or on earth, so long as we abide in him. There may arise, possibly there will arise, wild fanatics who will again spread alarming news about wars and rumours of wars, and select some fatal year as the end of all things. Well, if such things should be, if crowds should go into the wilderness or into the city to look for the coming of Christ, believe them not, but sit ye still in peace and tranquillity of spirit and say, " My soul loves him and he loves me. He cannot mean ill to me whether he destroys the earth or spares it. Though the heavens pass away and the earth itself melt with fervent heat, my heart is resting in her Lord and knows herself to be secure." Thus the Lord saves his people from the disturbance caused by false teaching.

There were also in the church disorderly characters, people that went about spreading idle tales and gossiping. They would not do anything for a living, and so they set people by the ears. But when the Lord gives a Christian man deep spiritual peace within, he soon puts aside the small nuisances of idle tongues and disorderly deeds. He refuses to be worried. Mosquitoes buzz around every Christian church, and blessed is the man who does not feel their bite or heed their buzzing; his soul shall dwell at ease. Peace from church troublers is a great blessing, and we ought to praise God for it when we are in the enjoyment of it, for strife within the church, like civil war, is the worst of warfare. O to live in holy love and unbroken concord in reference to all our fellow Christians. May the Lord of peace grant us this.

Thus, you see, the peace which is here spoken of has many sides to it. May you possess it in all its forms, modes, and phases, and may your spirit enter into the peace of God which passeth all understanding.

II. Now, secondly, let us note THE SPECIAL DESIRABLENESS OF PEACE. It is a very great thing for a soul to realize perfect peace, for if it does not do so, it must miss the joy, and comfort, and blessedness of the Christian life. God never meant his children to be like thistledown, wafted about with every breath, nor as a football, hurled to and fro by every foot. He meant us to be a happy, restful, established people. The cattle crop the grass, but they are not fattened till they lie down and ruminate in peace: the Lord makes his people to feed and to lie down in quietness. You do not know the gospel, dear friends, if you have not obtained peace through it; peace is the juice, the essence, the soul of the gospel. Doctrines are clusters, but you have never trodden them in the wine vat, you have never quaffed the flowing juice of their grapes if you have not peacefully considered divine truth in the quiet of your heart.

Without peace you cannot grow. A shepherd may find good pasture for his flock, but if his sheep are hunted about by wild dogs, so that they cannot rest, they will become mere skin and bone. The Lord's lambs cannot grow if they are worried and harried; they must enjoy the rest wherewith the Lord maketh the weary to rest. If your soul is always sighing, and moaning, and questioning its interest in Christ, if you are always in suspense as to what doctrine is true and what is false, if there is nothing established and settled about you, you will never come to the fulness of the stature of a man in Christ Jesus.

Neither without peace can you bear much fruit, if any. If a tree is frequently transplanted you cannot reasonably look for many golden apples upon its boughs. The man who has no root-hold, who neither believes, nor grasps, nor enjoys the gospel, can never know what it is to be steadfast, unmovable, neither will he be always abounding in the work of the Lord.

We know, too, some who, because they have no conscious peace with God, lack all stability, and are the prey of error. That doctrine can soon be driven out of a man's head which affords no light and comfort to his heart. If you derive no sweetness from what you believe, I should not marvel if you soon begin to doubt it. The power of the gospel is its best evidence to the soul; a man always believes in that which he enjoys. Only make a truth to be a man's spiritual food, let it be marrow and fatness to him, and I warrant you he will believe it. When truth becomes to a proud carnal mind what the manna became to murmuring Israel, namely, light bread that his soul abhorreth, then the puffed up intellect cries after something more pleasing to the flesh; but to the mind which hungers and thirsts after righteousness the gospel is so soul-satisfying that it never wearies of it.

Brethren, you must have peace for your soul's wealth. What a difference there is between a soul at peace and a soul continually tossed about! I have seen one man's heart like a country whose hedges are broken down, whose walls are laid level with the ground, where irrigation is neglected, where tilling has ceased, where the vines are untrimmed, where the fields are unploughed, and all because there is a perpetual sound of war in the soul, and the song of peace is never heard. Such a soul may be likened to the Holy Land beneath Turkish rule, where no man has rest, and consequently the highways lie waste, and the gardens are a desert. But I have seen another man's life which has grown up under the influence of holy peace, from whom God has kept back the wandering Arabs of doubt and fear, and to whom he has given a settled government of grace and an establishment in steadfastness and quiet assurance, and, lo, that man has been as the land which floweth with milk and honey. As war spends and peace gathers the riches of nations, so does inward strife devour us, while spiritual peace makes the soul fat. Even as Palestine when it abounded in corn and wine and oil could nourish Tyre and Sidon, which border thereon, even so does the man who is rich towards God through internal peace become a feeder of other souls, till even they who are but borderers upon Immanuel's land obtain a blessing. Beloved, I would that every Christian knew this soul-enriching peace to the full. I am sorry to meet with so many who "hope" they are believers, and "trust" they are saved, but they are not sure. Ah, brethren, in these matters we must get beyond mere hopes, we must reach to certainties. "Ifs" and "buts" are terrible in the things which concern the soul and eternity. We must have plain and unquestionable security here, divine security applied to the soul itself by the Holy Ghost. Friend, you are either saved this morning or you are not saved; either you are in the love of God, or you are not; either you are secure of heaven, or you are not—one of the two. I beseech you, do not let these things be in jeopardy; chance anything rather than your soul. Cry mightily to God that you may have these things fixed, certain, positive, beyond all dispute, for then shall your soul enjoy peace with God, and so shall you become strong, useful, and happy.

III. Now, thirdly, we shall get into the very heart of our text while we consider for a minute or two THE SOLE PERSON FROM WHOM THIS PEACE MUST COME,—" Now the Lord of peace himself give you peace." Who is this "Lord of peace" but the Lord Jesus, the Prince of peace, born into the world when there was peace all over the world? It was but a little interval in which the gates of the temple of war were closed, and lo, Jesus came to Bethlehem, and angels sang, "Peace on earth." He came to establish an empire of peace which shall be universal, and under whose influence they shall hang the useless helmet high and study war no more. "The Prince of peace!" How blessed is the title! So was it written of old by Esaias, and Paul, the true successor of Isaiah, changing but a word, now speaks of "the Lord of peace." This is he who, being in himself essential peace, undertook to be the Father's great Ambassador, and having made peace by the blood of his cross, ended the strife between man and his offended Maker. This is he who is our peace, who hath made Jew and Gentile one, and broken down the middle wall of partition which stood between us. This is the Lord who, when he stood in the midst of his disciples, gave them peace by saying, "Peace be unto you"; and this is he who in his departure made his last will and testament, and wrote therein this grand legacy— "Peace I leave with you, my peace I give unto you; not as the world giveth give I unto you." This is that Lord of peace to whom it is part of his nature and office to give peace.

I want to call particular attention to the apostle's words in this place. He does not say "May the Lord of peace send his angel to give you peace." It were a great mercy if he did, and we might be as glad as Jacob was at Mahanaim, when the angels of God met him. He does not even say, "May the Lord of peace send his minister to give you peace." If he did we might be as happy as Abraham when Melchizedec refreshed him with bread and wine. He does not even say, "May the Lord of peace at the communion table, or in reading the word, or in prayer, or in some other sacred exercise give you peace." In all these we might well be as refreshed as Israel was at Elim where wells and palm trees gladdened the tribes; but he says "the Lord of peace *himself* give you peace," as if he alone in his own person could give peace, and as if his presence were the sole means of such a divine peace as he desires.

"The Lord of peace himself give you peace." The words are inexpressibly sweet to me. If you will think for a minute you will see that we never do obtain peace except from the Lord himself. What after all in your worst times will bring you peace? I will tell you. "This man shall be the peace." To me it has often afforded great peace to think of his mysterious person. He is a man tempted in all points like as I am, a man who knows every grief of the soul and every pain of the body, hence his tender sympathy and power to succour. Have you not often derived peace from that sweet reflection? You know you have. His person then is a source of peace. And have you not been rested in your soul by meditating upon his death? You have viewed him wounded, bleeding, dying on the tree; and, insensibly to yourself, a wondrous calm has stolen over your heart, and you have felt pacified concerning all things. Yes, Jesus is himself that bundle of myrrh and spice from which peace flows like a sweet perfume. When he comes very near your heart and lays bare his wounds, and speaks his love home to you, making you feel its divine fervency, when he assures you that you are one with him, united to him in an everlasting wedlock, which knows of no divorce—then it is that your soul is steeped in peace. This is an experimental business and no mere words can express it. "The Lord of peace himself give you peace,"—this, I say, he does mainly by manifesting himself to the heart of his servants.

Then notice that the text says, "*give* you peace," not merely offer it to you, or argue with you that you ought to have peace, or show you the grounds of peace, but "give you peace." He has the power to breathe peace into the heart, to create peace in the soul, and lull the spirit into that sweet sleep of the beloved which is the peculiar gift of heaven. "I will give you rest," said he, and he can and will do it.

"*The Lord be with you all*": as much as to say, "That is what I mean." I pray that Jesus may be with you, for if he is present you must enjoy peace. Let the sea rage and let every timber of the ship be strained; yea, let her leak till between each timber there yawns a hungry mouth to swallow you up quick; yet when Jesus arises he will rebuke the winds and the waves, and there will be a great calm. "It is I, be not afraid," is enough to create peace at once. May you always know this peace which Jesus alone can give.

IV. Now I must conclude with the fourth head, which is a consideration of THE SWEEP OF THE PRAYER—"The Lord of peace himself give you peace *always*."

What! *always* at peace? Yes, that is what the apostle desires for you. May you have peace given you *always*. "Well, sir, I feel very happy on Sabbath-days. I have such peace that I wish I could have a week of Sundays." May the Lord himself give you peace *always*, on all the week days as well as on the Lord's days. "Truly, I have been very happy of late," says one, "God has prospered us and everyone has been very loving in the family; but I do not know how I should be if I had an awkward husband and unruly children." Sister, I will tell you what I want you to be,—I would have you restful under all circumstances,—"The Lord of peace give you peace always." "I enjoy such peace in the prayer-meeting," says one. I want you to have peace in the workshop also. "I do have peace when I get alone with my Bible," cries another. We pray that you may have equal peace when you are troubled with the ledger, and tired with those unpaid bills, and dull trade, and cross currents of business. You need peace always. Our friends who are commonly called Quakers have, as a rule, set us a fine example of calm, dignified quietness and peace. How undisturbed they generally appear. Whatever they fail in they certainly excel in a certain peacefulness of manner which I hope is the index of calm enjoyed within. Numbers of professors are very fretful, excitable, agitated, hasty, and fickle. It should not be so, brethren; you ought to have more weight about you, more grace, more solidity. Your soul's affairs are all right, are they not? All is right for ever, everything is signed, sealed, and delivered; the covenant is ordered in all things and sure, and everything is in divine hands for our good. Well, then, why not let us be as happy as the angels are? Why are we troubled? Is there anything worth shedding a tear for now that all is well for eternity? Our want of peace arises from the fact that we have not realized the fulness of our text. "The Lord of peace himself give you peace always." He can always give you peace, for he never changes; there is always the same reason for peace; you may always go to him for peace, and he is always ready to bestow it. Oh that we might always possess it!

Notice, again, it is written—"May the Lord of peace give you peace always *by all means*." Can he give us peace by all means? I know he can give us peace by some means, but can all means be made subservient to this end? Some agencies evidently work towards peace, but can he give us peace by opposing forces? Yes, certainly: he can give peace by the bitter as well as by the sweet, peace by the storm as well as by the calm, peace by loss as well as by gain, peace by death as well as by life. For, notice there are two grand ways of giving us peace: and one is by taking away all that disquiets us. Here is a man who frets because he does not make money, or because he has lost much of his wealth. Suppose the Lord takes away from him all covetousness, all greed of gain, all love of the world—is he not at once filled with peace? He is at peace not because he has more money, but because he has less of grasping desire. Another man is very ambitious, he wants to be somebody, he must be great, and yet he never will be, and therefore he is restless. Suppose the grace of God should humble him and take away his lofty aspirations, so that he only wishes to be and to do what the Lord wills. Do you not see how readily he rests? Another man has an angry temper, and is soon put out: the Lord does not alter the people that are round about him, but he changes the man himself, makes him quiet, ready to forgive, and of a gentle spirit. What peace the man now feels! Another person has had an envious eye—he did not like to see others prosper, and if others were better off than himself he always thought hardly of them. The Lord wrings that bitter drop of envy out of his heart, and now see how peaceful he is—he is glad to see others advanced, and if he is tried himself it helps to make him happy to think that others are more favoured. It is a great blessing when the Lord removes the disturbing elements from the heart. Even curiosity may be a source of unrest. Many are a great deal worried by curiosity. I have sometimes wanted to know why the Lord does this and that with me. Blessed be his name, I am resolved not to question him any more in that fashion. Somebody prayed the other day that I might see the reason why the Lord has lately afflicted me. I hope the brother will not pray that any more, for I do not want to know the Lord's reasons—why should I? I know he has done right, and I will not dishonour him by catechising him and wanting him to explain himself to a poor worm. This is where the mischief has been with most of us, that we have wanted to see how this and that can be right. Why should we? If God conceals a thing let us be anxious to keep it concealed. A servant was passing through a street with a dish that was curiously covered. There met him a fellow who said, "I am most anxious to know what thy lord has put in that dish, for he has so carefully covered it." But the servant said, "Therefore shouldst thou not desire to know, for seeing my lord has so carefully covered it, it is clear that it is no business of thine." So whenever a providence puzzles you take it as a sign that the Lord does not mean you to understand it, and be content to take it upon faith. When curiosity and other restless things are gone peace is enjoyed.

Then the Lord has ways of giving us peace by making discoveries of himself. Some of you do not know as yet the things which would give you peace. For instance, if you did but know that he loved you from before the foundation of the world, and that whom once he loves he never leaves, you who are now afraid that you have fallen from grace would obtain strong consolation. Ay, and if you understood the grand doctrine of the divine decree, and saw that the Lord will not fail nor be discouraged, nor turn aside from one jot or tittle of his purpose, then you would see how you, poor insignificant believers though you be, are one stitch in the great fabric that must not be suffered to drop, or else the whole fabric will be marred. You would understand how the eternal purpose ordered in wisdom, and backed up with sovereign power, guarantees your salvation as much as it does the glory of God, and so you would have peace.

Many a soul has not the peace it might have, because it does not fully understand the atoning blood. The great doctrine of substitution is not seen in all its length and breadth by some minds. But when they come to see Christ standing in the place of his chosen, made sin for them, and the chosen standing in Christ's place, "the righteousness of God in him," then will their peace be like a river. The grand truth of the union of the saints with Christ, if it be once understood, what a means of peace it is! He that believeth in Christ is one with him, a member of his body, of his flesh, and of his bones, one with Christ by eternal and indissoluble union, even as the Father is one with the Son. If this be known, together with the doctrine of the covenant, the attribute of immutability, the eternal purpose, and the marriage union between Christ and his elect, deep peace must be enjoyed, like the calm of heaven, like the bliss of immortality.

But there are some to whom this peace cannot come, some concerning whom the Lord saith "What hast thou to do with peace?" "There is no peace, saith my God, unto the wicked." Your works, your prayers, your repentances, none of these can bring you peace. As for the world and the pleasures thereof, they are destructive to all hope of peace. Come ye this day and believe in the great sacrifice which God himself has prepared in the person of his crucified Son. Come look into Emanuel's face and read where peace is to be found. Come to the great gash in Jesus' side and see the cleft of the rock where God's elect abide in peace. Trust in Jesus and you shall begin a peace which shall widen and deepen into the peace of God which passeth all understanding, which shall keep your hearts and minds by Christ Jesus. Amen.

5 The Peace of God

"And the peace of God, which passeth all understanding, shall keep your hearts and minds through Christ Jesus."—Philippians iv. 7.

"PEACE" is a heavenly word. When at the advent of our Lord angels came to sing among men a midnight sonnet their second note was "Peace on earth." Would God the shining ones would chant that song again till yonder Balkans heard the strain, and shook off the sulphurous cloud which now hangs around them. Those who have ever seen war, or even come near the trail of its bloody march, will be thankful to God for peace. I am almost of his mind who said that the worst peace is preferable to the very best war that was ever waged, if best there can be where all is bad as bad can be. Peace is most pleasant when religion sits beneath its shade, and offers her joyful vows to heaven. How grateful we ought to be that we can meet together to worship God after that form which best satisfies our consciences without any fear of being hunted down by the authorities of the land. We have no watchman on the hill tops looking out for Claverhouse's dragoons. We put none at the front door of our conventicle to watch lest the constable should come to take off worshipper and minister, that they may suffer imprisonment or fine. We worship God in unlimited liberty, and we ought to be exceedingly glad of the privilege, and infinitely more grateful for it than we are. Do we not sit every man under his own vine and fig tree, none making us afraid? Blessed is the land in which we dwell, and blessed are the days in which we live, when in all peace and quietness we worship God in public and sing his high praises as loudly as we please. Great God of peace, thou hast given us this peace, and in remembrance of our hunted forefathers we bless thee with our whole hearts!

We have met to-night for the purpose of hearing the gospel of peace, and many of us are afterwards coming to that sacred festival which celebrates peace, and is to all time the memorial of the great peace-making between God and man. And yet it may be that even all believers here are not quite at peace. Possibly you did not leave your family in peace this afternoon. Jars occur even among loving hearts. Alas! even Sabbaths are sometimes disturbed, for evil tempers cannot be bound over to keep the peace, but are riotous even on this sweet restful day. Do Christian men ever permit angry feelings to rise within them? If they do, I am sure that even in coming away from home to the house of God, they come with a disturbed mind. Ah, how insignificant a matter will mar our peace of mind: some little thing that happened in getting to your pew—some trifling incident even while you are in it, waiting for worship to begin, may, like dust in your eye, cause you the greatest distress. Such poor creatures are we that we may lose our peace of mind even by a word or a look. Peace, in the form of perfect calm and serenity, is a very delicate and sensitive thing, and needs more careful handling than a Venice glass. It is hard for the sea of our heart to remain long in a smooth and glassy state, it may be rippled and ruffled by an infant's breath. Perhaps, too, some of my brothers and sisters here have not been walking near to God; and if so their peace will not be perfect. It may be, my brother, that during the week you have backslidden somewhat from your true standing; and if so, your peace has fled. Your heart is troubled, and though you are believing in Christ for salvation, and are therefore safe, yet for all that your inward rest may be broken; therefore would I turn the text into a prayer, and pray for myself and for every believer in Jesus Christ—that the peace of God which passeth all understanding may now keep our hearts and minds through Christ Jesus. May you all know the text by experience. He who wrote it had felt it; may we who read it feel it too. Paul had oftentimes enjoyed the brightness of peace in the darkness of a dungeon, and he had felt living peace in prospect of a sudden and cruel death. He loved peace, preached peace, lived in peace, died in peace, and behold he hath entered into the fruition of peace, and dwells in peace before the throne of God.

Looking at the text, and thinking how we might handle it best to our profit, I thought we would notice first of all *the unspeakable privilege*—"the peace of God, which passeth all understanding." Then, secondly, I thought that we might gather, from its connection, *the method of coming at it*; for the preceding sentences are linked on to our text by the word "and," which is not an incidental conjunction, but is placed there with a purpose. Paul means to say that if we do what he bids us do in the fourth, fifth, and sixth verses, then the peace of God shall keep our hearts and minds. When we have looked at that matter for a few minutes, I shall want your careful attention, in the third place, to *the power of its operation*—for the peace of God "*shall* keep your hearts and minds"; and then we shall close, in the fourth place, by noticing *the sphere of its action*, namely "in Christ Jesus": the word should have been "in" rather than "through"—"shall keep your hearts and minds in Christ Jesus." May the Holy Spirit, who is the spirit of peace, now lead us into the centre and secret of our text.

I. First, then, here is AN UNSPEAKABLE PRIVILEGE—one of which it is very hard to speak, because it passeth all understanding, and therefore, you may be sure, it must pass all description. It is one of those things which can be more readily experienced than explained. Good Joseph Stennett was right when he spoke of those who

> "Draw from heaven that sweet repose
> Which none but he that feels it knows."

We may talk about inward rest, and dilate upon the peace of God, and select the most choice expressions to declare the delicacy of its enjoyment, but we cannot convey to others the knowledge at second hand; they must feel it, or they cannot understand it. If I were speaking to little children I would illustrate my point by the story of the boy at one of our mission stations who had a piece of loaf sugar given him one day at school. He had not before tasted such essence of sweetness, and when he went home to his father, he told him that he had eaten something which was wonderfully sweet. His father said, "Was it as sweet as such a fruit?" "It was far sweeter than that." "Was it as sweet as such and such a food?" which he mentioned. "It was much sweeter than that. But father," said he, "I cannot tell you." He rushed out of the house back to the mission house, begged a piece of sugar, got it, and brought it back, and said, "Father, taste and see, and then you will know how sweet it is." So I venture to use that simple illustration and say, "O taste and see that the peace of God is good," for in very deed it surpasseth all the tongues of men and of angels to set it forth.

What is the peace of God? I would describe it first by saying it is, of course, *peace with God*, peace of conscience, actual peace with the Most High through the atoning sacrifice. Reconciliation, forgiveness, restoration to favour there must be, and the soul must be aware of it: there can be no peace of God apart from justification through the blood and righteousness of Jesus Christ received by faith. A man conscious of being guilty can never know the peace of God till he becomes equally conscious of being forgiven. When his consciousness of pardon shall become as strong and vivid as his consciousness of guilt had been, then will he enter into the enjoyment of the peace of God which passeth all understanding. Dear brothers and sisters in Christ—you that have believed in Jesus—there is perfect peace between you and God now: "Therefore being justified by faith, we have peace with God." Your sin was the ground of the quarrel; but it has gone, it has ceased to be, it is blotted out, it is cast into the depth of the sea. As far as the east is from the west, so far hath he removed our transgressions from us. Our divine scapegoat has carried our iniquities into the wilderness. Our Lord and Master has finished transgression, made an end of sin, and brought in everlasting righteousness. The cause of offence is gone, and gone for ever: Jesus hath taken our guilt, hath suffered in our stead, hath made full compensation to the injured law, and vindicated justice to the very highest; and now there is nothing which can excite the anger of God towards us, for our sin is removed, and our unrighteousness is covered. We are reconciled to God by Christ Jesus, and accepted in the Beloved.

Now this actual reconciliation brings to the heart a profound sense of peace. O that all of you possessed it now! O that those who know it knew it more fully! Remember, O soul, if Christ did indeed suffer in your stead and was made a curse for thee, justice can never require at thy hands the penalty which thy Surety has discharged: for this would be to dishonour his sacrifice by making it of none effect. If Jesus stood as thy Substitute, and bore what God required as the vindication of his law, then thou art clear, beyond all hazard clear for ever, saved in the Lord with an everlasting salvation. If it were not so, why was there a Substitute permitted? Did God design to tantalize mankind by permitting an ineffectual substitution? What did that Substitute accomplish after all if he did not save those for whom he died? What meaning is there in the gospel if it does not reveal an effectual atonement? But truly the Lord Jesus was made sin for us, and the chastisement of our peace was upon him, and by his stripes we are saved. Here the soul rests: at the foot of the cross it finds a peace it never could have found elsewhere. I hope that many of you are now able to sing

> "Jesus was punish'd in my stead,
> Without the gate my Surety bled
> To expiate my stain:
> On earth the Godhead deign'd to dwell,
> And made of infinite avail
> The sufferings of the man.
>
> "And was he for such rebels given?
> He was; the Incarnate King of Heaven
> Did for his foes expire:
> Amazed, O earth, the tidings hear;
> He bore, that we might never bear
> His Father's righteous ire."

There take your full of peace, for by this sacrifice a covenant of peace is now established between you and your God, and it is sealed by atoning blood.

"The peace of God, which passeth all understanding" also takes a second form, namely, that of *a consequent peace in the little kingdom within.* When we know that we are forgiven and that we are at peace with God things within us come to a sudden and delightful change. By nature everything in our inner nature is at war with itself: it is a cage of evil beasts all rending and devouring each other. Man is out of order: out of order with God, with the universe, and with himself. The machinery of manhood has fallen into serious disorder; its cogs and wheels do not work in due harmony, but miss their touch and stroke. The passions, instead of being ruled by reason, often demand to hold the reins; and reason, instead of being guided by the knowledge which God communicates by his word, chooses to obey a depraved imagination, and demands to become a separate power and to judge God himself. There is not a faculty of our nature which is not in rebellion against God, and consequently in a state of confusion with regard to the rest of our system. A cruel internal war often rages among our mental powers, animal instincts, and moral faculties, causing distress, fear and unhappiness. There is no cure for this but restoring grace. O man, you cannot get your heart right, you cannot get your conscience right, you cannot get your understanding right, you cannot bring your various powers to their bearings and make them act in true harmony till first you are right with God. The King must occupy the throne, and then the estate of Mansoul will be duly settled, but till the chief authority has due eminence rebellion and riot will continue. When the Lord breathes peace into a man, and the Holy Spirit descends like a dove to dwell within the soul, then is there quiet: where all was chaos order appears, the man is created anew, and becomes a new creature in Christ Jesus; and though rebellious lusts still try to get the mastery, yet there is now a ruling power which keeps the man in order so that within him there is "the peace of God, which passeth all understanding."

This leads on to *peace in reference to all outward circumstances* by reason of our confidence that God ordereth them all rightly, and arranges them all for our good. The man who believes in Jesus and is reconciled to God has nothing outside of him that he needs to fear. Is he poor? He rejoices that Christ makes poor men rich. Does he prosper? He rejoices that there is grace to sanctify his prosperity lest it become intoxicating to him. Does there lie before him a great trouble? He thanks God for his promise that as his day his strength shall be. Does he apprehend the loss of friends? He prays that the trial may be averted, for he is permitted so to pray, even as David begged for the life of his child; but, having so done, he feels sure that God will not take away an earthly friend unless it be with kind intent to gather up our trust and confidence more fully to himself. Does there lie before him the prospect of speedy death? The hope of resurrection gives peace to his dying pillow. He knows that his Redeemer lives, and he is content to let his body sleep in the dust awhile. Is he reminded by Scripture of a day of judgment when all hearts shall be revealed? He has peace with regard to that dread mystery and all that surrounds it, for he knows whom he has believed, and he knows that he will protect him in that day. Whatever may be suggested that might alarm or distress the believer, deep down in his soul he cannot be disturbed, because he sees his God at the helm of the vessel holding the rudder with a hand which defies the storm. This is peculiarly advantageous in days like these when all things wear a dreary aspect. The storm signals are flying, the clouds are gathering, flashes of lightning and grumblings of distant thunder are around us. If you read the papers, wars and rumours of wars are incessant; your eyes light upon narratives of famine and drought; you see distress here, slackness of business there, and poverty and starvation in many places, and the fear creeps over you that there are dark days yet to come, and seasons in which faces will grow pale and hands hang heavy. Brethren, it is for the believer in such a case to feel no dismay, for our God is in the heavens, and he doth not forsake the throne; his purposes will be fulfilled and good will come out of evil, for at this very moment God sitteth in the council-chambers of kings, and ordereth all things according to the counsel of his will. We are not children whose father has gone to sea and left them at home without a guardian. We read just now the words, "I will not leave you comfortless: I will come to you," and we believe that gracious word. God is most near us, and we are most safe. Though we cannot see the future, and do not wish to pry between the folded leaves of the book of destiny, we are absolutely certain that nothing is written upon the unopened page of the future which can contradict the divine faithfulness so conspicuous in the past. We are sure that all things work together for good to them that love God, to them that are the called according to his purpose, and therefore our soul as to all external circumstances casts anchor and enjoys the peace of God, which passeth all understanding.

Nor is this all. God is pleased to give to his people peace *in reference to all his commands.* While the soul is unregenerate it rebels against the mind and will of God. If God forbids, the unrenewed heart longs for the forbidden thing. If God commands, the natural mind, for that very reason, refuses to do it. But when the change takes place, and we are reconciled to God by the death of his Son, then, beloved, we drop into the same line with God, and our deepest desire is to abide in full harmony with him. His will becomes our delight, and our only sorrow is that we cannot be perfectly conformed to it. There is no precept of God which is grievous to a gracious heart. His statutes are our songs in the house of our pilgrimage. We also feel perfect peace *with regard to God's providential doings,* because we believe that they are helping us to arrive at conformity with him, and that is just what we want. Oh that we could never have a thought or wish henceforth that would be disagreeable to the Lord. We now love him, we love his ways, we love his people, we love his word, we love his day, we love his promises, we love his precepts—we are altogether agreed with him through his rich grace; and in this sense we have a peace towards God which passeth all understanding.

What a wonderful description that is of this peace—*it "passeth all understanding."* It is not only beyond a common understanding, but it passeth *all* understanding. Some have said it means that the ungodly man cannot understand it; that statement is true, but it is not a tithe of the whole meaning, for even he who enjoys it cannot understand it. It is deeper, it is broader, it is sweeter, it is more heavenly than the joyful saint himself can tell. He enjoys what he cannot understand. What a mercy that such a thing is possible, for otherwise our joys would be narrow indeed! Reason has limits far narrower than joy.

Truly this peace is hid from the eyes of the ungodly and the unbelieving; it is far above, out of their sight. Now, there are kinds of peace in the world which the ungodly man can understand. There were the Stoics, who schooled themselves to apathy; they would not feel, and so they attained a senseless peace: their secret is easily discovered, it does not pass understanding. Many a Red Indian has been as stolid as the greatest Stoic, and has, perhaps, surpassed him, in hardening himself so that he would not groan if pierced with arrows or burned with fires. Some men have had such mastery over themselves that it has seemed a matter of perfect indifference whether they suffered pain or not. But Christianity does not teach us stoicism, nor does it point in that direction; it cultivates tenderness, and not insensibility. Its influence tends to make us sensitive rather than callous, and it gives us a peace consistent with the utmost delicacy of feeling, yea, with a sensitiveness more intense than other men know, since it makes our conscience more tender, and causes the mind to be deeply distressed by the slightest frown of heaven. Our peace is not the peace of apathy, but one of a far nobler sort. Others have aimed at the peace of levity, which the world can readily understand. They count it one of the wisest things to drive dull care away, and whatever happens of ill they drown reflection in the flowing bowl and laugh over it—making mirth when misery devours their souls. Christians do not atttempt to get rid of the trials of life in that fashion. The world, therefore, cannot understand the believer's peace, since he is neither apathetic nor frivolous.

Whence comes this peace? The jaunty answer of many a worldling is, "Oh, it comes from some fanatical delusion." But, indeed, we are not deluded. The grounds of a Christian's peace are rational, logical, and well grounded. They are to be justified by common sense. A person who has been in debt, and who is still in debt, ought not to be at peace; but suppose a man is found to be perfectly at his ease, who can blame him if he can say, "I have a right to be so, for my debt is paid"? No one can challenge such an argument. He who believes that Christ Jesus suffered in his stead that which was due to God's justice, has a rational argument for being at peace which he may plead anywhere he pleases. God has forgiven for Christ's sake all his iniquity, why should he not be at peace? And if it be indeed so—that the Christian has become the child of God, ought he not to be at peace? If God his Father rules all things for his good, ought he not to be at peace? If for him there remains no hazard of eternal death—if for him there is prepared a glorious resurrection, and if he is ultimately to shine with Christ in eternal glory, why should not the man have peace? It is far more difficult, I should think, rationally to blame him for his happiness than it would be to justify him if he were in alarm. We are not victims of delusion, but speak the words of truth and soberness when we claim to be the most favoured of mankind; the folly and the fanaticism lie with those who neglect God and eternity, and make a mock at sin.

Hence the worldling does not understand our peace, and frequently sneers at it because he is puzzled by it. Even the Christian is sometimes surprised at his own peacefulness. I know what it is to suffer from terrible depression of spirit at times; yet at the very moment when it has seemed to me that life was not worth one single bronze coin, I have been perfectly peaceful with regard to all the greater things. There is a possibility of having the surface of the mind lashed into storm while yet down deep in the caverns of one's inmost consciousness all is still: this I know by experience. There are earthquakes upon this earth, and yet our globe pursues the even tenor of its way, and the like is true in the little world of a believer's nature. Why, sometimes the Christian will feel himself to be so flooded with a delicious peace that he could not express his rapture. He is almost afraid to sing, lest even the sound of his voice should break the spell; but he says to himself,

"Come, then, expressive silence, muse his praise."

Satan has breathed a whisper into the mind—"It is too good to be true;" but the spirit, firmly believing in the truthfulness of God, has repelled the insinuation, and rested, in the faithfulness of God, in the eternal covenant, in the finished work of Christ, in the love of God manifested towards his people in Christ Jesus. This is the peace of God. "So he giveth his beloved sleep." It is a rest with an emphasis, rest in Jesus' sense when he said, "Come unto me, all ye that labour and are heavy laden, and I will give you rest"—rest in the most golden sense that we can ever give to the word, and much more. It passeth understanding, but it does not surpass experience. Do you know it? Pray answer the question each one for himself, for I must come back to where I started from. It is not to be described: it must be tested to be known.

II. Now, I must, in the second place, with very much brevity, indicate, beloved friends, HOW THIS PEACE IS TO BE OBTAINED.

Now, mark you, the apostle was addressing himself only to believers in the Lord Jesus, and I must beg you to take heed to the limitation. I am not now addressing myself to the ungodly: I speak to Christians alone. You are always at peace with God, though you do not always enjoy the sense of it; but if you wish to realize it, how are you to do so? The connection tells you. In the fourth verse Paul says, "*Rejoice in the Lord alway; and again I say, Rejoice.*" If you want to have peace of mind make God your joy, and place all your joy in God. You cannot rejoice in yourself, but you ought to rejoice in God. You cannot always rejoice in your circumstances, for they greatly vary, but the Lord never changes. "Rejoice in the Lord alway." If you have rejoicing in earthly things you must indulge it moderately ; but rejoicing in the Lord may be used without the possibility of excess, for the apostle adds, "Again I say, Rejoice"—rejoice, and rejoice again. Delight yourselves in the Lord. Who has such a God as you have ? " Their rock is not as our Rock, our enemies themselves being judges." Who has such a Friend, such a Father, such a Saviour, such a Comforter as you have in the Lord your God ? To think of God as our exceeding joy is to find "the peace of God, which passeth all understanding."

Go on to the fifth verse, where the apostle says, "*Let your moderation be known unto all men*"; that is to say, While all your joy is in God, deal with all earthly things on the principle of caution. If any man praises you, do not exult ; if, on the contrary, you are censured, do not let your spirit sink. If you have prosperity, thank God for it, but do not be sanguine that it will continue. If property be yours, take it, but do not let it become your treasure or the chief consideration of your mind. Do you suffer adversity ? Pray God to help you, but do not be so cast down as to despair. Drink of earthly cups by sips; do not be foolish like the fly which drowns itself in sweets. Use the things of time as not abusing them. Do not wade far out into the dangerous sea of this world's comfort. Take the good that God provides you, but say of it, "It passeth away," for indeed it is but a temporary supply for a temporary need. Never suffer your goods to become your god. Rejoice in God alone, and as for all else, come or go, rise or fall, let it neither distress you nor make you exult. Take matters quietly and calmly, and if you do that you will have peace. If you idolize any earthly good your peace will depart, but keep the world under your feet, and the peace of God shall keep your heart and mind.

Three rules are then added by the apostle, which you will be sure to recollect. He tells us to *be careful for nothing, to be prayerful for everything, and to be thankful for anything.* Anyone who can keep these three rules, with the other two, will be quite sure to have a peaceful mind. "Be careful for nothing"; that is—leave your care with God. Having done your best to provide things honest in the sight of all men, take no distressing, disturbing, anxious thought about anything, but cast your burden on the Lord. Then pray about everything, little as well as great, joyous as well as sad. "In every thing by prayer and supplication let your requests be made known unto God." That which you pray over will have the sting taken out of it if it be evil, and the sweetness of it will be sanctified if it be good. The tribulation which you pray over will become bearable, even if it be not changed into a subject for rejoicing. A trouble prayed over is a dead lion with honey in the carcase.

And then we are bidden to be thankful for anything, for the apostle says, "In every thing with thanksgiving let your requests be made known unto God." Thankfulness is the great promoter of peace; it is the mother and nurse of restfulness. Doubtless, our peace is often broken because we receive mercies from God without acknowledging them : neglected praises sour into unquiet forebodings. If we render to the Lord the fragrant incense of holy gratitude we shall find our soul perfumed with the sweet peace of God.

Take those five things, then, as the connection sets them before you. Pile up all your joy into the sacred storehouse of your God, and be glad in the Lord. Next, leave, as much as you can, the things of this world alone; touch them with a light finger—"Let your moderation be known unto all men." And then pray much, care for nothing, and bless God from morning to night. In such an atmosphere shall peace grow as rare flowers and fruits bloom beneath sunny skies in well-watered gardens. May the Holy Spirit work these things in us and cause us to rest.

III. This brings me to the third point of our subject to-night, which was THE OPERATION OF THIS BLESSED PRIVILEGE UPON OUR HEARTS.

It is said that the peace of God will keep our hearts and minds. The Greek word is *phroureo*, which signifies keeping guard, keeping as with a garrison : so completely and so effectually does the peace of God keep our hearts and minds. Look, then : our *hearts* want keeping, keeping from sinking, for our poor spirits are very apt to faint, even under small trials. They also want keeping from wandering, for how soon are they beguiled! What feeble charms are able to attract us away from the altogether lovely One! Our hearts need keeping up, and keeping right. The way to keep the heart, according to the text, is to let it be filled with the peace of God which passeth all understanding. A quiet spirit, calm, restful, happy, is one that will neither sink nor wander : how can it? If the peace of God be in you, what can cause you distress? You will be like those great buoys moored out at sea, which cannot sink; it matters not what storms may be raging, they always rise above all. Our souls, moored fast and rendered buoyant with peace, will be as fixed marks whereby others may know their way. Moreover, a man who has his heart full of peace is not likely to wander, for he says to himself, "Why should I wander? Where can such sweetness be found as I have tasted in my Lord? Why should I seek elsewhere?" The best way to keep a person in your service is to make it worth his while to stop; and if he is so happy and so content that he feels he could not better himself, you are likely to retain him for many a long day. Now, our Lord and Master has made his service such that we could not better ourselves. When he said to some of his servants "Will ye also go away?"

they said, "To whom shall we go?" Ah, indeed! to whom could we go? Eyes, will you leave the light for the thick darkness? Ears, will ye turn away from the music of Jesus' voice? Heart, wilt thou leave a faithful lover for a deceiver? Understanding, wilt thou go abroad after novelties when thou hast found the old, sure, satisfactory truth? Conscience, wilt thou burden thyself again with thy former load? When thou art so perfectly satisfied with the work and person of Christ wilt thou not stay where thou art? Oh yes, the heart is held with bands as strong as they are tender when it is full of the peace of God which passeth understanding. You young people get tempted, I know, and who among us does not? And the world has many charms for you. I recommend you, therefore, to pray the Lord to maintain your happiness in Christ, your joy in the Lord, for if you get out of heart with regard to your Lord and Master, it may be the devil may catch you when you are bad tempered and cross-grained towards your great Lord, and entice you away from your allegiance; but if your heart is always peaceful you will have a strength about you with which to resist the suggestions of the evil one. Rivets of peace are good fastenings for Christian loyalty. It is a very serious thing for a Christian to be in an uncomfortable state, for he is then weak in an important point. "Comfort ye, comfort ye, my people," are God's words to his prophets, because he knows that when we lose comfort, or lose peace, we lose one of the most valuable pieces of armour of which our panoply is composed.

But the text also adds that this will keep our *mind* as well as our heart. Now in all ages we find that the minds of Christians have been apt to be disturbed and vexed upon vital truths. I think sometimes that this is the worst age for error which has ever darkened the world. I get distressed and bowed to the earth as I see the treachery of ministers, professed ministers of Christ, who deny the inspiration of Scripture and lay the axe at the very root of all the doctrines which we hold dear, while yet they continue to occupy Christian pulpits. But when I look back all through history I find it was always so. From the days of Judas Iscariot until now there have been traitors and there have been men of ready speech and of quick thought who have used both fair speech and subtle thought to turn away simple minds from the gospel, insomuch that they would deceive, if it were possible, the very elect. But why are not the elect deceived? As a rule it is because they find such peace —such perfect peace—in the truths which they have received, that deceivers vainly attempt to entice them away from it. "Ah," cries the restful believer, "I cannot give up the gospel. It is my life, my strength, my solace, my all. It was the comfort of my dying mother, and it remains the mainstay of my aged father. It was that which brought me to a Saviour's feet and gives me grace to remain there. It has helped me in the hour of trial again and again. I feel I want its consolations, and therefore I can never part with it." And so he grows indignant with the man who casts a doubt thereon, especially if he be of the clerical order, and a pretender to the Christian ministry. Brethren, we cannot move one single inch from the truth which we have been taught by the Holy Ghost in our soul, and it is only such truth as that which can bring into the heart the peace of God which passeth understanding. When the Lord has brought his own truth into our minds by his own power and made the sweet savour of it to pervade our frame, and given us to drink thereof till we have been filled with joy and peace unutterable, we cannot, then, depart from it. Truth taught us by man we may forget, but that which the Holy Ghost engraves upon the inmost heart we cannot depart from. So help us God, we *must* stand to it, even if we die for it.

And what are the inventions they offer us instead of the choice things of the covenant of peace? They are trifles light as air. If they were true they would not be worth propagating: they might be left among the minor matters which are of no practical value to the sons of men. They bring us no new grounds of solid peace or fresh discovered arguments for holy joy. The negative theology promises no blessings to mankind; it is an empty-handed plunderer, robbing us of every solace, but offering nothing in return. If modern thought could be proved to be true the next thing that ought to be done would be to hang the world in sackcloth, because such vanity of vanities has taken the place of the delightful truth which once gladdened the hearts of men. It were the saddest of all facts if we were assured that the doctrines of grace are after all a fiction. But they are not so. They cannot be: they bear their own witness within themselves. Some of us can speak about them as Christian replied to Atheist, when Atheist said, "Go back: go back!" Christian's reply was, "We are seeking the Celestial City." "Oh," said Atheist, "but I have gone farther than any of you, and I tell you that there is no such place. I have met with many learned men who have studied the whole matter, and it is all a delusion. Go back: go back." Then Christian said, "What! No Celestial City? Did we not see it from the top of Mount Clear, when we were with the shepherds and looked through the telescopic glass?" So we say—No atonement? Have we not felt the peace with which it soothes the conscience? No regeneration? Are we not ourselves the living evidence that men are made new creatures in Christ Jesus? No answers to prayer? Surely then we are not sane men at all, and our senses have failed us. No final perseverance? What then has kept us to this day? No work of the Holy Ghost? What? Are we asleep? Is even our existence a delusion? No, as we rub our eyes we feel that we have not been dreaming, but we feel sure that some other people are dozing and doting, and we pray that God in mercy may end their dream, and bring them to know those glorious and substantial verities which fill us with the peace of God which passeth all understanding, and in so doing keep our hearts and minds. We are bound to the cross for ever, nailed to the wood with Christ for ever. The blood-red colours of the atonement are fastened to our masthead, to fly there till our vessel sinks, if sink it must, but never to be struck, though man or devil, priest or philosopher, fire hot shot into our vessel. We dare not change, but stand faithful to that which Jesus has taught us, at whose feet we sat in our youth, and who continues to teach us still. His peace keeps our heart and mind, and therefore we will with heart and mind keep his truth, come what may.

IV. Lastly, let us observe THE SPHERE OF ITS ACTION.

The text says, "In Christ Jesus." Now, beloved, I beg you to note this with interest. The apostle never mentions the name of Jesus too often. You cannot say that he drags it in, but he mentions it as often as ever he can, for he delights in the sound of it. "In Christ Jesus." These words touch every point of our text all the way through. Are we speaking of ourselves? We are in Christ Jesus. Our faith has realised our union with his sacred person. He is our head, and we are his members; he is the corner-stone, and we are built upon him. There is nothing about ourselves worth thinking of apart from him; and it will be well if we dismiss the thought.

Then if we dwell upon the peace of God, we still think of our Lord Jesus, for it is all in him. No peace is to be found out of Christ. No peace can warm our heart while we forget Christ. "He is our peace." Never go, dear brethren and sisters, for your peace to the law or to your own experience, to your own past achievements, or even to your own faith. All your peace is in Jesus.

And then our hearts and our minds, mentioned in the text, must all be in Jesus: the heart loving him, and loved of him; the mind believing him, resting in him, using its faculties for him,—all in him. If I leave that last thought with you it will be the best ending for my sermon: namely, that to get peace, and to get your hearts and minds kept, the grand necessity is to be in Christ—in your dying, risen, reigning Lord. Let him be upon your thoughts now and always. His table is now spread, come hither to commune with him. Come hither with your Master, to see your Master, and to eat his flesh, and drink his blood, after a spiritual fashion, at his own table.

A word to you who do not know our Lord. How I wish you did know him. You can never possess peace till you possess Christ. What a blessed beginning of Sabbaths it would be to your souls if you were to seek Christ to-night. You have not far to go to find him. He is not far from any of us. Cover your eyes and breathe a prayer to him. Stand behind one of the columns outside, or get into the street and let your heart say, "Saviour, I want peace, and peace I can never have till I have found thee. Behold, I trust thee. Manifest thyself to me at this moment and say unto my soul, 'I am thy salvation.'" God grant you may so pray. It seems to me very wonderful that we should need to persuade men to think of their own interests, and to care for their own selves. In other things they are always sharp enough to look after what they call "number one," but when it comes to the most solemn concern, the greatest blessing, and the purest happiness that can be had, they are so foolish as to let all things else attract them more than the Lord Jesus. The Lord save you all for his infinite mercy's sake. Amen.

6 The Reason Why Many Cannot Find Peace

"Submit yourselves therefore to God. Resist the devil, and he will flee from you. Draw nigh to God, and he will draw nigh to you. Cleanse your hands, ye sinners; and purify your hearts, ye double minded. Be afflicted, and mourn, and weep: let your laughter be turned to mourning, and your joy to heaviness. Humble yourselves in the sight of the Lord, and he shall lift you up."—James iv. 7—10.

WE frequently meet with persons who tell us that they cannot find peace with God. They have been bidden to believe in the Lord Jesus, but they misunderstand the command, and, while they think they are obeying it, they are really unbelievers; hence they miss the way of peace. They attempt to pray, but their petitions are not answered, and their supplications yield them no comfort whatever, for neither their faith nor their prayer is accepted of the Lord. Such persons are described by James in the third verse of the chapter now open before us—"Ye ask, and receive not, because ye ask amiss." We cannot be content to see seekers in this wretchedness, and hence we endeavour to comfort them, instructing them again and again in the great gospel precept, "Believe and live"; yet as a rule they get no further, but linger in an unsatisfactory condition. They assure us that they believe in Jesus, but we see none of the fruits of faith in them, neither can they themselves say that they derive any spiritual benefit from the faith which they profess. Now I fear that comfort is misplaced in these cases. When we have endeavoured to cheer such people, I fear we may have been filming over a wound which needs a sharp knife rather than a soft bandage, a keen lancet rather than a healing liniment. We shall try at this time to show certain uneasy souls why they do not obtain peace, and what they must be brought to by the Holy Spirit before they can rightly claim that they are saved. Though our words may be somewhat caustic they will be uttered in loving faithfulness, and may the Lord our God make them effectual to the ending of the inner strife and the establishment of settled peace.

I fear that many who profess to be Christians are in a very questionable condition: they have no joy of their faith and no success in their prayers. Whether they are Christians or not is a moot point, and the practical James does not waste time in discussing the doubtful question, but speaks to them from both sides of their apparent condition. In his previous chapters he calls them "my brethren," and even "my beloved brethren," and he draws no line of demarcation when he afterwards addresses them as "sinners," whose hands must be cleansed, and as "double-minded" persons, whose hearts must be purified. They were both these: they were professedly brethren, but they were at heart unchaste to Christ; they indulged in grievous sins of contention and malice, and their hearts were divided between the love of sin and the hope of salvation. We will not, therefore, raise personal questions, or try to discriminate where certainty is hard to reach, but we will speak to suspicious characters without determining whether they are believers or not. If such persons claim to be called brethren, we will address them as such, but it will be in a sentence like this, "My brethren, such things ought not to be." On the other hand, we will use no condemnatory title, but leave the question between God and each man's own conscience. We will go to the root of the matter, and set forth the reason for the lack of peace and salvation of which some complain. May the sacred Spirit help us to point out the fatal failure which keeps the soul from rest. If any man be not sure that he is in Christ, he ought not to be easy one moment until he is so. Dear friend, without the fullest confidence as to your saved condition, you have no right to be at ease, and I pray you may never be so. This is a matter too important to be left undecided. Instantly should every man of prudence make assurance doubly sure; and bind all things fast that he may find them fast for eternity—for eternity I say, for thus saith the Lord. Never risk your souls, for your souls are yourselves, your real selves, and nothing can make up for their loss. If you lose your own souls, it will be no recompense to have gained the whole world. Be careful, then, leave nothing insecure, carefully measure and weigh every important step; consider and examine, lest being so near to the kingdom any of you should seem to come short of it. To help you to a settled peace, let me first of all urge upon you to obey *the comprehensive command* of our text—"Submit yourselves therefore to God"; and then, secondly, let me further press upon you to practise the *other precepts which follow*, such as "Resist the devil," "Draw nigh to God," "Cleanse your hands," "Purify your hearts," and "Be afflicted, and mourn, and weep;" and "Humble yourselves in the sight of the Lord."

I. First hearken to THE COMPREHENSIVE COMMAND—"*Submit yourselves therefore to God.*" According to the connection, the fighting spirit within many men shows that they have not submitted themselves to God; lusting, envy, strife, contention, jealousy, anger, all these things declare that the heart is not submissive, but remains violently self-willed and rebellious. Those who are still wrathful, proud, contentious, and selfish, are evidently unsubdued. There are some men to whom the very idea of submission is distasteful; they will be *sub* to no one, but wish to be their own gods, and a law unto themselves. "Submit" is a galling word to them. They say in their hearts, "Who is the Lord that I should obey his voice?" They are willing enough to accept his favours, willing enough after their fashion to say "Thank God," but as to submission, they will have none of it, it suits not their high mightiness. They strive for the mastery, they push for the front place, aiming to advance their own interests, and make great I to be lord paramount. The apostle quietly indicates in the words of our text that many Christian professors need to submit, for at present their unhumbled nature leads them to lustings and strivings, and effectually prevents their asking so as to receive at the Lord's hands.

A want of submission is no new or rare fault in mankind; ever since the fall it has been the root of all sin. When the heart submits to God in sincerity the work of grace is begun, and when it submits perfectly the work is complete; but for this divine grace must display its power, for the heart is obstinate and rebellious. From the moment when our mother Eve stretched out her hand to pluck the forbidden fruit, and her husband joined her in setting up the human will against the divine, the sons of men have universally been guilty of a want of conformity to the will of God. They choose their own way, and will not submit their wills; they think their own thoughts, and will not submit their understandings; they love earthly things, and will not submit their affections. Man wants to be his own law, and his own master. This is abominable, since we are not our own makers; for "it is he that hath made us and not we ourselves." The Lord should have supremacy over us, for our existence depends on his will. I have heard much of the rights of man: but it were well also to consider the rights of God, which are the first, highest, surest, and most solemn rights in the universe, and lie at the base of all other rights. The Lord has an absolute right to the beings whom he has fashioned, and it is shameful that the great mass of men seem never even to recollect that he exists, much less to ask themselves what is due to him. Alas, great God, how art thou a stranger even in the world which thou hast thyself made! Thy creatures, who could not see if thou hadst not given them eyes, look everywhere except to thee. Creatures who could not think if thou hadst not given them minds, think of all things except thee; and beings who could not live if thou didst not keep them in being, forget thee utterly, or if they remember thine existence, and see thy power, are foolhardy enough to become thy foes! The hemlock of sin grows in the furrows of opposition to God. When the Lord is pleased to turn the hearts of opposers to the obedience of the truth, it is an evident token of salvation; in fact, it is the dawn of salvation itself. To submit to God is to find rest.

The rule of God is so beneficial that he ought readily to be obeyed. He never commands us to do that which, in the long run, can be injurious to us; nor does he forbid us anything which can be to our real advantage. Our God is so kind, so wise, so full of loving forethought, that it must ever be to our best interest to follow his lead. Even if we could be left to choose our own way, and were under no bonds of duty, it would be wise and prudent to choose the way of the Lord, for it is the path of pleasantness and safety. Beloved, the Lord is far too great to have any need to deal unjustly, or unkindly, with his creatures; indeed, he is so great that he cannot desire any personal advantage from his government, but he condescends to govern us because without his rule and guidance we should be utterly undone. It is for our good that like a father in his family he commands us this or forbids us the other.

It is wanton cruelty to ourselves when we break away from the liberty with which Jesus makes us free to place ourselves under the tyranny of selfishness and the baser passions of the mind. It is madness to forsake the honourable service of the great King to become the slave of Satan. O that men would submit themselves unto God and be willing to be blest.

All resistance against God must, from the necessity of the case, be futile. Common sense teaches that rebellion against omnipotence is both insanity and blasphemy. The Lord's purpose must stand, and his pleasure must be done; his power will assuredly crush all opposition, and it is idle to raise it. Why, then, should a man contend against his Master? Wisdom as well as righteousness call upon him to submit himself unto God.

And then let it always be known that submission to God is absolutely necessary to salvation. A man is not saved until he bows before the supreme majesty of God. He may say, "I believe in Jesus," but if he goes on to follow out his own desires, and to gratify his own passions, he is a mere pretender, a wolf in the clothing of a sheep. Dead faith will save no man; it is not even as good as the faith of devils, for they "believe *and tremble*," and these men believe in a fashion which makes them brazen in their iniquity. No, salvation means being saved from the domination of self and sin; salvation means being made to long after likeness to God, being helped by divine grace to reach to that likeness, and living after the mind and will of the Most High. Submission to God is the salvation which we preach, not a mere deliverance from eternal burnings, but deliverance from present rebellion, deliverance from the sin which is the fuel of those flames unquenchable. There must be conformity to the eternal laws of the universe, and according to these God must be first and man must bow to him: nothing can be right till this is done. *Submit* is a command which in every case must be obeyed, or no peace or salvation will be found.

Now, it is generally in this matter of submission that the stumbling-block lies in the way of souls when seeking peace with God. It keeps them unsaved, and as I have already said, necessarily so, because a man who is not submissive to God is not saved; he is not saved from rebellion, he is not saved from pride, he is still evidently an unsaved man, let him think whatever he will of himself. Perhaps by a few personal remarks I may hit upon the reason why certain of my hearers cannot get the peace which the gospel so freely sets before them. There is a want of submission in some point or other. Now, in the saved man there is and must be a full and unconditional submission *to the law of God*. He must consent unto the law that it is good. If your mind has aforetime cavilled against the law, you must end the contest, for it is impossible that you should be right while you quarrel with the law of righteousness. If you set yourself up to be a judge of the law, you judge the lawgiver himself, and what is this but the blackest presumption? Traced to its real meaning, the thought of judging the law is treason, and would dethrone God and reign in his stead. How sad to see a sinful mortal criticizing the perfect law of his Maker! Dare you do this? If you say in your heart, "He is too strict in marking sin, and too severe in punishing it," what is this but condemning your Judge? If you say, "He calls me to account for idle words, and even for sins of ignorance, and this is hard," what is this but to call your Lord unjust? Should the law be amended to suit your desires? Should its requirements be accommodated to ease your indolence? If you ask for this you are not saved, for a saved person delights in the law of God after the inward man; he says of it, "the law is holy"; though he weeps as he adds, "but I am carnal, sold under sin." He honours the law as he bows before it and confesses his shortcomings.

Yes, and before a man can have peace with God he must submit himself *to the sentence of the law.* Though that law in its severity searches the reins and tries the heart, arraigns us before the bar of God, and pronounces sentence upon us, we must own it to be just. Grace working in the heart brings the penitent to plead guilty to the sin, and to own that the penalty is deserved. In my own case I unreservedly own that when the law in my conscience condemned me to hell, I dared not lift a finger nor even think a thought by way of disputing the sentence. The conscience is not divinely quickened, nor the soul renewed, nor the man saved, unless he cries, "I acknowledge my transgressions: and my sin is ever before me. Against thee, thee only, have I sinned, and done this evil in thy sight, that thou mightest be justified when thou speakest, and be clear when thou judgest." You must submit yourselves to the righteousness and severity of God, or he will resist you as he doth all the proud. There can be no pardon for a man unless he will honour the law by hearty submission. If your plea be "not guilty," you will be committed for trial according to justice, but you cannot be forgiven by mercy. You are in a hopeless position; God himself cannot meet you upon that ground, for he cannot admit that the law is unrighteous and its penalty too heavy. The Lord cannot be at peace with you while you defy his law. He declares that you are guilty and you dispute this declaration, hence between you and himself there is a quarrel which never can be ended till you own your error and beg for pardon. He can deal with you in mercy when you once stand where mercy can meet with you, namely, in the sinner's place, but if you say "I am not guilty," and begin to vindicate or excuse yourself, you are on a ground which the Lord cannot recognise. If you are professedly righteous how can the Lord deal with you except in justice? And if he deal with you in justice he will readily enough summon his witnesses, and prove you guilty, and condemn you everlastingly. Submit, then, unto God, and say, "Guilty, Lord: I throw down the weapons of my rebellion, and own that I stand condemned before thee, and if saved at all it must be by thy free forgiveness, by thine unmerited mercy, by thy boundless love."

A man must next submit himself *to the plan of salvation by grace alone.* God meets the sinner on the footing of grace. "I cannot exonerate you," he seems to say, "but I can forgive you; I cannot tolerate your denial of guilt, but if you confess your sin I am faithful and just to forgive you your sin, and to save you from all unrighteousness." Now, are you willing, my dear hearer, are you sure that you are willing to be saved by grace alone and to owe your deliverance from sin and its punishment entirely to the free favour of God? Will you yield to that? I trust you will. But there are some who will not, for they go about to establish their own righteousness and do not submit themselves to the righteousness of God. They think that so much chapel-going, church-going, sermon-hearing, prayer-meeting attending, Bible reading, and so on, will certainly work up something like a claim upon God. O, sirs, have done with claims. If you come with anything like a claim the Lord will not touch the case at all, for you have no claim, and the pretence of one would be an insult to God. If you fancy you have demands upon God, go into the court of justice and plead them, but the sentence is certain to be against you, for by the deeds of the law no flesh can be justified. Try the other way. Come to God with no claim, and appeal to his pity, saying, "Lord, I cry for mercy. Gladly will I accept thy free grace if thou wilt but give it me." You will be accepted on that footing; for the Lord is gracious and casts out none who come to him confessing their sins.

You must also submit yourselves *to God's way of saving you through an atoning sacrifice* and by means of your personal faith in that sacrifice. You must receive his Son as divine, and you must believe in that atoning blood which was shed for many for the remission of sins. Surely there should be no difficulty about surrendering the mind to this. Salvation by the great Mediator is such a delightful way of salvation, so just to God, so safe to man, that we ought to clap our hands for very joy to think that such a royal road to heaven is opened for us. What say you, dear hearers? Does the Holy Ghost incline you to trust in the blood of Jesus?

And then there must be a full submission *to God in the matter of giving up every sin*. Numbers of persons pray for mercy, but they continue in their sins. Such men cannot be saved, because salvation is salvation *from* sin—not *in* sin. How can we be saved from sin if we are its slaves? If you come to God and cry, "Lord, deliver me, and have mercy upon me," and yet you practise private drinking, and tipple yourselves into semi-drunkenness, how can you be saved? If you keep on cheating in business, or telling lies, or indulge a malicious or angry temper in the family, or are proud and unkind, selfish and miserly, how can you be saved? I warn you, sirs, that faith itself cannot save you while these things are so, for if your faith were a saving faith it would rescue you from these evils. This, indeed, is salvation, namely, deliverance from the power and habit of sin. Many prayers are semi-hypocritical; there is a kind of sincerity about them, but there is no whole-hearted desire after holiness, and therefore they will never gain a comfortable answer from God. O seeker, art thou willing to give up every sin? Come, drunkard, thou prayest to be forgiven, but art thou willing to abjure the intoxicating cup once for all? Thou, my brother, askest to be pardoned; it is well, but art thou at the same time desirous to cease from your transgressions? Yes or no! Art thou anxious to search out every false way, and abandon it as soon as it is discovered? Dost thou wish to have a holy, truthful, godly tongue? Dost thou long to be saved from every lust and secret vice? If so, believing in the Lord Jesus Christ, thou art already saved; thy sigh to be delivered from evil is the commencement of the work of sanctification. But if thou dost say, "I would be saved from every wrong way except my one indulgence, my one secret iniquity," then thou art in the gall of bitterness and in the bonds of iniquity; thy prayers will come back into thy bosom unanswered, and thy pretended faith in Christ will condemn thee. Thy fancied faith cannot save thee, seeing thou huggest thy sin. A certain man has been accustomed to eat of a certain dish which is bad for his health, and when he calls in a physician their talk is after this fashion: "If you trust in me," says the doctor, "I can cure you." "Yes," replies the patient, "I do trust in you heartily." The doctor proceeds, "That dainty of yours must be given up, for it is the cause of your disease, and so long as you eat it you must suffer in consequence." "Well, doctor," he says, "I trust in you, but I cannot give up my favourite food." Is it not apparent to everybody that he is not trusting in the physician at all? Even so when a man declares, "I trust in Christ to save me from sin," and then continues in his wickedness: he mocks the Good Physician, and is in danger of sudden destruction. Either you must cast sin out of your heart or it will keep you out of heaven. This point must be insisted on: receiving Christ is impossible without at the same time renouncing sin.

If we would be saved there must be submission *to the Lord as to all his teachings;* a very necessary point in this age, for a multitude of persons, who appear to be religious, judge the Scriptures instead of allowing the Scriptures to judge them. Hear, O ye wise men, "Except ye be converted, and become as little children, ye shall not enter into the kingdom of heaven." Submission to the infallible authority of the inspired word is absolutely required of every disciple of Jesus, but this age delights in the opposite spirit. Even some of those who call themselves ministers of the gospel persistently indulge a spirit which is precisely the reverse of the childlike faith which saves the soul. They industriously endeavour to excite rebellion against the teachings of Christ, and cry it up under the name of "honest doubt." They do not wish men to believe, but to *think*, and their gospel, practically, is, "Doubt, and do not be baptized, and you shall be saved." Shame upon them! Now our gospel is, "He that believeth, and is baptized, shall be saved"; and we are content to teach what Jesus Christ our Lord told his disciples to preach to all nations. If I will never yield my reason, if I will never believe what I cannot understand, if I will carry an open knife about with me to cut and hack at texts of Scripture, if I will not sit at Jesus' feet with Mary, but want him to sit at my feet that I may tell him what his religion ought to be, and what he ought to have said, how can I be saved? If, after all, we are personally infallible, and are to spend all our days in selecting our opinions, how can we know Christ? If instead of yielding my judgment to the plain teachings of my Lord I must needs revise his doctrines, how can I be saved? If I have not submitted my intellect to God, what peace can there be? Mark this well, ye wise young men who know so much more than your fathers, and are too intellectual to reverence your fathers' God.

And, now, I must ask another question of you who desire peace and cannot find it: have you submitted yourselves *to the providential arrangements of God?* I know persons who often sit in this house of prayer who have a quarrel with God. He took away a beloved object, and they not only thought him unkind and cruel at the time, but they think so still. Like a child in a fit of the sulks, they cast an evil eye upon the great Father. They are not at peace, and never will be till they have owned the Lord's supremacy, and ceased from their rebellious thoughts. If they were in a right state of heart they would thank the Lord for their sharp trials, and consent to his will, as being assuredly right. I fear that unsubmission on this point affects a great number of persons. They cannot succeed in business, and therefore they are out of temper with God. He knows very well that they are not fit to be made rich, and could not be trusted with a large business; and, therefore, he does not grant their suicidal desires. Some men would never win the race of life if they had an ounce of gold to carry; the only hope for their running at all lies in keeping them unencumbered. We know, also, thoughtful young men who cannot pursue their studies because of failing health: they want to be famous, but they are not strong enough to continue their work for the examination, and so they are vexed with the Lord. Or, it may be, they have less talent than ambition, and they rebel because their Maker has not given them intellects as capacious as that of Solomon. Let them be satisfied to use the talent they have, and cease from contending with their Creator. Many men have a sort of private pique with providence, and sit down like Jonah under their withered gourd and mutter, "We do well to be angry even unto death." Now, if such be the case with any before me, I would say to them,—leave off quarrelling with your God. What can be the use of it? The very best and wisest thing for you is to make friends with him, and let his will be yours. After all he deals well with you, if you would but see it. Depend upon it there is something to be made out of the position you occupy: gain will come to you out of all those losses, profit will arise even from those sad bereavements, if you will stand still and see the salvation of God. Acquaint yourselves with God and be at peace, for thereby good shall come unto you; for unless you do this you may say, "I believe," but you have no faith in God. How can a man believe in God when he charges God with treating him wrongly? Faith begets resignation and submission, but where there is strife and enmity, unbelief is still supreme. Until you submit yourselves to God it cannot be well with your souls, for he resisteth the proud, but giveth grace unto the humble.

This is the long and the short of it: you must, as a guilty sinner, cast yourself at God's feet and say, "Have mercy upon me, O Lord, and have mercy upon me in thine own way. I dictate not to thee, but I implore thy grace? I humbly beg forgiveness, be pleased to pity me. I yield up myself to thee, asking thee to make me holy. I do from my very heart give up the love of sin. I fear I shall sin, help me to loathe myself when I do so; make me what thou wilt have me to be, and then deal as thou wilt with me. I make no terms nor conditions; mine is an unconditional surrender. Only for thy mercy's sake renew me, make me thy child and save me. As thou biddest me trust thy Son, I do trust him. "Lord, I believe; help thou mine unbelief." You will have peace when your heart is brought to this point. At present your wound does not heal, because it needs washing, for the grit of pride has fallen into it and is causing a wretched irritation. When pride is gone and you are fully submissive then shall the wound heal and your broken bones shall rejoice. I am not asking you to submit to a priest, I am not asking you to submit to a mere man, but I speak very earnestly when I say, "Submit yourselves unto God": it is natural, it is right; it is good in itself, and fraught with the highest good to you. Submission is essential to salvation, therefore bow before the Lord at once. May the Lord bend that stubborn will and conquer that wayward heart. Yield yourselves unto God, and pray to be delivered from future rebellion. If you have submitted, do so yet more completely, for so shall you be known to be Christians when you submit yourselves unto God. If you will not submit, your faith is a lie, your hope is a delusion, your prayer is an insult, your peace is presumption, your end will be despair. Rebellion is as the sin of witchcraft, and stubbornness is as iniquity and idolatry. "But God shall wound the head of his enemies, and the hairy scalp of such an one as goeth on still in his trespasses."

II. But now, secondly, having thus spoken upon the great duty of submission, let us consider the other and FOLLOWING PRECEPTS. I think I am not suspicious without reason when I express a fear that the preaching which has lately been very common, and in some respects very useful, of "only believe and you shall be saved," has sometimes been altogether mistaken by those who have heard it. Cases occur in which young persons go on living light, frivolous, giddy, and even wicked lives, and yet they assert that they believe in Jesus Christ. When you come to examine them a little you find that their belief in Christ means that they believe that he has saved them, although everybody who knows their character can see clearly that they are not saved at all: now, what is their faith but the belief of a lie? They are living just as they did live, and hence it is clear that they are not saved from their former foolish conversation, nor from their bad tempers, nor from their old sins; and yet they try to persuade themselves that they are saved. Now, true faith never believes falsehoods: presumption lives upon lies, but faith will only feed on truth. My faith does not teach me to believe I am saved when straight before my very eyes I have the evidence that I am not saved, since I am living in the very sin I pretend to be saved from. Though we would not for a moment cast a doubt upon the doctrine of justification by faith and free salvation, we must also preach more and more that parallel truth, "Ye must be born again." We must bring to the front the grand old word which has been thrown into the background by some evangelists, namely, "Repent." Repentance is as essential to salvation as faith: indeed there is no faith without repentance except the faith which needs to be repented of. A dry-eyed faith will never see the kingdom of God. A holy loathing for sin always attends upon a childlike faith in the Sin-bearer. Where the root grace of faith is found other graces will grow from it.

Now notice how the Spirit of God, after having bidden us submit, goes on to show what else is to be done. He calls for a brave resistance of the devil. "*Resist the devil, and he will flee from you.*" The business of salvation is not all passive, the soul must be aroused to active warfare. I am to fall into the arms of Christ, that he may save me, and trust in him entirely; but when I depend upon him I receive life, and the very first effort of that life is to smite with all its might the adversary of Christ and of my own soul. I am not only to contend with sin, but with the spirit which foments and suggests sin. I am to resist the secret spirit of evil as well as its outward acts. "Oh," saith one, "I cannot give up an inveterate habit." Sir, you must give it up; you must resist the devil or perish. "But I have been so long in it," cries the man. Yes, but if you truly trust Christ your first effort will be to fight against the evil habit. Ay, and if it is not a habit merely, nor an impulse, but if your danger lies in the existence of a cunning spirit who is armed at all points, and both strong and subtle, yet you must not yield, but resolve to resist to the death, cheered by the gracious promise that he will flee from you. You shall in the name of Jesus overcome temptation, master evil habit, and escape from bondage: only strike for freedom and disdain the chain of sin. If you are to have peace with God there must be war with Satan; you cannot rest in your spirit and know the peace which faith gives unless you wage war to the knife against every evil and against the patron and prince of evil, even Satan. Are you ready for this? You cannot have peace unless you are.

Next the apostle writes, "*Draw nigh to God, and he will draw nigh to you.*" He who believes in Christ sincerely will be much in prayer; yet there are some who say, "We want to be saved," but they neglect prayer. They cannot make out how it is that they have no enjoyment of religion; but why need they be puzzled? Ask your neglected closet, ask your own heart, how you can be happy and prosperous and blessed in divine things if you do not pray. Recollect that the mere saying of prayers is not praying. The essence of prayer lies in the heart drawing near to God: and it can do that without words. Prayer is the feeling that God is present, and the desire of the soul to come near to him, so as to own his influence, to know his love, to feel his power, and to be conformed to his will. This kind of praying can be continued by the power of God's Holy Spirit all the day long. We must know something of this. "Behold he prayeth" is one of the first marks of a saved soul; and if you think that by some momentary act of faith which you suppose you exercised you are therefore saved, while your heart remains at a distance from God, prayerless and careless, you are fatally deceived. Such is not the teaching of Scripture, and there is no warrant for it in the promises of God. If prayer be utterly neglected, the soul is dead.

The next precept is, "*Cleanse your hands, ye sinners.*" What! does the word of God tell sinners to cleanse their hands and purify their hearts? Yes, it does. Some brother whispers "Ah, that is Arminianism." Who art thou that repliest against God's word? If such teaching is in this inspired book, how dare we question it? It comes with a "thus saith the Lord,"—"Cleanse your hands, ye sinners." When a man comes to God and says, "I am willing and anxious to be saved, and I trust Christ to save me," and yet he keeps his dirty black hands exercised in filthy actions, doing what he knows is wrong, does he expect God to hear him? Do I need spend even so many as a half-dozen words to show that this man does not believe and is not really honest before the Most High? "Cleanse your hands, ye sinners." Can you ask God to be at peace with you while your hands grasp your sins with loving embrace and are full of bribes, or are foul with lust, or are smiting with the fist of anger and wrath? If you do the devil's work with your hands, do not expect the Lord to fill them with his blessing. It cannot be, you must break off your sins by righteousness, and as Paul shook off the viper from his hand into the fire, so must you. By the power of faith, if it be a real faith, you will be able to purge your outward life. Why, when men talk about being spiritual, and are not even decently moral, it makes us sick to hear them. How dare they talk about being Christians when they do not live as well as Mohammedans or heathens? Oh ye dogs, howling out your shame, what portion have you among the children so long as you bite and devour and love your filthiness? It is idle to talk about salvation while sin is hugged to the heart with both hands. Away with such hypocrisy!

Then it is added, "*Purify your hearts, ye double-minded.*" Can they do this? Assuredly not by themselves, but still in order to peace with God there must be so much purification of the heart that it shall no longer be double-minded. He who would have salvation must seek it with all his heart, must so seek it that he is resolved to give up anything, and to endure anything, so that he may but be rescued from sin. "Purify your hearts, ye double-minded." Get rid of that leering eye of yours towards uncleanness, and that cross eye which squints towards worldly gain; for till your whole heart cries after the Most High he will not hear you. When you can say with David, "My heart and my flesh cry out for the living God," you shall find the Lord. When you cease trying to serve two masters, and submit yourselves unto God, he will bless you, but not till then. I believe that this touches the centre of the mischief in many of those hearts which fail to reach peace; they have not given up sin, they are not whole-hearted after salvation.

Then the Lord bids us "*be afflicted, and mourn, and weep: let your laughter be turned to mourning, and your joy to heaviness.*" I grieve to say that I have met with persons who say, "I cannot find peace, I cannot get salvation," and talk very prettily in that way; but yet outside the door they are giggling one with another, as if it were matter of amusement. The Sabbath day is spent in vain, idle, frivolous conversation—seriousness they do not seem even to have felt. The whole matter appears to be a mere sport. Some converts seem to jump into religion as people do into a bath, and jump out again about as fast; they never weigh the matter, they have no thought, no sorrow for sin, no humiliation before God. Stop that laughter if you are an unsaved soul—for decency's sake, stop that laughter. For you to laugh whilst in danger of being lost sounds to me as ghastly and as grim as if the fiends of hell were to set up a theatre and act a comedy in the pit. What right have you with laughter while sin is unforgiven, while God is angry with you? Nay, go to him in fitter form and fashion, or he will refuse your prayers. Be serious, begin to think of death, and judgment, and wrath to come. These are not trifles, sirs, nor things to make sport about, neither is true religion a thing that is to be attended to as easily as when one snaps his finger and says, "Heigh presto! Quick. It's done!" By no manner of means. If you are saved your mind is solemnly impressed by eternal realities and you are serious about matters of life and death; the very thought of sin pains you, and since you meet with it in your daily life you have cause for daily humbling, and are afflicted because of it. Many, I fear, fail to get peace because it is not a solemn matter at all, they trifle with it as if it were a game for boys and girls to play at, and not for the heart and spirit to enter upon with deep concern.

Then the Lord sums up his precepts by saying, "*Humble yourselves in the sight of God.*" With that I close. There must be a deep and lowly prostration of the spirit before God. If you happen to have a boy who shows a high rebellious spirit against you, and you have chastened him for it, and yet he stands out, you tell him that there must be a humbling of himself before you can forgive him. If he is a wise child, and wishes to escape your anger, he makes a dutiful confession, acknowledges that he was wrong, and appeals to your love, and you freely pardon him: but in many who pretend to come to God there is no humbling. They do not own that they ever did anything particularly wrong, and they do not care if they did: still they hear there is such a thing as believing in Jesus, and they profess to believe, not because there is any need for it, as they think, but for fashion sake. Ah, sirs, Jesus Christ did not come to heal the whole, but the sick, neither did he die to bind up those who are not broken, nor to make alive those who were never killed. There must be in you, and may God give to you, a brokenness of spirit; a broken and a contrite heart he will not despise.

If your heart has never been broken, how can he bind it up? If it was never wounded, how can he heal it? These are weighty matters, and I speak them weightily lest anyone among you should be deceived. God help you to cry, "Search me, O God, and know my heart: try me, and know my thoughts: and see if there be any wicked way in me, and lead me in the way everlasting."

This is the way of salvation, that ye believe in Jesus Christ whom God hath sent. But remember that he saves us *from* our sins, not *in* our sins. Faith in Jesus Christ does save and will save all who have it, but it is by purging out sin. It assures us that we are pardoned, and thus it makes us love the Christ by whom we are forgiven: this love leads us to abhor ourselves for our sins, and we endeavour to purify ourselves from them by his Spirit. Faith without works is dead, being alone; and though a man is justified by faith and not by works, and by faith alone, and not even in part by his works, yet the faith which saves is a faith which produces good works, and leads into the way of holiness. He who doth not seek after righteousness and true holiness, let him pretend what he may, is dead while he lives. The Lord have mercy upon you, for Christ's sake. Amen.

7 Peace: A Fact and a Feeling

"Therefore being justified by faith, we have peace with God through our Lord Jesus Christ."—Romans v. 1.

WONDERFUL is the power of faith. In the Epistle to the Hebrews our apostle tells us of the marvellous exploits which it has wrought in subduing kingdoms and obtaining promises, in quenching the violence of fire and stopping the mouths of lions, in braving perils and doing deeds of prowess. Still, to us personally one of the most wonderful of its effects is that it brings us justification and consequent peace. "Being justified by faith, we have peace with God." If we know the justifying power of faith, and the way in which, like a hand, it puts upon us the matchless garment of the Saviour's righteousness, we shall value that faith as our first parents did the gracious hand of God which made for them coats of skins and therewith covered their nakedness. The little faith we have will make us crave for more; and every need we feel will make us long to prove its virtue in our own souls to meet our own personal case, by the operation of the Holy Ghost.

Now, faith brings to the soul, according to the text, two blessings. It is not the creator of these things, but the conveyance, the channel, the conduit pipe through which these favours come to us. First, *it brings us a state of peace*—"being justified by faith"; and, secondly, *it brings us a sense of peace*—"we have peace with God through our Lord Jesus Christ."

I. Our first thoughts shall cluster about that most important of all matters—A STATE OF PEACE WITH GOD.

Naturally we have no peace. God is angry with us because we are sinful, and we are at variance with God because he is holy. God cannot agree with us—"Can two walk together except they be agreed?" And we cannot agree with God, for "the carnal mind is enmity against God: for it is not subject to the law of God, neither indeed can be." There is a breach between the rebellious creature and the righteous Creator. Sad that it should be so, but such is the case by nature with every man that is born of woman. We are set against the Lord. We kick against his providence, we rebel against his commands, we resist his Holy Spirit, we reject his love as manifested in the death of Christ, and we should live and die in this hostility if it were not for his almighty grace. Before ever we can enjoy peace within our hearts there must be a state of peace established between us and God. We must submit ourselves to the Lord, and he must forgive the past, and make with us a covenant of peace, or else there is no peace for us; for "there is no peace, saith my God, unto the wicked."

Let me briefly explain to you the way in which we come to possess peace with God. We are criminals condemned, though we do not consider ourselves to be in such a critical condition. We persist that we are righteous, we decline to acknowledge the jurisdiction of the law, and we refuse to own the justice of its sentence. Therefore or ever we can have peace with God we must be brought into court, hear the indictment preferred against us, and be put on our trial. When thus arraigned we must put in our pleading. Dost thou say "Not guilty"? Then, man, thou challengest thine accuser to bring forward the evidence which will soon spoil thy conceit, and crush thee with its weight. But before there can be peace between us and God *we must with all our hearts plead "guilty."* We must confess the truth, for God will never agree with liars, nor with those who indulge self-deception. He is a God of truth, and dissemblers can have no communion with him. Being guilty, we must take the place of the guilty: it is our proper position, and it is due to the judge of all the earth that we take it; to refuse to do so is contempt of court. There is mercy for a sinner, but there is no mercy for the man who will not own himself a sinner. "If we confess our sins he is faithful and just to forgive us our sins"; but if any man say that he has no sin he is a liar, and the truth is not in him, and there cannot be peace between him and God while he is in that humour.

It seems a stern demand, and very galling for our pride, to have to stand in the dock, and in answer to the question, "Guilty or not guilty?" to reply, "Guilty, Lord, guilty. Whatever the consequences may be, guilty." But to some of us it no longer seems to be hard, because we could not now plead otherwise. We are so conscious of our guilt that we cannot escape from a sense of it. "If I wash myself with snow water, and make my hands never so clean, yet shalt thou plunge me in the ditch, and mine own clothes shall abhor me." We cannot look upon a single day without being convinced of sin; and in reviewing our past lives from our childhood, we are over and over constrained to blush at the memory of our waywardness and our wilfulness, our perverseness and our provocation. The faults and the follies that have tracked our course haunt us, till our very looks would tell the truth though our tongues were silent. To plead guilty has now become a positive though a painful relief to us; it is the ending of a vain show which we found it hard to keep up; it is coming to the bottom of the matter, and knowing the worst of our case. Dear hearer, before thou canst have peace with heaven thou must take up thy true position, and plead guilty. I pray the Holy Spirit to lead thee to do so. It is his work to convince us of sin, and if he shall exercise his divine office upon any of us we shall no longer profess like the Pharisee that we are not as other men, but like the publican we shall heartily pray, "God be merciful to me a sinner."

Supposing that with confusion of face, contrition of heart, and aroused conscience we own and acknowledge our inexcusable guilt, *the next thing requisite to our peace is that we should admit the justice of the divine sentence,* and reverence instead of reviling the Judge of all the earth, against whom we have so grossly revolted. There are men who will say, "Yes, I am guilty and sinful, but still the penalty is out of proportion to my criminality; I cannot believe that God will deal so severely with the offences of his creatures." Now, however rational such reflections may sound they certainly are not acceptable with God. Of this thing, my friend, I warrant thee: if the Holy Spirit has ever shown thee sin in its natural hideousness and deformity, thou wilt think nothing too bad for it. Thou wilt cry from the depths of thy soul, "Let it be condemned, let it be punished." I would not, if I could, lift a finger to prevent God from punishing sin. Whatsoever a man soweth, that must he reap: the result of sin must follow its commission. The foundations of society would be undermined and there would be no living in the world if there were no laws, or if laws might be violated with impunity. There would indeed be no proof that there was a great Judge of all the earth if he did not do right; and if he does right, he must punish sin, for it ought to be punished. Were I the judge of quick and dead the first thing that I would do would be to condemn myself, for I deserve condemnation and punishment. Neither would it yield my heart the least comfort to be told that God could wink at sin. I want not such a God, neither could I endure to think that the law of righteousness was thus relaxed. My conscience would not be relieved of a sense of obligations I could not deny, nor of impurities I could not cleanse, nor of wrongs I could not rectify, by a suspicion that the Majesty of heaven had threatened a damnation which did not exist. I pray the Spirit of God to bring you, my hearer, not only to be convinced of sin, but of righteousness and of judgment to come. God is righteous in fixing a day in which he will judge the world by the man Christ Jesus, according to our gospel.

This appears to be a painful process, to be bound to confess your guilt, and then to bare your neck to the sword of vengeance, and to say, "Thou wilt be justified when thou judgest, and wilt be clear when thou condemnest; for against thee, thee only have I sinned, and done this evil in thy sight;" yet, there cannot be any peace with God till we come to it: because there can be no peace with the God of truth where there is any prevarication. Lasting peace must be founded upon everlasting truth. The fact is, we are guilty, and we deserve the punishment which God apportions to guilt, and we must agree with that truth, grim as it looks, or else we cannot be friends with God.

The next essential to our receiving justification is this: the prisoner is guilty, sentence is pronounced, and he admits the righteousness of it; he is asked if he has anything to say why the sentence should not be executed, and he stands speechless: and now comes in the abounding mercy of *God, who, in order to our peace, finds a substitute to bear our penalty, and reveals to us this gracious fact.* He puts his Son into the sinner's place. Voluntarily doth the divine Saviour take upon himself our nature, and come under the law, and by a sovereign act Jehovah lays upon him the iniquity of us all. That sin having been laid on Christ, he has borne it and carried it away. In his own body he bore it on the tree. The transgressions of his people were made to meet upon his devoted person: those five wounds tell what he suffered, that marred countenance bears the tokens of his inward grief, and that cry, "My God, my God, why hast thou forsaken me?" indicates to us, as far as we are able to understand it, what he endured when he stood in the sinner's stead, the sin-bearer and the sacrifice.

When the Lord enables the soul to perceive that Christ stood in its stead, then the work of appropriating the justification is going on. Christ died "the just for the unjust, that he might bring us to God;" for he "made him to be sin for us, who knew no sin; that we might be made the righteousness of God in him." He was "made a curse for us: as it is written, Cursed is every one that hangeth on a tree." Christ hath once suffered for sin, and this is the foundation of our peace.

The point wherein faith comes into contact with pardon is when faith believes that the Son of God did come and stand in the sinner's stead, and when faith accepts that substitution as a glorious boon of grace, and rests in it, and says, "Now I see how God is just, and smites Christ in my stead. Seeing he condemned me before I had personally sinned, because of Adam's sin, I see how he can absolve me, though I have no righteousness, because of Christ's righteousness. In another did I fall, and in another do I rise. By one Adam I was destroyed: by another Adam am I restored. I see it. I leap for joy as I see it, and I accept it as from the Lord."

This is not quite all, for now here stands the guilty one, who has owned the sentence, and he has seen the sentence executed upon another. What then? *He takes his place as no longer liable to that sentence.* The penalty cannot be exacted twice. It were neither in accord with human or divine righteousness that two individuals should be punished for the same offence unless both were guilty. When God devised the plan of substitution the full penalty demanded of the guiltless surety was clearly intended to bring exemption to the guilty sinners. That Jesus should suffer vicariously and yet those for whom he paid the quittance in drops of blood should obtain no acquittal could not be. When God laid sin upon Christ it must have been in the intent of his heart that he would never lay it on those for whom Christ died. So then there standeth the man who was once guilty, but he is no more condemned, because another has taken upon him the condemnation to which he was exposed. Still more, inasmuch as the Lord Jesus Christ came voluntarily under the law, obeyed the law, fulfilled the law, and made it honourable, according to the infinite purpose and will of God the righteousness of Christ is imputed to the believer. While Christ stands in the sinner's place, the believing sinner stands in Christ's place. As the Lord looked upon Christ as though he had been a sinner, though he was no sinner, and dealt with him as such, so now the Lord looks upon the believing sinner as though he were righteous, though indeed he has no righteousness of his own; and he loves him, and delights in his perfect comeliness, regarding him as covered with the mantle of his Redeemer's righteousness, and as having neither spot nor wrinkle nor any such thing.

This is wonderful doctrine, but it is the doctrine of the word of God. It is the doctrine whereon faith can feed and rest; and when faith receives it she says to the soul, "Soul, thou art free from sin, for Christ has borne thy sin in his own body on the tree. Soul, thou art righteous before God, for the righteousness of Christ is thine by imputation." Without any works of thine own thou art yet justified according to the righteousness of faith, even as faithful Abraham, of whom it is written, "He believed God, and it was counted unto him for righteousness." This is a wonderful exchange, the putting of Christ where the sinner was, and of the sinner where Christ was. And, now, what does the court say? The court says, "Not guilty; absolved; acquitted." And what is the condition of the man towards God? Why, he can say—

> " ' Now freed from sin, I walk at large;
> My Saviour's blood's my full discharge.
> At his dear feet my soul I lay,
> A sinner saved I'll homage pay.'

Now do I love the Lord, and I know that the Lord loveth me."

By this process we have come to the truth before God, and we have dealt with each other on the line of truth. There has been no fabrication or falsehood. Justice has been vindicated, mercy has been magnified, and we are justly forgiven. Strange fusion of vehement grace and vindictive wrath! Behold how judgment and mercy have linked hands together in the person of the dying, bleeding, rising Son of God. This is the way by which we obtain justification.

The soul may well have a settled peace when it has realized and received such a justification as this, seeing it is a peace consistent with justice. The Lord has not winked at sin; he has not treated sin as if it were a trifle; the Lord has punished transgression and iniquity. The rod has been made to fall, and the blessed shoulders of our Lord have been made to smart under the infliction. If justice had never been satisfied the human conscience would not have been content. The proclamation of unconditional mercy would never have satisfied a human mind. If we had to preach to you that God forgave you irrespectively of an atonement, no awakened conscience would welcome the tidings; we should still have to confront the question, "Where is justice, then?" We should be unable to see how the law could be vindicated, or the moral government of God maintained. We are quite at rest, when we see that there is as much justice as there is mercy in the forgiveness of a believing soul, and that God is as glorious in holiness when he passes by sin as he would have been if he had cast the whole race into the abyss of unfathomable woe.

Nor need there be any morbid apprehension as to whether all the evidence that could be produced against us at our trial has been brought forward. Nobody can come in and say "Though you have been exonerated upon a partial trial, upon a more searching investigation your guilt could have been proved." We can reply, " But it was proved." There was the best of evidence to prove it, for we confessed it. There was no other evidence wanted, and nothing further could have been brought, since we pleaded guilty to every charge. If you bring any further accusation, we can only say that we pleaded guilty without reserve. It was all in the indictment; we did not attempt for a moment to cloak or conceal any guilt we had incurred. We confessed it all before the

Lord, and owned to it; and since the Lord Jesus Christ took it all there is no cause for reopening the proceedings. There cannot be a second trial through a writ of error: the case is thoroughly disposed of; the prisoner has pleaded guilty to the capital charge, and has borne the utmost penalty of the law by his Substitute, which penalty God himself has accepted. His acquittal is such as he can rest upon with implicit reliance.

Moreover we know that, being justified, we are now at peace with God, because there cannot be any more demands made against us. All that was against us Christ took away. "The blood of Jesus Christ his Son cleanseth us from all sin." The death of our great Redeemer has abounding merit in it, seeing that he was the Son of God. All the transgressions and iniquities that could ever be raked up against us were all laid to his charge, and his atonement by one offering has put an end to them all. We are not afraid, therefore, that anything fresh will be raised against us.

Again, our acquittal is certified beyond all question, and the certificate is always producible. Somebody might say to a prisoner "How do you know that you were acquitted?" He cannot produce any writing. On the record of the court it stands; and yet, mayhap, he has no means of access to the court record. But, beloved, you and I have a writ of acquittal which is always visible. Faith can see it to-night. "What is that?" say you. It is the risen Christ, for Jesus Christ "died for our sins, and rose again for our justification." You all know how that was. He was cast into the prison of the grave until it had been certified that our liabilities were fully discharged, and

> "If Jesus ne'er had paid the debt
> He ne'er had been at freedom set."

He was our hostage, and his body was held in durance till it was certified that there was no further claim against any one of his people. That done, he rose again from the dead for our justification. He is at the Father's right hand, and he could not be there if any of our iniquity remained on him. He took our sin, but he has our sin no longer, for on the cross he discharged and annihilated it all so that it ceased to be, and he has gone into the glory as the representative and the substitute of his people, cleared from their imputed liabilities—clean delivered from anything that could be brought against him on their account. So long as we see the Lord Jesus sitting in the throne of glory, we may boldly ask, "Who is he that condemneth? Christ has died, yea rather, hath risen again, who is even at the right hand of God, who also maketh intercession for us." We know our justification to be for ever complete, and beyond challenge, for Jesus keeps the place of acceptance for us.

And lastly, on this point, it was a justification from the very highest court. You know how it is in law: a matter may be decided in your favour, but there is an appeal to a higher court; and such are the glorious uncertainties of law that a sentence which has been confirmed in several courts may after all be reversed when it comes before the highest authorities. But you and I pleaded guilty *before God*. There is no higher authority than that of God himself. When Jesus stood in our stead *we* we did not put him there; nor did he put himself there; it was the act and deed of the Eternal Father. Is it not written—"The Lord hath laid on him the iniquity of us all." It is not only true as a matter of personal faith that

"I lay my sins on Jesus,"

but as a matter of fact of a far earlier date the Lord laid them on him. There is no higher authority than the Lord's; and therefore do we cry, "it is God that justifieth, who is he that condemneth?" We have been taken into the highest court of all, and there we have been cleared through Jesus's blood; have we not cause to be fully at peace with God, "being justified by faith"? Precious doctrine! Oh to rest in it with a childlike confidence henceforth and for evermore!

II. I now come to the second part of the subject, which is this. Faith brings us into the state of peace which I have explained, and afterwards FAITH GIVES US THE SENSE OF PEACE. "Therefore being justified by faith, we have peace with God."

Will you please to notice that the sense of peace follows upon the state of peace. We do not get peace before we are justified, neither is peace a means of justification. No, brethren, we are justified first. "While we were yet without strength, in due time Christ died for the ungodly." God justifies the ungodly. We have no peace till that is done. At least there may seem to be peace, a horrible peace—the peace of death and of daring presumption—when a man says, "Peace, peace," when there is no peace, and talks about rest when he has a conscience seared as with a hot iron—and a mind drugged with presumption, so that he sleeps that awful sleep which is the presage of waking up in hell. From such peace may God deliver us! But real peace—the peace of God—and peace with God must spring out of our being justified in the way which I have been trying to describe. The man who is justified, according to the text, at this moment has a sense of peace with God, but this is only true of those who by faith are justified.

Here I want you to observe—for every word is instructive—that we have peace with God "through Jesus Christ our Lord." Many children of God lose their peace in a measure, and part of the reason of it is because they begin to deal with God absolutely. None of us will ever experience true peace with God except through Jesus Christ. I like that strong expression of Luther, bald and bare as it is, when, in commenting on the Epistle to the Galatians, he says, "I will have nothing to do with an absolute God." If you have anything to do with God absolutely, you will be destroyed. There cannot be any point of contact between absolute deity and fallen humanity except through Jesus Christ, the appointed Mediator. That is God's door; all else is a wall of fire. You can by Christ approach the Lord, but this is the sole bridge across the gulf.

Whenever you, dear soul, begin to deal with God according to your own experience, according to your own frames and feelings, or even according to the exercises of your own faith, unless that faith keeps its eye on Christ, you will lose your peace. Stand out of Christ, and what a wretched creature you are! Have you attempted to approach the Eternal King without his chosen ambassador? How presumptuous is your attempt! The throne of divine sovereignty is terrible apart from the redeeming blood. Peace with God must come to us by the way of the cross. Through our Lord Jesus Christ we gain it, and through him we keep it.

There be some among you who, I trust, are really believers in Christ, who are constantly prone to fret and say, "I have no lasting peace. I am a believer in Jesus, and I have a measure of peace at times, but I do not enjoy fulness of peace." Well, now we must look at this a little, and the more closely we inspect it the more convinced we shall be that peace is the right of every believer. What is there now between him and God? Sin is forgiven. What is more, righteousness is imputed. He is the object of eternal love; he is more than that; he is the object of divine complacency. God sees him in his Son, and loves him. Why should he not be at peace? "Let not your heart be troubled; ye believe in God," said Jesus, "believe also in me." Christian, there is no ground of quarrel between you and your heavenly Father. God for Christ's sake has forgiven you. To you the Lord virtually says, "Come now and let us reason together, though your sins be as scarlet, I have made them as wool. Though they be red like crimson, I have already made them as snow." When he says, "They shall be," he is speaking to the sinner; but to you they *are* so. You are justified. Why have you not peace, then? You have a claim to it, and you ought to enjoy it. What is the reason why you do not possess it? I will tell you. It is your unbelief. You are justified by faith, remember; and it is by faith that you obtain peace with God; and when you are doubting and fearing instead of simply believing—when you are questioning and grumbling, then it is that you lose your peace; but in proportion as your faith stands so will your peace with God abide.

I feel certain that the text tells us that every justified man has peace with God; and if so how is it that I hear poor souls crying, "I do believe, but I do not enjoy peace." I think I can tell you how it is. You make a mistake as to what this peace is. You say, "I am so dreadfully tempted. Sometimes I am drawn this way, and sometimes the other, and the devil never lets me alone." Listen. Did you ever read in the Bible that you were to have peace with the devil? Look at the text—"Therefore being justified by faith, we have peace *with God.*" That is a very different thing from having peace with Satan. If the devil were to let you alone and never to tempt you I should begin to think that you belonged to him; for he is kind to his own in his own way, for a while. He has a way of whispering soft things into their ears, and with dulcet notes and siren songs he lures them to eternal destruction. But he worries with a malicious joy those whom he cannot destroy; for in their case he hath great wrath, knowing that his time is short. He expects to see you soon in heaven out of gunshot of him; and so he makes the best of his opportunities to try if he can distress and injure you while you are here. You will soon be so far above him that you will not be able to hear the hell-dog bark, and so he snaps at you now to see if he can hurt you, as once he did your Master when he wounded his heel. You never had a promise of being at peace with the prince of darkness, but there is another promise which is far better: it is this—"The Lord shall bruise Satan under your feet shortly." A bruise it shall be when we have him under our feet; we will triumph like our Master in the breaking of his head. Till then depend upon it the enmity between the seed of the serpent and the seed of the woman will continue, and there will be no truce to the war.

Do I hear another tried one saying, "Alas, it is not the devil; it is myself that I fear. I feel the flesh revolting and rebelling. Lusts that I thought were slain have a terrible resurrection. When I would do good, evil is present with me. Sin assails me with an awful power by reason of the weakness of my spirit and the strength of my flesh, and I cry, 'O wretched man that I am!'" Hearken again. Did the Lord ever promise that you should have peace with the flesh? Oh no, the moment you were converted there began a battle between the flesh and the spirit, and that battle will last till that flesh of yours shall lie low in the dust from whence it came, and your spirit, delivered from its bondage, shall ascend to God. You must not suppose that as long as you are in this body the flesh will help you. Ah no, you will cry with Paul, "O wretched man that I am, who shall deliver me from the body of this death?" You are harassed and hampered by the rising corruption of your nature, and it will still rise. Your brethren will still say of you, "What will ye see in the Shulamite? As it were the company of two armies." The flesh is striving against the spirit, and the spirit against the flesh; and though the lion shall one day lie down with the lamb, the flesh will never agree with the spirit. As the Lord hath war with Amalek for ever and ever, so there is war between the spirit and the flesh so long as the two are in the same man. There is no promise of peace with the flesh, then; but we have peace with God.

"Ah," says another, "I have little peace, for I am surrounded by those that vex me. When I serve the Lord they malign and misrepresent me with scoff and slander. They take up an evil report against me. Woe is me that I sojourn in Mesech, that I dwell in the tents of Kedar. My soul is among lions, even amongst them that are set on fire of hell. They give me no rest." Yes, but I smile as I think of it. Did you ever dream of having peace with the wicked, peace with such as turn aside to their crooked ways, peace with the workers of iniquity? Vain thought! Peace in this world where your Lord was crucified—peace with those that hate you for his sake? Why, did he not say to you at the first, "If the world hate you, ye know that it hated me before it hated you. If ye were of the world, the world would love his own: but because ye are not of the world, but I have chosen you out of the world, therefore the world hateth you." What! do you expect to wear a crown of gold where he wore a crown of thorns? The confessors and martyrs of ancient times never reckoned upon peace with the world. Nor did the apostle Paul, for he said, "The world is crucified to me, and I unto the world." You have no promise of the world's love, but you have a promise of this sort, "These things have I spoken unto you, that in me ye might have peace. In the world ye shall have tribulation: but be of good cheer; I have overcome the world." "And this is the victory which overcometh the world, even our faith." I pray you, then, do not misconstrue the text. It does not say that you shall either have peace with the devil, or peace with the flesh, or peace with the world; but it does say that you have peace with God, which is infinitely better.

"Still," says one, "I find every day that I sin, and I hate myself for sinning. I cannot get to my bed at night but I feel grieved in my soul that I am not more like Christ, and that I cannot grow in grace as I desire. I do not seem to make the advance in the divine life that I hoped I should, and I am full of sin. Whatever I do is stained with defilement. Wherever I go I seem to fall one way or another into something that wounds my conscience and hurts me." Yes; and the Lord never said that you should have peace with sin. I am delighted to find that sin stings you, and that you hate it. The more hatred of sin the better. A sin-hating soul is a God-loving soul. If sin never distresses you, then God has never favoured you. Unless you hate sin you do not love holiness; and if you hate sin you cannot have any peace with it. You will never be satisfied till you are perfect, and when will you be perfect? Why, when you wake up in your Lord's likeness. That will be the hour of your perfection, but till then sin will vex you. Then shall you have no Canaanite to harass you, and there shall be war with Amalek no more, when the last enemy is slain, when sin is extirpated, and you shall be near and like your God. You have no promise of peace with sin, nor need you wish for one, but you have peace with God.

To come back again to what is promised, and indeed to what is not only promised but really bestowed and communicated to us—" Being justified by faith, *we have peace with God.*"

Most assuredly we do enjoy peace with God in this respect—that *we know he loves us.* He would not have given his Son to die for us if he had not. He would not have devised this matchless plan of justification if he had not loved us. Moreover, we feel a fervent love to him in return. We do not love him as we wish to do, nor as we hope to do, but we do love him for all that. We can say, " Lord, thou knowest all things; thou knowest that I love thee."

> " Yes, I love thee and adore,
> Oh for grace to love thee more."

Of the excellence and virtue of this peace we make daily, hourly proof; for now *we are not afraid to go to our covenant God* for all necessary things, and to seek his face for help in time of trouble. Why, to some of us this resorting to God has become so habitual, that we speak with him every hour of the day. Nothing happens but we fly to him for counsel or for succour. We no longer ask leave to do so, for he has given to us the private key and the perpetual permit of access. We have not always such settled peace with our fellow creatures, for at times we so much lack confidence in them that we could not divulge to them our troubles; but we have peace with God; such an amity that we can always have recourse to him, assured of his sympathy and his readiness to come to our relief in every time of need. Our habitude of prayer proves that we have peace with God; we should not think of praying to him if we believed that he was our adversary, or if we doubted his goodwill. If we felt any enmity in our hearts to him we should not go to him as we do, with a childlike hope, in time of distress.

This peace with God makes us *delight in him.* I am sure that every soul here that has been justified by faith delights in God. You do not always feel him equally near, but when he is near it is the joy of your spirit. What are the best and happiest moments you ever know? Are they not those in which you have communion with God? What days can you reflect upon with the greatest satisfaction and ardently wish to have repeated? Are they not those in which his majesty and mercy have been so revealed to your spirit that with mingled awe and sweetness you have realized intensely his power and his presence? Oh, what a good God he is! Bad as we are, how good he is! Now, take care that you indulge this delight very often. If you delight in anything else you will be an idolater, but he has said, "Delight thyself in the Lord, and he will give thee the desire of thy heart." You cannot be too delighted with your God. Is he not perfection itself? Are we not, in all respects, rejoiced to have such a God? We would not have one attribute changed; nor one appointment of his sovereign will in the least degree moved from its order. Let him be as he is, and do as he pleases, and our souls shall delight in him. "Yea, though he slay me, yet will I trust in him." Now, when you can delight in God, though you cannot delight in yourself, it shows that you have peace with him, and are justified.

Then, brethren, this peace also shows itself in our *acquiescing in all that he does in his rough providences.* You know that a hypocrite is like a strange dog that will follow a man as long as he casts him a bone or a bit of meat; but a true believer is like a man's own dog that will follow him when he gives him nothing, and even when he deals him a cuff or a blow. A true believer says, "Shall I receive good from the hand of the Lord, and shall I not also receive evil? If he chasten me, I would sooner be chastened by my Father than I would be caressed by Satan." It were better to smart till one were black and blue under the rod of God, than to be set upon a high throne by the world or the devil. When he offers thee the kingdoms of this world be sure that thou say to the foul fiend, "Get thee behind me"; but when the Lord hands thee the bitter cup be sure to say, "Thy will be done," and take it cheerfully at his hands. If we feel an agreement with our Lord's will it shows that we are at peace with him.

One more evidence of being at peace with God is when you can *with confidence look forward to the time of your departure* out of this world and say, "I can die, if thou, O Lord, be with me." When you can fall in with the words of the hymn we were singing just now—

> "Bold shall I stand in that great day,
> For who aught to my charge shall lay?
> While through thy blood absolved I am,
> From sin's tremendous curse and shame,"

We are not afraid of the day of judgment because we have peace with God, and hence we are not afraid to die.

There is concord and harmony between the righteous God and his redeemed people, and hence fear is banished. He has given to us his Spirit to dwell in our hearts, and now we desire that each rising wish may be prompted by his will. Our mind is agreed with the mind of God. He wishes us to be holy, and we wish to be holy. He would kill sin in us, and we long to have it killed. He wishes us to obey, and we desire to obey. He would have us seek his glory, and we desire that he should be glorified in us, in our whole spirit, soul, and body. The lines of our life run parallel with the life of

God, though upon a lower level: we can never be as he is in the glory of his nature, but still we desire to be holy as he is holy. The life within us is divine, for we have been begotten again by himself, and henceforth we are in Christ, and Christ in us, and so we are at peace with God.

Go your way, my brethren, and swim in this peace. Bathe your weary souls in seas of heavenly rest until you come to the place where not a wave of trouble shall ever roll across your peaceful breasts ; and the very God of peace sanctify you wholly, and preserve you blameless unto the coming of our Lord Jesus Christ. Faithful is he that calleth you, who also will do it. Amen.

8 Rare Fruit

"I create the fruit of the lips; Peace, peace."—Isaiah lvii. 19.

"THE fruit of the lips"! The lips are neither trees of the orchard nor herbs of the garden. What fruit can they bear? The scattering of Babel came of human speech when languages were multiplied, and the united race split up into fragments. Wars and fightings, and hatred and bloodshed have sprung of talk and bluster: these are deadly fruits, the very mention of which brings pain to the heart,—surely it is in vain to look for much that is worth gathering to mouths and tongues. Great talkers are proverbially little doers, and the more talk the less work. We may come for years looking for fruit on this fig-tree and find none. "Nothing but leaves" will be gathered by those who look to the lips for a harvest to fill the barn. This is most true. If you let the lips alone they produce mischief and trouble, and not much else. An unrenewed tongue is worse almost than an unregenerate heart, because bad as the heart may be there is heart in it; the tongue is often heartless, a mere sounding sham with no reality to support its brazen noise. Too many speak with the lips, and their heart is not in what they say. If the lips become the instruments of hypocrisy, and if the fruit of the lips be *only* the fruit of the lips, it is comparable to the apples of Sodom. The lips, moreover, cause pain and evil all around, which the heart alone cannot do. The heart is as an oven closed up; the tongue is a fire raging abroad, setting on flame the course of nature when it is itself set on fire of hell. The lips of the wicked are like the upas tree, which drips poison.

We could readily dispense with the fruit of the lips as it comes from uncircumcised and unclean lips. Go out and gather a basketful of the fruit of the lips,—gossiping, bickering, fault-finding, murmuring, nonsense, vanity, falsehood, boasting, infidelity. I will not tell you all that I might put into that basket. Certainly, if it were to be shred and poured out into the broth of daily life, we should soon have to say as they did who threw the wild cucumber into the pottage, " O thou man of God, there is death in the pot." The fruit of the lips tendeth to vanity, to poverty, to sorrow, to shame, to death. The fruit of the lips is just what the root of an unrenewed, unregenerate heart causes it to be. You know Æsop, and how wisely he kept his master's command when he bade him provide for dinner the best things he could, and when they came together he set out tongues—nothing else but tongues. His master was pleased with his wit, though I am afraid the guests did not relish it, and he ordered him the next time to provide for dinner the worst things he possibly could. Tongues again—nothing else but tongues! Truly Æsop was wise there, for the fruit of the lips is sometimes the best thing in the world, and sometimes the worst thing in the world: it is a blessing and a curse, according to the man whose tongue speaketh. The fruit of the lips may be compared to Jeremiah's figs—the good, very good, but the bad, exceeding bad, exceeding naughty figs, that cannot be eaten. Fruit of the lips, what shall I say about thee? It might seem that the less we said the better, lest in our case also the fruit of the lips should add to the useless heap.

Our text tells us that God creates the fruit of the lips; but this must be understood, of course, with a reservation. He does not create the fruit of the lips as we commonly see it, but the good fruit, the true fruit, the fruit worth gathering, that which *should be* the fruit of the lips—of this God is the Creator. Because the natural fruit is so evil it needs the Creator again to step in, and make us new creatures, and our fruit new also, or else it will remain so bad that the verdict upon it must be "Vanity of vanities, all is vanities." And what is that fruit which the Creator produces from a source which is naturally so barren? First of all, it is the sacrifice of *thanksgiving*—"the fruit of our lips giving thanks to his name." (Heb. xiii. 15.) The fruit of the lips which God creates should be, above all things, *praise*. We ought to delight to praise God: it should be our element, our occupation, our recreation, our very life. We are as much and as evidently intended to praise God as angels are. When I look at a bird, if I study it awhile, I am convinced that it was made to sing. When we look at an angel, and study his formation and character, we are certain that he was ordained to praise God; and he that studies man, if he can see beyond the defects which the fall has brought upon every organ, will be forced to see that he is a creature adapted for the praise of God. Our tongue is the glory of our frame, and it is given us that we may give glory to him who framed it. Articulate speech, which is denied to birds and beasts, is given to us for this major reason—that we may articulately and distinctly praise and magnify the name of the Most High. O man, however eloquent in oratory or charming in song thy lips may be, they are fruitless if thou dost not therewith extol thy Maker! Thy lips are as dry Sahara sand, or as the salt deserts, where not a blade of grass can live, if from them there never springs the sweet flower of gratitude to God, fragrantly expressing itself in words of love. Thy lips should drop as the honeycomb; a gentle dew of thankfulness should distil from them. They should be like the rose, sending forth perpetual perfume; each word should be a fragrant leaf, scattering a sweet smell of adoration. The lips should be the gates of thankfulness, and from between them there should continually pour forth a wealthy traffic of song, bearing abroad the products of a grateful heart, wrought in the forges of glowing thankfulness to God.

Another fruit of the lips should never be forgotten, and that is *prayer*. This should be the fruit of renewed manhood at every age ; the lips of little children can compass prayer, and the mouth of the aged may not fail to utter it. This is a God-created fruit ; he that abounds in it is as a vine which God has blessed. Woe unto the mouth which is silent at the mercy-seat, for it will one day be dumb at the judgment-seat! Those lips are cursed that never pray. Those lips shall blister with unutterable pain that never pray. "Behold, he prayeth," is an absolutely necessary sign of the possession of grace in the heart. True praise never flowered from those lips upon which prayer has never blossomed. Be ye sure of this, that prayer and praise are grapes of the same cluster, and the lips which are barren of the one are bare of the other. These two fruits of the lips God creates wherever his grace enters.

Furthermore, when there is prayer and praise in us, another fruit of the lip is *testimony*. Do you produce this, dear friends? Has God created it from your lips? It is the bearing witness to others of what God can do, because you have received it in your own experience. God blesses us on purpose that we may tell other poor souls how he can bless the sons of men ; and yet there are Christians—at least, I hope they are Christians—who appear to have received great mercy from God, but they keep the matter hidden. Oh! be not such, I pray you. If you have good tidings in your heart, bring forth the fruit of the lip and tell it. "I should stammer," says one. There is a great beauty in the stammering of earnestness. "I could never be eloquent," says one. Yet there is much true eloquence where there is no appearance of it: when a man cannot speak his heart, it matters not if you can read in his face that he would speak with the tongues of angels if he could, for he feels that his theme transcends his utmost ability. Fine words are not forceful ; it is the heart which prevaileth. Tell thy neighbour that Jesus died ; tell thy neighbour that Jesus came into the world to save sinners ; tell thy neighbour he is welcome to Christ ; tell thy neighbour Christ hath saved *thee*. Do not hesitate to tell him of thine own tasting and handling of the good word of life, for this is a most profitable fruit of the lips. What is so likely to prevail with a man as brotherly testimony? How can we so surely attract men to Canaan as by showing its Eshcol clusters, setting them forth with earnest speech, as the Holy Ghost enables us? These discourses of mine are the fruit of my lips. I cannot tell you how much I wish they were more worthy of my Master's honour ; but, such as they are, you all have the benefit of them, and they lay you under an obligation to yield your fruit unto others. I am not called to bear witness alone, and when I have borne my fruit, and you are refreshed, it is your bounden duty to go and bring forth the like fruit for the refreshment of others. Thus much about the threefold fruit of the lips.

Now, there is one renowned topic upon which the lips ought always to be able to speak, and that blessed subject is summed up in the two words of my text, "Peace, peace." "I create the fruit of the lips ; Peace, peace." The lips ought to be occupied with the subject of peace ; this should be their breath : as Saul breathed out threatenings, so should we breathe out peace, and yet again peace, a double peace from our two lips. From the mouth of truth should come kisses of peace, words of peace, the breath of peace. This is the best lip-salve— " Peace, peace." Nothing can so sweeten the breath as " Peace, peace." Nothing can so flavour the palate and delight the heart as this " Peace, peace," felt within, and breathed without. No teeth of ivory, nor lips of coral, are complete in loveliness till over all there glistens the brightness of peace. Fierce speech becomes not loveliness, and threatening and clamour destroy beauty, but the charm of the lips is peace. So I am going to take those two words and recommend them to you as a fruit of the lips which God creates ; and may the Lord help us all to go out of this place with this on our lips—" Peace, peace."

I. We shall employ these words in four ways, and we shall commence by using them as THE CRY OF THE AWAKENED.

When men are awakened by the grace of God into a consciousness of their true condition they find themselves at war with God and at war with their own consciences, and consequently they begin to cry, " Peace, peace": longing eagerly to end the dreadful conflict in which they find themselves engaged. While a man is dead in trespasses and sins, where nature left him, and where the devil keeps him, he has a deadly calm of mind. He is not troubled; he has no bonds in his death, should he die, and none in his life while he is drunken with sin. He is like a brute beast, looking no further than to the pasture in which he feeds: he lives for the present, and, as long as his bodily wants are satisfied, he is content. When the Spirit of God arouses in him thoughts about higher things, the whole matter is changed; he thinks of God, and laments that he has forgotten his Maker. He thinks of that Maker's law, and perceives that he has constantly broken it; indeed, he has never regarded it, but treated it as a thing of nought. He thinks of death, and he says, " I must die, but I am unprepared." He thinks of eternity, of that other world, that lasting world beyond time, that world where we must dwell for ever, and he cries, " Where shall I dwell? and where will my portion be?" He feels it cannot be amongst the sanctified, for he is not one of them. He cannot hope to see the face of God with joy, for he has never sought that face, nor cared for the knowledge of God's ways. As he begins thinking of these high themes, conscience sets before his mind the day of judgment: he sees the heavens on a blaze, and the great Judge calling all men to account: and he is sore troubled. He sees heaven open and all its glory, but he fears that he will be excluded, for he has been a rebel against the Lord; he looks down to hell with all its terror, and it seems to gape for him, as for one most suitable to be its everlasting prey. Do you wonder, then, if the man is tormented with intestine strife, and with horror of a war without ? He has no rest, and he cries " Peace, peace": the cry only echoes in his ear, for what peace can there be to him? Very likely a worldling comes along and says, " You are melancholy. Do not give way to such low spirits. I count it one of the wisest things to drive dull care away. Come with me where they make merry." He goes; but, somehow or other, he sees that all the gold is gilt, and all the finery is flimsy, and that there is nothing in the mirth. The sport is tame and dull to him, and he himself is duller than ever.

He does not enjoy what once was the delight of his eyes; he comes away, and when they ask him to visit their haunts again he says, " No, no. My heart seems heavier there than when I am alone." "As vinegar upon nitre, so is he that singeth songs to a sad heart." There is no suitability in worldly merry-making to ease a tortured spirit. The awakened sinner cries, " Peace, peace. Oh that I had peace."

Then there visits him one who knowingly whispers, " You need not disturb yourself. These things are not so. Do you not know that these are all bugbears of a past generation? We men of modern thought have made great discoveries, and changed all the fears of our benighted ancestors into a brave unbelief. You can live at ease. Do not fret yourself about sin, or heaven, or hell, or eternity." Vain are these stale scepticisms, the man is too much in earnest to be drugged with such soporifics. Boastful unbelief has small power over an agonized soul. God himself has convinced this man of sin, of righteousness, and of judgment, and though he tries to disbelieve he cannot. Conviction haunts him, follows him into his chamber, robs him of his rest, and he cries, "I fain would be an unbeliever if I could, but I cannot. Oh that I had peace! Oh that I had peace!"

Mr. Worldly Wiseman calls upon him, with his friend Dr. Legality, and his assistant-surgeon Mr. Civility, and these try their Balm of Conceit, and Plaister of Natural Goodness. Dr. Legality finds his patient disturbed with the threatenings of the gospel and the doctrines of Holy Writ, and he says, "These things are quite true, but you need not worry, because you have not been so bad as a great many, and if it goes hard with you it will go very hard with the most of people. You are all right, for you have been honest, obliging, generous, and religious." Ay, but if God has been dealing with this man, he will say, " But I am not all right. I feel that I deserve the wrath of God, and that goodness is not in me. You may think it is so, but I know myself, and I have looked into my heart, and I find all manner of evil there. Oh that I had peace! Oh that I had peace!" Self-righteousness is too short a bed for an awakened sinner to stretch himself thereon, neither can flatterers cajole him into a peace based upon forgetfulness of the divine law.

Then comes the priest, and he exclaims, " Come with us, and undergo ceremonies, and take sacraments, and we will ease you of your burden." Perhaps the poor man tries this, but though he tries it he finds no rest whatever. No, the leprosy lies deep within, and no outward form can cleanse away the deep-seated pollution. The burden presses on his heart, and therefore no manipulation of outward rites can remove the heavy load from him. His cry is, " Peace, peace, peace, peace! Oh that I could get it! Oh that I could get it! I would search through earth, and sea, and air, and hell itself, if I might find it, and bless the grave if it would give it me." Dear heart, I sympathize with you. I remember when I would have gone to the utmost verge of this green earth if I could have found peace. I tell you, racks and tortures I would have boldly endured; prison-houses and dungeons I would have bravely entered, and battle and death I would have gladly encountered, if I could have found peace from my accusing conscience; but I found none. I was like that serpent which is said to sting itself to death.

"My thoughts," as George Herbert says, "were all a case of knives." Every motion of my mind seemed to drive a dagger into my heart. A volcano had burst up within my soul, and the burning lava of despair flowed over all. I was no fool, nor was I under a delusion. I think I was never saner than at that dread period of my life; certainly I was never more seriously in earnest. I was not a simpleton scared at his own shadow, but I had cause to be disquieted, for actual guilt was upon me; not that I was worse than others in outward sin, but that I had such a sight and sense of my guiltiness that I could only cry out, "Woe is me! Oh, wretched man that I am!" Then my daily prayer was, "Peace, peace!" but I could not find it. This is a good cry, however, for every awakened spirit. I would put it into the mouth of every penitent: rather may the Lord himself create it there as the fruit of the lips. "Peace, peace."

II. Secondly, our theme is much more cheerful when we see that this is THE ANSWER OF THE SAVIOUR.

It is the fruit of the Saviour's lips, whose lips are as lilies dropping sweet smelling myrrh. It is he that comes to a soul and says, "Peace, peace." Oh, did you ever see him *as dying of sin?* If you have never seen him with the eye of faith you do not know what peace means. After this fashion he shows himself. He looks upon the sinner, troubled and tossed to and fro, and he says, "What aileth thee?" "My sin," says the sinner, "has utterly condemned me." "Dost thou not know that I bore it eighteen hundred years ago and more, in my own body on the tree?" "Yes, Lord, I have heard that thou didst something of the kind, but didst thou bear it so that I need not bear it?" Then the Redeemer shows that he bore the burden of guilt effectually and carried it away into the land of forgetfulness: and, moreover, he makes clear the truth that if he took our sin, it can never be laid on us, for it is not consistent with the Father's justice first to punish the Substitute for sin and then to punish the offender also. That were to make a mockery of Christ Jesus by making him a Substitute and then punishing those for whom he stood as a Surety. Dost thou see that, poor soul? Is it not clear enough that if the Surety is sued for the debt, and is made to discharge it, the original debtor is free? Rest in the fact that this is the believer's case.

"But," says the heart, "my Lord, I know that thou didst die. I see thy wounds, I mark thy open side, but tell me, didst thou die for me in particular?" "Wilt thou trust me, soul? Wilt thou trust me wholly?" "Ah! that I will, my Lord." "Then I bore thy sin. I was punished in thy stead. Thy iniquity has ceased to be. Thy sins I have cast into the depths of the sea. Thy transgression shall never be mentioned against thee any more for ever. Go, and sin no more. Peace, peace!" What can break a peace like this? Why need I fret about sin which is hurled into oblivion? Why should I despair because of my guilt, and reckon myself condemned? I am not condemned, for Jesus was condemned for me—even he in whom my spirit fixes all her trust. He paid my debts, and discharged my liability to justice, and therefore my soul is clear. Peace, peace! Was there ever peace like this? Glory be to my Redeemer for such rest. Truly a God has given us this repose.

> "O thou who didst thy glory leave
> Apostate sinners to retrieve
> From nature's deadly fall,
> Me thou hast purchased with a price,
> Nor shall my crimes in judgment rise,
> For thou hast borne them all."

But did you ever see Christ as he is *risen from the dead?* Here is another vision of consolation, another fount of peace. The poor heart lies prostrate at the Saviour's feet and cries, "I see thee, my Lord; I see how thou hast put away my sin, and I am at peace; but alas! I am a poor fool, and shall sin again, and I have a wayward, wandering heart that will soon be away over the mountains leaping into sin again. How can I hope to enter heaven?" To this the Lord Jesus replies most sweetly, "Dost thou not know that I am risen from the dead? I am he that liveth, though once I died for sin. I am that great Shepherd who lives to take care of his own flock. Because I live thou shalt live also. I am able also to save them to the uttermost that come unto God by me, seeing I ever live to make intercession for them." Do you know the peace which the resurrection of the Lord Jesus brings into the spirit? If so, you find rich fruit hanging upon Jesus' lips. He who knows the virtue of the living Lord at once concludes that the future is as safe as the past. The slain Saviour has slain our past sin, and the living Saviour lives to take care of our eternal life, and to bring us to God's right hand at the last. See how Jesus says, "Peace, peace, peace! All is well."

Did you ever see Jesus as he sits there *triumphant at the Lord God's right hand*? I hope you have; because a poor, tried spirit is greatly comforted by that sight. The downcast one exclaims, "My Lord, I know thou wilt take care of me here, for I perceive that thou livest to provide for me; but I shall have to die, and what shall I then do? My Lord, I am afraid to die. It is grim work—dying. It is a path I never trod before. What shall I do in the swellings of Jordan?" Jesus answers such fears in his own sweet fashion by saying, "Dost thou not know that I am risen from the dead, and that I have gone into the glory to prepare a place for thee? I will come to thee at the last, and I will take thy spirit away to dwell with me for ever. Thou needest not fear to die, for he that liveth and believeth in me shall never die. He that believeth in me, though he were dead, yet shall he live. I will help thee. Death shall be no death to thee. I will catch thy soul away and thou shalt never know it till thou seest me face to face. As for thy poor dust, it shall lie in the grave a little while, but I will take care of every atom of it, and when I shall descend in the latter day upon the earth, my archangel shall sound his trumpet, and thy poor body shall rise again, only more fair and beautiful than when thou hadst it in its best estate below, and so thou shalt be for ever with the Lord, both as to body and soul." Does not this breathe, "Peace, peace, peace"?

> "Sure the last end
> Of the good man is peace How calm his exit!
> Night dews fall not more calmly on the ground,
> Nor weary worn out winds expire so soft.'

If I were to go on picturing our glorious Lord Jesus Christ in any, and all of his relationships to us, we should in each case hear him say, "Peace, peace." His voice is the sovereign balm which heals every wound, the cordial which removes every fear. No distress or amazement can seize upon you, for which in Christ there is not a peace that passeth all understanding, to keep your heart and soul against all dread and downcasting. This is the fruit of the lips of the Well-beloved —peace, peace, peace. If you do not come to him, you will receive no peace; if you do not keep near him, you will retain no peace; and if you do not come growingly nearer and nearer to him, you will miss much of peace that you might have. Abide in Christ Jesus, and let him abide in you, and you shall have abundance of peace so long as the moon endureth.

A soldier in the Crimean war, as he lay dying, was visited by a worthy missionary. The young man asked his visitor to read a chapter to him, and the chapter chosen was John xiv. When he came to this verse— "Peace I leave with you," the soldier was almost in the article of death, but he said to the reader, "Sir, that is the peace which I enjoy. I have had it for years." "Peace I leave with you." "Now," he said, "if I have known this peace—and I have had it for years—I shall not lose it *now*, but shall die triumphantly." And so he did. Can you, my hearer, say to-night that you have that peace? If you have it now you shall have it in your dying hour. Could you say what Dr. Watts said to his host, Sir Thomas Abney? He said, "Sir Thomas, I thank God that for many a month I have been able to say, 'It is a matter of perfect indifference to me, when I fall asleep at night, whether I wake up in this world or in another.'" I well remember reading the old story of a Methodist, who was pressed into the army some fifty or sixty years ago, who had his leg carried away in battle, and lay bleeding on the ground. When they carried him off the field he said, "I am as happy as a man can be while out of heaven." They said he was mad. O for more of such glorious madness. To be able to say when your limb is shot away, and you are bleeding away your life, "I am as happy as a man can be out of heaven," why there is something in that surely! This must be the finger of God. Where else can such triumph over pain and weakness be found? What voice but that of Jesus can in such a storm command a heavenly calm? Jesus, Master, whose message to thy people is always "Peace, peace," speak thou that divine word to me, and to all thy troubled ones. Stand in our midst and say, "Peace be unto you," and peace shall be ours.

III. Thirdly, I am going to use these words as THE SONG OF THE TRUE BELIEVER.

He who has really seen Christ, and placed his trust in him, can now sing, "Peace, peace, peace." What a thrice accursed thing is war! I believe with Benjamin Franklin that there never was a good war, and there never was a bad peace. War is unmitigated mischief from end to end, and peace is a thing to rejoice at, take it in whatever light you will. Killing and slaying, devastating and burning, are sport for fiends, and for fiends alone. True men, if once called to battle, are the last persons who would lightly enter upon it again. It is an awful and terrible thing. I recollect reading that when the last great war was over—I mean the great war of all, in which we were so long engaged with the Buonapartes—news of the peace came to a certain town. It was only gently whispered that there was peace, but it was all over the town in a few minutes. Everybody ran through the streets. Bread had been sent up to an awful price by the war, and everybody was weary with the taxes, the slaughter of soldiers, and the perpetual fear of invasion. A man ran down the street shouting, "Peace, peace, peace, peace," and everybody was glad. All manner of good things were wrapped up in the one word "peace": families would no more be divided, trade would no longer be crippled, famine would no more devour the land. Now the loaf would be within the reach of the poor and the hungry; and the widow might keep her sons at home, safe from the cannon's mouth. "Peace, peace," they cried; and within an hour there were bells ringing from every steeple, and as the sun went down there were candles in every window. Everybody must have an illumination because peace had come. Now, if peace be so precious as to temporal things, it is equally precious as to eternal things; and if a man has once seen Jesus Christ, it is the joy of his life to sing, "Peace, peace." Here stands the reconciled man, and he looks up to heaven through the pure blue air, past yon stars, endless leagues beyond imagination's utmost stretch: he looks up, and his mind conceives of God, and his heart feels, "I am at peace with him. Though he be a consuming fire, I am at peace with him. With the great Father I am at peace. Though it is very tempestuous round about him, yet I am at peace with him. I am at peace with the eternal Son: though he shall break his enemies with a rod of iron, he will never break me; I am at peace with him. I am at peace with the Holy Ghost, for though to blaspheme him is death without hope of mercy, yet I am at peace with him: he will never destroy me." What a peace is this!—peace with God, the peace of God, perfect peace. Having this peace, every angel is my friend, every cherub is my guardian; and all the hosts in glittering ranks above, of spirits angelic and unfallen, and of spirits human, saved and washed in the blood, are all my friends, for I have peace with the armies of heaven if I have peace with the Lord of hosts. How delightful to look all around you, and to feel confident that providence is on your side! The wheels are stupendous, and the results that come of their revolution are mysterious and terrible ; but let the wheels revolve, they cannot hurt a child of God. All things work together for good to them that love God, to them that are the called according to his purpose. There is peace in all events when there is peace with heaven. The beasts of the field are in league with us, and the stones of the field are at peace with us, when we are at peace with God. It is most sweet to feel that wherever you are everything is at peace with you ; and then to look inside into this little world where there once raged such fierce battles, and there also to feel the sprinkled blood— this, this is joy! Conscience is quiet, fear has subsided, the deadly dread is gone, all is quiet, and all is well.

To feel that you have forgiven every enemy if you have any, that you do not bear a recollection of an injury, this also is a brave easement of the heart. As the tablets of the Romans when they had written upon the wax were afterwards rolled over with a hot iron to produce a complete erasure, so by grace we are enabled to smooth out of the soul every angry line, and to begin life anew as to our fellow-men. Revenge and malice are unknown among true Christians. I have no more memory of ill towards any man that liveth than a babe unborn. This is a clear atmosphere to live in! How different from the thunder-charged air of envy, malice, and hate! "Ye shall go out with joy, and be led forth with peace: the mountains and the hills shall break forth before you into singing, and all the trees of the field shall clap their hands." Blessed are the men who live in this peace,—peace of God's giving; peace of the Holy Ghost's working; peace above and peace below, peace within and peace around: peace, peace, the blessed fruit of the lips.

IV. I close by using my text in a fourth way, practically, by saying that this should be THE MOTTO OF EVERY BELIEVER.

It has been his song for himself,—now let it be his motto in dealing with other people. This should be his spirit and desire *in the church*— "Peace, peace." I thank God that we have enjoyed peace as a church these many years, but I have known certain churches where peace would be a novelty, a novelty which I recommend them to try. Some little churches seem to think that they must have an angry discussion every month, or else they are living beneath their gospel privileges. This leads to heart-burnings, and promotes splits and divisions, and these are as frequent among them as fights at an Irish wake. They want a new minister every now and then, for they consider their want of prosperity to be the minister's fault: and then they want a fresh set of deacons, for the evil is thought to be the deacons' fault. By-and-by they discover that some leading man, or, what is worse, some leading woman, is at the bottom of the evil, and they must get rid of him or her, and then all will go right; and they practise the process of dismemberment, cutting off one part of the body, and then another, till they think the smaller they become the better they will be. What a mistake! Do they think to find peace by breaking into pieces? The more Christians are divided the more they can subdivide, and the smaller the sect the more prepared is it for another schism. Brethren, whenever you fall a-quarrelling I shall know that the Spirit of God has gone from you. Hitherto we have put up with one another very well, by God's grace, and I hope we shall continue to do so. I do not suppose you ever thought that I was perfect: if you did, you did not know much about me. I knew very well that you were not perfect. I never flattered you from the very beginning, and therefore I am not disappointed in you. We have gone on wonderfully well with each other, considering how imperfect we are; and I trust that the grace of God, which has kept so large a multitude together in love and peace, will continue to do it, to his own glory.

Now, especially when I am away, if any enemy brings strange fire to set the church alight with it, I pray you who are older and wiser than others to keep your buckets full of water, and stand ready to quench the first spark of ill feeling. You, good brothers and sisters, who are rather fond of talking, if you see a little blaze beginning, leave off your talking, for fear you should be adding fuel to the flame. Do not repeat what you have heard against a brother, but ring the curfew, and cover the fire. Pull the logs all apart, and throw the holy water of love over the hot ashes. Do not let the fire of anger burn. Why should we? We have to live together in heaven for ever, we may as well enjoy happy fellowship here. May the Lord grant us to feel the force of those heavenly principles, which will enable us to live in peace and quiet for many and many a year to come! I would like every member of the church to go about saying within himself, "Peace, peace. I am a peace-maker in the church, and if I ever must be a peace-*breaker* it shall not be in the house of God, among the family of the Lord Jesus."

We should labour to carry out the same quiet spirit *in the family*. When you get home do not change "Peace, peace," into scolding and nagging. "If it be possible, as much as lieth in you, live peaceably with all men." The apostle says, "If it be possible," because he knew that it would be a very difficult thing always to be peaceable with everybody, for some people are so unreasonable that they are never at peace till they are at war, and never quiet till they are making a disturbance. Be it ours under great provocation still to cry, "Peace, peace." Put up with a great deal: bear, and bear, and bear, and bear, and bear—I have not time to repeat the word—till seventy times seven. They will most surely conquer who can most completely submit, for in this world he that would be greatest must be least, and he that can stoop the lowest shall rise the highest. I do not think there is much in a heritage worth fighting for compared with brotherly unity. Family peace and love are worth more than a disputed will can ever yield. The game of quarrelling is not worth the candle. When I have had to compose family differences I have usually found that the misunderstanding began about nothing, and went on about nothing; and yet the mischief done is frequently terrible. When I have to make peace, I like to have some *real* injury, injustice, or wrong to deal with: something that I can handle, judge, and condemn; but an invisible, misty, indefinable suspicion is hard to overcome. When there is nothing in the squabble, peace-making is difficult work. There is a great tingle-tangle over nothing. You cannot get at it. It is a sort of stinging jelly-fish, which you feel but cannot grasp. Loving bonds are broken, and there is ill-blood between Christian men and Christian women who ought to love one another, and all about—about—nothing! Now, you Christian people, go about with this as your pass-word— "Peace, peace, peace, peace." This will quiet the worst termagant of a wife that ever wearied a man—peace, peace. This will sober the most outrageous husband that ever tried a woman—peace, peace. Cultivate peace in the home garden whatever you do elsewhere.

When peace reigns in your own family, go *into the world* with the same watchword—"Peace, peace." Do not set dogs by the ears, but tame lions and tigers. Compose differences, and make people friends. If certain persons were dropped into the garden of Eden, they would be the serpent in it; but there are others who, if you were to set them down in a village distracted with strife and contention, they would be lumps of love to sweeten every bitterness. Try and be just such. Members of the Tabernacle, especially, let your motto always be, "Peace, peace," amongst your neighbours, for the glory of God.

What a difference there will be when this is taken up among all Christian sects—when there shall be no more envying and strife between this denomination and that, but each one shall be saying in Christ's name, "We are brethren—peace, peace." How silly it is for one clique of good people to be setting up Mr. So-and-so as "the greatest preacher that ever lived." How idle for others to reply, "No, he is not. So-and-so preaches better." Let all this be silenced while we cry, "Peace, peace." None of us who are ministers preach as well as we ought to do, and none of you who are hearers live as you ought to live. When you hear anything like crying up of such poor mortals as we are, cry, "Peace, peace," to such nonsense! We are all servants of one Master; and may the Lord make us all better servants! Let peace ring the death-knell of petty jealousies, and may all the saints be visibly one in Christ Jesus!

May the day come when, all the world over, there shall be peace; peace to Afghan and to Zulu, as it is to-day to Prussian and to Frenchman and to Englishman. Let us wish "Peace, peace" to all of woman born. May this blessed word be rung out as a clarion note beneath these heavens till men shall recognise that they make one family, and God is the one great Father. Ye nations, learn war no more! "Peace, peace, peace." Catch the words, ye winds, and waft them—"Peace, peace, peace." Hear the words, ye stars, and shine them out to-night—"Peace, peace." Rise up, O sun, in the morning, and over all rejoicing lands pour forth, with thy light and warmth, peace and quietness! May peace be with you, my brethren, henceforth and for ever. Amen and amen.

9 The Song of a City, and the Pearl of Peace

"Thou wilt keep him in perfect peace, whose mind is stayed on thee: because he trusteth in thee."—Isaiah xxvi. 3.

THIS is no dry, didactic statement, but a verse from a song. We are among the poets of revelation, who did not compose ballads for the passing hour, but made sonnets for the people of God to sing in after days. I quote to you a stanza from "the song of a city." Judah has not aforetime thus chanted before her God, but she has much to learn, and one day she shall learn this psalm also:—" We have a strong city; salvation will God appoint for walls and bulwarks." Into the open country the adversary easily advances, but walled cities are a check upon the invading foe. Those people who had been hurried to and fro as captives, and had frequently been robbed of their property by invaders, were glad when they saw builded among them a city, a well-defended city, which should be the centre of their race, and the shield of their nation.

This song of a city may, however, belong to us as much as to the men of Judah, and we may throw into it a deeper sense of which they were not aware. We were once unguarded from spiritual evil, and we spent our days in constant fear; but the Lord has found for us a city of defence, a castle of refuge. We have a burgess-ship in the new Jerusalem which is the mother of us all; and within that strong city we dwell securely. Let us sing this morning, "We have a strong city." The man that hath come into fellowship with God through the atoning sacrifice, hath gotten into a place of perfect safety, where he may dwell, ay, dwell for ever, without fear of assault. We are no longer hunted by hosts of fears, and trodden down by dark despairs; but "We have a strong city" which overawes the foe, and quiets ourselves. Our gospel hymns are the songs of men who, in the truest spiritual sense, have seen an end of alarm, by accepting God's provision against trouble of heart.

Observe how the song goes on to dilate upon the city's strength. "Salvation will God appoint for walls and bulwarks." Our refuge will repay a close examination. We are doubly defended. Its lofty walls are the mainstay of a city's security; when they are strong, and high, they keep out the foe, whether he assail by scaling-ladder, or battering-engine. Outside the wall, on the other side of the moat, lies what is called the bulwark; the earthwork where, in times of peace, the citizens delight to take their walks. The bulwark of their confidence is the *boulevard* of their communion. The Lord our God has set ring upon ring, defence upon defence, around his people. All the powers of providence and of grace protect the saints. Material and spiritual forces alike surround her. The Lord keeps his people doubly fenced by walls and bulwarks, and hence he speaks of a double peace. " Thou wilt keep him in peace, peace," saith the Hebrew. God does nothing by halves, but everything by doubles. His salvation is decreed and appointed, and this is made the basis for the unbroken serenity of all his chosen.

The song, however, does not end with verses concerning the city, but it conducts us within its walls. " Open ye the gates, that the righteous nation which keepeth the truth may enter in." Entrance into this grace, wherein we stand, is a choice privilege. The greatest joy of true godliness lies in our being able to enter into it. If the City of God were shut against us, it were sad, indeed, for us. If, to-day, you and I were outside of her, of what value would her walls and bulwarks be to us? Whatever God has done to his people, it is just so much additional sorrow rather than increased joy to ourselves if we are not partakers therein. That there should be a Christ, and that I should be Christless; that there should be a cleansing, and I should remain foul; that there should be a Father's love, and I should be an alien; that there should be a heaven, and I should be cast into hell, is grief embittered, sorrow aggravated. Come, then, let us sing of personal entrance into the City of God. The music and the feasting are not outside the door: to enjoy them we must enter in. Our citizenship is now in heaven. Nothing is barred against us, for the Son of David has set before us an open door, and no man can shut it. Let us not neglect our opportunities. Let it not be said, "They could not enter in because of unbelief." No, let it be ours to sing of salvation because we enjoy it to the full. Let our music never cease.

Now, when we get as far as this,—a strong city, and a city into which we have entered, we are still further glad to learn who the keeper and garrison of that city may be, for a city needs to be kept while there are so many foes abroad. To render all secure there needs to be some leader and commander for the people, who has strength with which to man the walls, and drive off besiegers. Our text tells us how securely this strong city will be held—so securely that none of her citizens shall ever be disturbed in heart,—" Thou wilt keep him in perfect peace, whose mind is stayed on thee: because he trusteth in thee."

Permit me to remind you again that my text is the verse of a song. I earnestly desire you to feel like singing all the time while I am preaching, and let the words of the text ring in your heart with deep mysterious chimes, as of a land beyond these clouds and tempests.—" Thou wilt keep him in perfect peace, whose mind is stayed on thee: because he trusteth in thee." I do not want you to be thinking, " I wish that the Lord would keep me in peace;" I would have you now enter into rest before the Lord. Do not say, " I am fretting and worrying, because I cannot reach this peace;" but pray to enjoy it this morning. O Lord and Giver of peace, vouchsafe it to our faith at once! O ye trustful ones, enter at once into the opened gates of the city of peace, and then bless God that you cannot be driven out again, for the Lord promises to be your garrison and safeguard. May the Holy Spirit, who is the Comforter, and whose fruit is peace, now work peace in each of us!

I. First, we are going to answer this question as best we can, WHAT IS THIS PERFECT PEACE? The text in the original, as I have told you, is—"Thou will keep him in peace, peace." It is the Hebrew way of expressing emphatic peace; true and real peace; double peace, peace of great depth and vast extent. Many of you know what it is; and you will probably think my answer a very poor one. I shall give the best I can, I can do no more; and if you try to make up for my deficiencies, our brethren will be gainers. I confess that I cannot to the full describe the peace that may be enjoyed if our faith is strong, and our confidence in God has reached its appropriate height. We are not limited as to quality or measure of this precious thing. Peace is a jewel of so rare a price that he only hath valued it aright who has sold all that he hath to buy it. Describe it? Nay, verily, there we fail.

This "peace, peace" means, I think, *an absence of all war, and of all alarm of war*. You who can imagine the full meaning of siege, storm, sack, and pillage, can also guess the happier state of things when a city hears no longer the tramp of armies, when from her ramparts and towers no sign of adversary can be discovered; but all is peace. That is very much the condition of the people of God when the Lord keepeth them in peace. God himself, at one time, seemed to be against us: the ten great cannon of his Law were turned against our walls; all heaven and earth mustered for battle; God himself was against us, at least, so conscience reported from her look-out. But, now, at this moment, having believed in Jesus Christ, we have entered into rest, and we have perfect peace as to our former sins. Who is he that can harm you, O ye that are reconciled to God? "If God be for us, who can be against us?" "Who shall lay anything to the charge of God's elect?" We have by faith arrived at a state of perfect reconciliation with God. The divine Fatherhood has covered us. We inherit the spirit of children, the spirit of love and of unquestioning confidence. Everything is quiet, for we dwell in our Father's house. Look upward, and you will perceive no seat of fiery wrath to shoot devouring flame. Look downward, and you discover no hell, for there is no condemnation to them that are in Christ Jesus. Look back, and sin is blotted out. Look around, and all things work together for good to them that love God. Look beyond, and glory shineth through the veil of the future, like the sun through a morning's mist. Look outward, and the stones of the field, and the beasts of the field, are at peace with us. Look inward, and the peace of God, which passeth all understanding, keeps our hearts and minds by Christ Jesus. The Lord leadeth us by still waters at such happy times, along that road of which we read, "No lion shall be there." If you who are believers in Jesus do not usually enjoy this peace, the blame must be laid to your own door: you make your own disquietude, for God saith to you, "Peace, peace," and he will keep you there if your mind is stayed on him. Happy is he whose conflict is ended, and whose warfare is accomplished by faith in Christ Jesus.

Further, *this perfect peace reigns over all things within its circle*. Not only is no enemy near, but the inhabitants of the city are all at rest, and all their affairs are happy. No man can be said to be at *perfect* peace who has any cause of disquietude at all. Yet the child of God has this perfect peace according to our Lord's own statement; and, therefore, it must be true that the believer is raised above all disquietude. "What," say you, "has he not an evil heart of unbelief?" Yes, and that demands his watchfulness, but should not create in him any kind of terror, for "God is greater than our hearts," and where sin abounded, grace doth much more abound. The flesh has received its death-warrant, and unbelief is but a part of the flesh doomed to die. The holy life within us must triumph. "If we believe not, yet he abideth faithful: he cannot deny himself." Though we be as yet like the smoking flax, we shall soon shine forth, and he will bring forth judgment unto victory. "Ah," saith one, "but I have disquietude in my family: I have a wild, unruly son;" or, "I have a sick, pining child, who will soon be taken away from me by consumption!" Yes, friend, but if your mind is stayed on God, and you can trust God with such matters, you should not lose your perfect peace even through this. For, what if your heart be troubled? Will that make the consumptive child any the stronger? Or will your melancholy be likely to restrain your rebellious son? No, but "The just shall live by faith," and shall triumph by faith, too. It shall be your strength to bring your sick, and lay them at Jesus' feet; it shall be your hope to bring your unruly one, and say, "Lord, cast out the devil from my child, and let him live unto thee." Nothing ought to avail to break the peace of the believer; the shield of faith should quench every fiery dart. For, observe, that your sin is forgiven you for Christ's sake, and that is done once for all. Observe, that Christ has taken possession of you, and you are his; neither will he lose you, but he will hold you single-handed against the world, and death, and hell. Observe, too, that your heavenly Father rules in providence, giving you what you need, for he has said, "No good thing will I withhold from them that walk uprightly." He reigns in power, anticipating every danger, for he hath declared, "No weapon that is formed against thee shall prosper; and every tongue that shall rise against thee in judgment thou shalt condemn." God's peace covers the whole extent of the territory. Tell it out through every street of Mansoul that the Prince Emmanuel has come, and to every creature within the city walls the peace of God is granted, to be possessed with gladness and delight.

We are getting some idea, I trust, of this peace, though words cannot fully convey it; we must know it for ourselves. Yet it is pleasant to note that this peace is deeply real and true. No perfect peace can be enjoyed unless *every secret cause of fear is met and removed.* Whisper it at the gates, and in the hostelries, that the city might be taken by surprise, and that spies had been seen in the meadows, down by the East gate; and straightway the city would be in a ferment. No; peace cannot breathe while suspicion haunts the streets. Our peace may be a false peace, a fool's peace; we may be lulled into a carnal security. Politically, nations have become self-confident, have dreamed of peace when the forges were ringing with the hammers of war; and so ill has happened unto them. Spiritually, there are multitudes of persons who think that all is right with their souls, when, indeed, all is wrong, for eternity. It is to be feared that some have received a "strong delusion, that they should believe a lie." Now, we cannot call that perfect peace which lies only on the surface, and will not bear to be looked into. We desire a peace which sits in open court, and neither blindfolds nor muzzles ambassadors. The peace which requires that there should be a hushing-up of this and of that is an evil thing. Such is the direct opposite of the peace of God. If there be any charge against God's people, men are challenged to bring it,—"Who shall lay any thing to the charge of God's elect?" The pardon which God gives us is not a smothering-up of our sins, nor a blinding of justice. God is as just in his pardons as in his punishments. It shall be seen at the last, when believers enter into their glory, that they rise there by law, just as surely as the lost sink down to hell by law: that is to say, that the Lord Jesus Christ hath rendered to the law such recompense by his perfect obedience, and his matchless atonement, that it shall be as just on God's part to save his elect as to condemn the unbelieving world. We claim that our peace is just and right. It may be examined and tested; for here we have NO FICTION. If truth is to be found beneath the stars, it is in the peace which comes through the precious blood of the Son of God. The peace which God gives goes to the very bottom of things, and brings us into the eternal harmonies.

We may gaze upon this truth with the most attentive eye, but we shall see only the more clearly that he that believeth in the Lord Jesus Christ hath salvation for walls and bulwarks. Under any light believers in Jesus are secure. You may be put in circumstances of a very trying kind, especially you may be brought to the brink of death, and near to the bar of God; and yet, dear friend, the God in whom you trust will not fail you. Your heart rests on his promises and faithfulness, and there is no reason why its peace should be broken.

Is not this a perfect peace? If I stood here to preach up a sort of enthusiastic confidence, which would not bear the test, I would be ashamed of myself; but in preaching this peace of God, which passeth all understanding, which has no back-reckonings to disturb it, which has nothing behind that can come in ultimately to break it up, I preach something worth the having. I do desire and pray that every man and woman here may know it as I know it; for I have peace with God, and therefore my heart is glad. Oh that all of you here present might now believe God, and stay yourselves upon him; then would you hear the Lord say "Peace! peace!"

One thing more, *peace in a city would not be consistent with the stoppage of commerce.* During perfect peace intercourse goes on with all surrounding places, and the city by its trade is enriched. Where there is perfect peace with God, commerce prospers between the soul and heaven. Good men commune with the good, and thereby their sense of peace increases. If you have perfect peace, you have fellowship with all the saints: personal jealousies, sectarian bitternesses, and unholy emulations are all laid aside. Oh, it is a happy state of mind when we have no prejudices which can keep an heir of heaven out of our heart, no peculiarities which can wall out the godly from fellowship with us! Oh, how blessed to say spontaneously, "If he is a child of God, I love him;

if he is a member of the heavenly family, he is my brother, and I welcome him!" When we are at one with all the people of God, we are quit of a world of wars.

Better still, there is a sweet peace between the heart and its God when from day to day, by prayer and praise, we commune with the Most High. Any peace that is linked with forgetfulness of God is a horrible thing: it is the peace of the miasma, which is brooding in quiet before it strikes with the arrow of death; it is that dead calm which precedes the cyclone or the earthquake. The perfect peace which God giveth sunneth itself in the presence of God; it is a tropical flower, which lives in the flaming sun-light; a bird with rainbow-wings, which is at home in the high-noon of heaven's summertide. God give us to know more and more of this perfect peace, by enabling us to plunge more and more completely into his own self! One with God in Christ Jesus, we have reached everlasting peace.

Further let me speak upon this peace that God gives to us. It consists in *rest of the soul*. You know how the body casts all the limbs upon the bed, and they lie at ease; so does our spiritual nature stretch itself at ease. The heart reclines upon God's love, and the judgment leans on his wisdom; the desires recline, the hopes repose, the expectations rest, the soul throws all its weight and all its weariness upon the Lord, and then a perfect peace follows. To this absolute recumbency add a *perfect resignation to the divine will*. If you quarrel with God, your peace is at an end; but when you say, "It is the Lord; let him do what seemeth him good," you have obtained one of the main elements of perfect peace. When the Lord's will is owned and loved, all ground for quarrel is over: the peace must be deep. It consists also in *sweet confidence in God*, when there is not the shadow of doubt about anything God does, for you are sure of this, if of nothing else, that he must be true, that he must be right and kind, and in all things better to you than you are to yourself. Then to leave everything with God, trusting in him for ever, because in him there is everlasting strength—this is peace. It means, in fact, the swallowing up of self in the great sea of God, the giving up of all we are, and all we have, so entirely to God that henceforth we cannot be troubled, or be disturbed, because that which could make trouble is already bound over to keep the peace. Then comes *a blessed contentment;* we want no more, we have enough. "The Lord is my portion, saith my soul; therefore will I hope in him." Having him, my desires all stay at home with him. Let me but know him better, and I shall grow even more satisfied with unutterable beauties, his indiscribable perfections.

I hope you know this peace; and if you do, I need not tell you it means *freedom from everything like despondency*. The mind cannot yield to mistrust, for the Lord's peace keeps it. The compass on board an iron steam-vessel is placed aloft, so that it may not be so much influenced by the metal of the ship: though surrounded by that which would put it out of place, the needle faithfully adheres to the pole because it is set above the misleading influence. So with the child of God, when the Lord has given him peace: he is lifted beyond the supremacy of his sorrowful surroundings, and his heart is delivered from its sad surroundings.

Thus we are *kept from everything like rashness:* resting in God, we are not in sinful haste ; we can wait God's time to deliver us, knowing that there is love in every second of the delay. We do not kick, as the untutored bullock kicks against the goad, but we push on the more eagerly with our furrow, toiling on to the end, till God shall appear for us. Thus we are saved from the temptations which come with our trials. We get the smelting of the furance without its smut. We endure the sorrow, but escape the sin, and this is joy enough for a pilgrim in this vale of tears.

O friends, he that hath this perfect peace is the richest man in the world ! What are broad acres if you have a troubled spirit ? What are millions of gold, laid by in the bank, if you have no God to go to in the hour of distress ? What would it be to be a prince, a king, an emperor, if still you had no hope for the hereafter, no treasure of eternal love ? I, therefore, charge you to get and keep this " peace,"—this perfect peace.

II. May the Lord strengthen me, in this time of painful weakness, while I speak upon another question. WHO ALONE CAN GIVE US THIS PEACE, AND PRESERVE IT IN US ? The answer is in the words of the song, "Thou wilt keep him in perfect peace." See, it is God himself that can give us this peace, and keep us in it. The answer is one and indivisible. I know that while I was speaking some of you were saying, " The pastor is setting forth a high style of living ; how can we reach to it ? " But if peace be God's gift, and if the Lord himself is to keep us in it, how easily can we attain it by putting ourselves into his hands ! To be striving after peace is hard work, for by our very anxiety to find it we miss its trail. How differently does the matter appear when we read, " Thou wilt keep him in perfect peace ! "

How does the Lord keep his people in peace ? I answer, first, *by a special operation upon the mind in the time of its trial.* We read in the 12th verse, " Lord, thou wilt ordain peace for us: for thou also hast wrought all our works in us." If this be so, we can understand how the Lord can work peace in us among all the other works. There is an operation of God upon the human mind, mysterious and inscrutable, of which the effects are manifest enough ; and among those effects is this, a quiet of heart, a calm of spirit, which never comes in any other way. " Thou wilt keep him in perfect peace." The Creator of our mind knows how to operate upon it by his Holy Spirit. Let the heart and will be allowed to be as free as you choose, yet is the Lord free to act upon them. As we can tune the strings of a harp, so can the Lord adjust the chords of our heart to joyous serenity. Not only by the Word of God, and by our meditation thereon, but by his own direct operation, the Lord can create peace within the land-locked sea of the human spirit. The Lord can get at men, and influence them for the highest ends, apart from outward means. I have noticed that, altogether apart from the subjects of my reflections, I have, on a sudden, received a singular calm and peace of spirit directly from God. I can remember occasions when I had been hurried through broken water ; the winds were wild, and my little vessel was at one instant lifted out of the water, and at the next beaten under the waves. Then, in a moment, everything was calm as a summer's evening, quiet as when the hush of Sabbath falls on a hamlet in the lone Highlands. My heart was royally glad, for it had entered into perfect peace. I think you must have noticed such matters in your own case. Generally, I grant you, we are led into this peace by the consideration of the promises of God; but sometimes, apart from that, without our knowing why or wherefore, we have upon a sudden glided from darkness into light, by the distinct operation of the Spirit of God upon the mind.

But usually the Lord keeps his people in perfect peace *by the operation of certain considerations, intended by his infinite wisdom to work in that manner.* For instance, if sin be before the mind, it may well disquiet us, but when a man considereth that Christ died for our sins, according to the Scriptures, he hath that before him which allayeth the disquietude. When he considereth that, in dying, the Lord Jesus rendered unto God a full and satisfactory atonement for all the sin of all his believing people, then the man is at once, by that consideration, brought into perfect peace. Or suppose that a temporal trial ruffles the mind; the uneasy one turns to Scripture, and he finds that affliction is not sent as a legal punishment, but only as a fatherly chastisement of love: then is the bitterness of it passed away. Let a man know that all his trials work together for his good, and every sufficient reason for discontent is removed. The man noteth that there is good in the evil which surrounds him; indeed, he perceives the Lord to be at work everywhere, and henceforth he accepts the arrangements of providence without mistrust, and his heart is at peace. Depend upon it, dear friend, if you are tossed up and down, like the locust, you will only find peace by flying to the fields of Scripture. In this garden of the Lord, flowers are blooming which yield a balm for every wound of the heart. Never was there a lock of soul-trouble yet, but what there was a key to open it in the Word of God. For our pain, here is an anodyne; for our darkness, a lamp; for our loneliness, a friend. It is like the garden of Eden: a double river of peace glideth through it. Turn you then to the Lord's Word, to communion with his people, to prayer, to praise, or some form of holy service, and God will thus keep you in perfect peace.

I believe, also, that the Lord keeps his people in perfect peace *by the distinct operations of his providence.* When a man's ways please the Lord, he maketh even his enemies to be at peace with him. By secret workings he can quiet foes so that they are as still as a stone till thy people pass over, O Lord. When one providence apparently fights against you, another will come in to deliver you. The Lord's thoughts towards his people are thoughts of good, and not of evil; and they shall see it to be so. Either the afflicted shall reach a place of rest, or else double strength shall be given for the double trial. God will allow no war in his providence against his own child, all must be for you there. If you are God's Jonah, and are thrown into the sea, a whale must wait upon you; and if you are God's servant, and are brought into the lowest dungeon in Egypt, Pharaoh's own self must send and fetch you out of it to sit upon a throne. Lift up now your eyes, O you that crouch among the ashes because of your daily fret! Be no longer grovellers in the dust! The Lord is your King; nothing can break your peace. The Creator of yon stars and clouds, Lord of the universe, Monarch of all nature: thinkest thou that he cannot speedily send thee deliverance? All these ages has he loved thee; canst thou mistrust him? Knowest thou not that he feeds the sparrows, ay, and the fish of the sea, and the myriads of living creatures which only his eye can see? There is no limit to his stores, nor bounds to his power. Canst thou not trust in him, that he will help thee through, and give thee rest? Thus, you see, our peace comes from God in some way or other; and I therefore the more earnestly ask you never to seek peace elsewhere. Do not seek peace by praying for the absence of trial. You may be just as happy *in* affliction as out of it, if the Lord be with you. Do not seek peace by cultivating hardness of heart, and indifference of spirit. No, when you are afflicted, you ought to feel it: God means you should; and you must learn to feel it, and yet be fully at peace. Do not imagine you can get peace by philosophy, or by considerations derived from reason, or by knowledge fetched from experience. There is but one well from which you can draw the sweet waters of perfect peace, and it bears about its rim this dainty inscription—"Thou wilt keep him in perfect peace, O Jehovah." Such peace as God giveth makes us like to God, it fills us with his love, it sets us acting according to his holiness; and, meanwhile, it prepares us for his palace, where everlasting peace perfumes every chamber, and covers the whole fabric with glory.

III. I have to answer another question this morning, and that is—WHO SHALL OBTAIN THIS PEACE? "Thou wilt keep him in perfect peace, whose mind is stayed on thee." The Hebrew is very involved and difficult to understand, but we shall not err if we permit it to teach us this,—that *the whole of our being is stayed upon God in order to this peace*. The word for "mind" is very vague, but it must include our thoughts. If your thoughts are stayed on God, you will have perfect peace: our misery comes from stray, vagabond, unsettled thoughts. If you will think of nothing except in connection with God, if you will only think of your sin in connection with a merciful God, if you will only think of tribulation in connection with a faithful God, if you will set the Lord always before you, so that he is at your right hand, you shall not be moved; but you certainly cannot be perfectly at peace till each thought, being held captive, learns to stay itself on him. This includes the imagination. The imaginations are most untamable wild beasts, and cause a world of terror in timid minds. Oh for grace to fasten up imagination in the Lord's own cage! We must not imagine anything to be possible which would make the Lord appear to be unkind or untrue. Pray that your imagination may be stayed on God, that you may never again imagine anything contrary to the grace, goodness, and love of your heavenly Father. What peace would rule if this were the case! I think our text includes especially the desires. Desires are very grasping things. It is utterly impossible to satisfy a worldly man's heart: if he had all he now wishes for, he would be sure then to enlarge his desires as hell, and ask for more. But you, dear friend, must stay your desires at some bound or other, and what more fit than to stay them upon God? Say, "I want nothing but what God wills to give me; I desire to have nothing but what he thinks is for his glory, and for my profit." When you once come to this point, when your imaginations and desires all pitch their tents within the compass of God himself, who is your heavenly portion, then you will be kept in perfect peace.

What else is meant by being stayed? Does it not mean rested? When your thoughts recline at their ease in God's revealed will, that is staying upon God. When your desires are filled, and no longer open their greedy mouths for more, because God has filled them, that is staying. Does it not mean stopping there? We speak of staying at a place. Well, when our minds are stayed on God, we just stop at God; we do not propose any further journeying; we do not wish to push on in advance of where he leads the way. Our heart is rooted and grounded in the great Father's love, and so we stay our souls on him.

Staying means upholding. We speak of a stay, and of a mainstay; it is something upon which we are depending. Such a person is the stay of the house,—its chief upholder and support. See, then, what it is to stay your souls on God, and mind that you daily carry it out. Some are staying themselves upon a friend, others are staying themselves upon their own ability, but blessed is the man who stays himself on God. We are to have no confidence except in the Almighty arm; our reliance must be placed there only. When in our God we live, and move, and have our being, this is the crowning condition of a creature. Oh, to feel to the utmost that we are wholly the Lord's, and that, whether his will appoints us joy or woe, we shall be equally satisfied, for we have come to lie down on his will, and go no further. I like staid persons— you know what they are and where they are. They are not easily put about, neither do they readily forsake a cause which they have espoused. He that is stayed upon God is the most staid person in the world; he is steadfast, grounded, settled, and he cannot be removed from the blessed hope of the gospel. He that is fully staid is the man that shall have perfect peace. Oh, whither away, ye undecided ones? Oh, whither away, poor hearts? Will ye wander over every mountain? Will ye never take up a lodging with your God, and dwell at ease in him? Of this be ye well assured, your souls are on the wing, and are bound to fly on and on for ever unless they make bold to settle down upon the Lord their God. In God is rest, but in none else. All earth and heaven, time and eternity, cannot make up a peace for a bruised spirit, and yet a word from the Lord bestows it beyond recall.

Observe, it says, "stayed *on thee.*" Dwell with emphasis upon that, for there are many ways of staying yourself, but you must mind that all your staying is on God; on your heavenly Father, who will withhold no good thing from you; on your divine Saviour, who pleads for you at the right hand of God; on the Holy Ghost, who dwells in you; on the triune God, who hath said, "I will never leave thee, nor forsake thee."

Now, instead of saying more, I should like, if God the Holy Spirit would help us, for each one to go through the mental act of rolling our care upon the Lord. Let us commit ourselves, and all that we are, and all that we have, and all that we have to do, and all that we have to suffer, to the guardian care of our loving God, casting all our care upon him, for he careth for us. Here we are in God, and here we mean to abide. We are not regretting the grace of yesterday, nor sighing for the grace of to-morrow. We stay where we are—at home with God.

Our anchor is down, and we do not mean to draw it up again. "My heart is fixed, O God, my heart is fixed: I will sing and give praise." "Oh," saith one, "you do not know my troubles!" No, but I remember the story of a poor Methodist at the battle of Fontenoy. He had both his legs shot away, and when the surgeon came to attend to him, he was evidently bleeding to death, but he cried, "I am as happy as I can be out of Paradise!" Well, if in the very article of death, and suffering as he was, he could overflow with happiness, surely you and I can rejoice in perfect peace. I want you all to be like Dr. Watts, who said that for many years he went to his bed without the slightest solicitude as to whether he should wake up in this world, or in the next. To rest in God's Word, to rejoice in God's covenant, to trust in the divine sacrifice, to be conformed to God's will, to delight in God's self—this is to stay yourself upon God, and the consequence of it is perfect peace.

IV. WHY IS IT THAT THE LORD WILL KEEP THAT MAN IN PERFECT PEACE WHO STAYS HIMSELF ON HIM? The answer is, "Because he trusteth in thee." Dear friends, that means surely this, that *in faith there is a tendency to create and nourish peace.* In all other ways of trying to live before God there is a tendency to produce uneasiness; but he that believes shall rest. Faith lays a cool hand upon a burning brow, and removes the fever of the fearful heart. Faith hath a voice of silver, wherewith she whispers, "Peace, be still." Nothing can conduce so much to a quiet life as a firm, unwavering confidence in the faithfulness of God's promise, and in the fact that what he has promised he is able also to perform.

Further, the text means this, that when a man stays himself upon God it is not only his faith that brings him peace, but *his faith is rewarded by peace*, which the Lord gives him as a token of approval. A kind of discipline is going on in our heavenly Father's family, not rewards and punishments such as judges award to criminals, but such as fathers give to their children. By this we are being trained for the many mansions in the Father's house above. If we will stay ourselves on God, we shall have peace; if we will not do so, we shall have no rest, but shall be in sore disquietude. "Let not your heart be troubled: ye believe in God, believe also in me." The pressure of the trouble comes with the decline of faith. If thou believest more, it may not make thee richer, but thou wilt not feel thy poverty so keenly. If thou believest more, it may not make thee healthy in body, but thou shalt not fret because of thy sickness: if thou believest more, it will not give thee back thy buried ones, but it shall fill thy heart with a still higher love. "All things are possible to him that believeth," and peace, peace is among those possibilities; but if thou wilt not believe, neither shalt thou be established, thine unbelief shall be a rod for thine own back, a bitter for thine own cup. If thou wilt not trust thy God, thou shalt wander into a weary land, seeking rest and finding none. Come, brothers and sisters, let us fly from such a fate, and win perfect peace as the reward of perfect confidence.

I think, lastly, this peace comes out of faith, because *it is faith's way of proclaiming herself.* If God gives you perfect peace, you will not need, when you go home, to shout to your friends, "I am a believer." They will soon see it. You have lost one that was very dear to you, and instead of fretting and repining, you kiss the hand of God, and go about your daily duties with patience. That is a very wonderful fruit of the Spirit, wrought by faith, and thus faith is seen. A man has had a fire, or some other form of loss, and his comforts are destroyed. If he is an unbeliever, we do not wonder that he tears his hair, and curses God, and rages and fumes. But if he has stayed himself on God, he will be at peace, and he will say, "The Lord hath done it. It is the Lord: let him do what seemeth him good." By this will you be known to be the disciples of Christ, when in patience ye possess your souls. Faith which only operates when all goes well, is the mockery of faith; the love that praises God when God gives thee according to thy desire is no more than the love of some dogs to their masters, who care just as much for them as the number of the scraps may be. Wilt thou have such a cupboard love as that? It were far better to get to this state, "Though he slay me, yet will I trust in him." If thou hast this faith within thee, then shall thy peace be like a river. The peace of God which passeth all understanding shall keep thy heart and mind by Christ Jesus.

I am very much concerned in leaving you, that you, dear friends, should aim much at the possession of this peace. It is a mode of propagating the gospel never to be despised. Multitudes of people have been converted by seeing the holy patience of God's people: they have been impressed by it, and have said, "There must be something in a religion that can give such a peace as this." When you are fretting and worrying, you are undoing your minister's work. When the people of God are over and above troubled, when they count life to be a burden to them because things are not as they would wish them to be, they are really slandering their heavenly Father, and they are preventing the wandering from coming back. The unconverted say, "Why should we go to God to be made miserable?" O ye banished seed, be glad! O ye troubled ones, rejoice! Though now for a season, if need be, ye are in heaviness through manifold temptations, yet lift up your heads, for your redemption draweth nigh. Within a short time you shall put on the garments of your excellency and beauty, and the weeds of your mourning shall be laid aside. Wherefore play the man: better still, play the Christian; and let all men know that where God is, and where the Lord rules the heart, there is, there must be, a deep and profound peace. May God bless you, for Jesus Christ's sake. Amen.

10 The Lover of God's Law Filled with Peace

"Great peace have they which love thy law: and nothing shall offend them."—Psalm cxix. 165.

THIS forms part of a devotional passage. It is not merely a statement that great peace comes to those who love the law of God, but it is uttered as part of a hymn of praise unto the Lord. We cannot praise God better than by stating facts concerning him and his Word. If you desire to praise God, you must speak of him as he is. If you would pour out an acceptable libation before him, you must fill the vessel from himself, as the well-head of all excellence. Our *Te Deums* are simply declarations of what God is: there can be no higher praise. His praises can only be the reflection of his own light. All glory is already in him, none can be added to him; and so, when we are adoring him for his law, and blessing him for giving us his Word, we cannot do better than observe how that law operates upon the heart, and praise him because it so works. We have no need to heap up flattering titles as men do with their kings; we have no need to invent exaggerated expressions; we have but to speak the simple truth concerning our God, and we have praised him.

By the word "law" here is intended, not only the law of the ten commandments, but the whole of divine revelation, as it was in David's time, and as it is now. Whatever God has revealed is loved by saintly men. This sacred Book, which we commonly call the Bible, contains the mind of God, so far as he has seen fit to reveal it to men. It is the law of holiness as the guide of our actions, and the law of faith by which we receive of his grace. Here we have the law of the kingdom of heaven, the law of life in Christ Jesus. As a law of works, this holy Book convinces us of sin; as a law of love, it leads us to Jesus, to find forgiveness through his blood. In David's day, the law was a smaller Book than ours, but he found great peace in the reading of it: it was even then competent for the highest spiritual ends. We have that Book at greater length, but it is one and the same. The same gospel is in Genesis as in Matthew. The

Old Testament was perfect in itself as the law of the Lord, and the New Testament is but an expansion of the same truth which the Old contains. We rejoice to find that our larger edition of the Word of God contains nothing which lessens that great peace which the earlier Scriptures were able to produce. As the light is clearer the joy is brighter, and the reasons for great peace are more clearly seen.

God's law comprises all his precepts, and in keeping these we have peace of conscience; it contains all his promises, and these are our great peace in the hour of need; and it comprehends all those great doctrines which surround the cross of Christ and the covenant of grace, and each one of these is a fountain of peace to our hearts. We take this Book as a whole, and in this way we have peace. We dare not rend it, we would not leave out any part of it, lest we miss the blessed effect which, as a whole, it is calculated to produce. Sitting as learners at the feet of Jesus, our Master, submitting our hearts and minds to the infallible teaching of the Holy Ghost, who leads us into all truth, we find that the peace of God, which passeth all understanding, keeps our hearts and minds by Christ Jesus.

Three things in the text are worthy of earnest attention. May the Spirit of God bless all we say! First, here is *a spiritual character*—"they which love thy law": secondly, here is *a special possession*—"great peace have they": and thirdly, here is *a singular preservation*—"nothing shall offend them": or nothing shall be a stumbling-block to them. Oh, that we may know our text experimentally!

I. First, here is A SPIRITUAL CHARACTER—"they which love thy law."

Love lies deep, it is in the heart: it is not a thing of the surface, it is of the man's own self. As a man loveth so is he. To love God's law is to have the very nature and essence of our manhood in a right condition. To love the Word is something more than to read it, even though we should study it day and night. It is more even than to understand it; for the cold light of the intellect is of little worth compared with the warm sunlight of love. Many, no doubt, perceive the truths which are taught in God's Word, and so become orthodox in their professed creed; but without love their faith is dead. You cannot learn the law of God as you learn the laws of nature; your heart must be affected by it, and you must obey it in your life, or you do not truly know it. Only he who does the will of God can know of the doctrine. Mere knowledge brings no peace to the man. The truth must go from the head to the heart before its power is known. Some even try to keep the law of the Lord, so far as to make the outward life conformable to morality and religion; but this falls far short of the love of the heart. To stand in slavish fear and dread of God is better than to be utterly indifferent, but it is a poor thing compared with love. Slaves obey their masters because of the lash, and so do many outwardly follow the Word because of the spirit of bondage which will not permit them to rebel; but there is a something lacking: nothing in religion is sound till the heart goes with it. God says, "My son, give me thine heart," and he cannot be satisfied with anything short of it. Search, then, my hearers, and see if you really love the law of the Lord.

He who loves the Word would not wish to have it altered, enlarged, or diminished: it reveals enough for him, and no more; for he is content with what God chooses to teach him. If he finds any want of conformity in his own thought to God's thought, he throws his own thought away, and sets up the divine thought in its place. As he is reconciled to God in Christ Jesus, so is his mind reconciled to the teaching against which he at first rebelled. He loves the law of the Lord just as he finds it; and instead of judging it, and daring to set himself up as a dictator of what it ought to be, he is humble and docile, and cries, "Speak, Lord; for thy servant heareth." He loves every truth which the Lord declares, ay, and the very style and method of the declaration. Every word of God's Book has in it music for his ear, beauty for his eye, honey for his mouth, and food for his soul. The teachings of God's Word are to the instructed believer, not only articles of faith, but matters of life. Our faith has imbibed them, and our experience has assimilated them. We could part with everything except what we have learned out of the Sacred Book by the teaching of the Holy Ghost; for that flows through our souls like the blood through our body, and it is intermixed with every vital part of our being. Like wool which has been made to lie long in scarlet, we are dyed ingrain. As certain insects take their colour from the leaves they feed upon, so have we become tinctured to the core of our nature with the living and incorruptible Word, which has proved its own inspiration by inspiring us with its spirit. Now we live in the Word as the fish in the stream; it is the element of our spiritual life. This may suffice to set before you the sort of people who obtain great peace from the law of the Lord, because, in the truest sense, they love it.

This inward and spiritual love to God's Word includes many other good things. Permit me to use the connection in order to help myself as to order, and to help you as to memory. Read the first verse of this octave—the one hundred and sixty-first verse: "Princes have persecuted me without a cause: but my heart standeth in awe of thy Word." The love of God's law includes a deep *reverence for it.* That man is blessed who trembles at God's Word. This Book is not to be compared with other books; it is not of the same class and order. It is inspired in a sense in which they are not; it stands alone, and is not one among other books. As towers an Alp above the molehills of the meadow, so Holy Scripture rises above the purest, truest, and holiest literature of man's composing. Even could all those other books be purged of error, and be corrected to the highest degree of human knowledge, yet would they no more reach to the degree of the Book of God than man can become God. It is supreme, and of another quality from all the rest of them. Other writings we feel free to criticize, but "My heart standeth in awe of thy Word." The man who loves God's Word does not trifle with it; it is far too sacred to be toyed with. He does not cavil at it; for he believes it to be God's Word. With a docility which comes of true sonship, it is enough for him that his Father says so. His one anxiety is, as far as possible, to know the meaning of his Father's words; and, that known, all debate is out of question. "Thus saith the Lord," is to every true child of God the end of the matter. I have often told you, my dear friends, that I view the difficulties of Holy Scriptures as so many prayer-stools upon which I kneel and worship the glorious Lord. What we cannot comprehend by our understandings we apprehend by our affections. Awe of God's Word is a main element in that love of God's law which brings great peace.

This advances to *rejoicing in it*. Read verse 162 : "I rejoice at thy Word, as one that findeth great spoil." As a conqueror in the glad hour of victory shouts over the dividing of the prey, so do believers rejoice in God's Word. I can recollect as a youth the great joy I had when the doctrines of grace were gradually opened up to me by the Spirit of truth. I did not at first perceive the whole chain of precious truth. I knew that Jesus had suffered in my stead, and that by believing in him I had found peace; but the deep things of the covenant of grace came to me one by one, even as at night you first see one star and then another, and by-and-by the whole heavens are studded with them. When it first became clear to me that salvation was all of grace, what a revelation it was! I saw that God had made me to differ from others: I ascribed my salvation wholly to his free favour. I perceived that, at the back of the grace which I had received, there must have been a purpose to give that grace, and then the glorious fact of an election of grace flowed in upon my soul in a torrent of delight. I saw that the love of God to his own was without beginning—a boundless, fathomless, infinite, endless love, which carries every chosen vessel of mercy from grace to glory. What a God is the God of sovereign grace! How did my soul rejoice as I saw the God of love in his sovereignty, immutability, faithfulness, and omnipotence! "Among the gods there is none like unto thee." So will any young convert here rejoice if he so loves the law of the Lord as to continue studying it, and receiving the illumination of the Holy Ghost concerning it. As the child of God sees into the deep things of God, he will be ready to clap his hands for joy. It is a delightful sensation to feel that you are growing. Trees, I suppose, do not know when they grow, but men and women do, when the growth is spiritual. We seem to pass into a new heaven and a new earth as we discover God's truth. A new guest has come to live within our mind, and he has brought with him banquets such as we never tasted before. Oh, how happy is that man to whose loving mind Holy Scripture is opening up its priceless treasures! We know that we love God's Word when we can rejoice in it. Fain would we gather up every crumb of Scripture, and find food in its smallest fragments. Even its bitter rebukes are sweet to us. I would kiss the very feet of Scripture, and wash them with my tears! Alas, that I should sin against it by a thought, much more by a word! If it be but God's Word, though some may call it non-essential, we dare not think it so. The little things of God are more precious than the great things of man. Truth is no trifle to one who has fought his way to it, and learned it in the school of affliction. "O my soul, thou hast trodden down strength!" and that which thou hast gained in the battle is thy joyful spoil.

Further than this, we receive Holy Scripture *with emotion*. David says, "I hate and abhor lying: but thy law do I love." He regards all that is opposed to the law of the Lord as hateful lying. Those are hard words, David! Surely you are sinning against the charity of our cultured age! Yes, but when a man feels strongly, he cannot help speaking strongly. "I hate," says he, and that is not enough; he says, "I hate and abhor lying." His whole being revolts at it. He means not only that lying with which in common life men would deceive their fellows, and that is hateful enough; but he refers especially to that kind of teaching which gives the lie to the law of the Lord; for he adds, "But thy law do I love." A good man's hate of falsehood is as intense as his love of truth; it must necessarily be so. He who worships the true God detests and loathes idols. In these days there are many men to whom the truths of Scripture are like a pack of cards, to be shuffled as occasion suits. To them peace and quietness are jewels, and truth is as the mire of the streets. It does not matter to them what this man preaches and what that man writes. Hold your tongue, it will be all the same a hundred years hence; and really nobody can be quite sure of anything! To the man that is loyal to his Lord, and faithful to his convictions, it can never be so; he hates the teaching which belies his God. He that has never felt his blood boil against an error which robs God of his glory does not love the law, nor will he know that great peace which comes by having the law enshrined in the heart.

One other virtue is included in the love of the Word. According to the context, *great gratitude to God* for his Word is formed in the believing heart. "Seven times a day do I praise thee because of thy righteous judgments." God's judgments written in his Word are matters of praise.

> "This is the judge that ends the strife
> Where wit and reason fail."

God's judgments actively going on in the world, which tally with those predicted in his Word, are also matters for adoring praise. The God of the word is the God of the deed. What he says he does, and every day and all the day we praise him for it.

Beloved, God may do what he wills, and we will praise him. He may say what he wills, and we will praise him. We read in his Word stern things, words of wrath and deeds of vengeance. Shall we try to soften them, or invent apologies for them? By no means. Jehovah our God is a consuming fire. We love him, not as he is improved upon by "modern thought," but as he reveals himself in Scripture. The God of Abraham, of Isaac, and of Jacob, "this God is our God for ever and ever: he will be our Guide, even unto death." Even when he is robed in the terror of his judgments, we sing praises unto his name; even as they did at the Red Sea, when they saw Pharaoh and his host swallowed up of the mighty waters: "Sing unto the Lord, for he hath triumphed gloriously: the horse and his rider hath he thrown into the sea." Our hallelujahs are "to him that slew mighty kings; for his mercy endureth for ever." It is not mine to improve upon the character of Jehovah, but to reverence and adore him as he manifests himself, either in judgment or in grace. I, who am less than nothing and vanity, dare not scan his work, nor bring him to my bar, lest I hear a voice saying, "Nay, but, O man, who art thou that repliest against God?" What am I that I should be the ultimate judge of truth, or of justice, or of wisdom? Whatever God may be, or speak, or do—that is right: it is not mine to arraign my Maker, but to adore him. Extenuations, explanations, and apologies may be produced from the best of motives; but too often they suggest to opposers that it is admitted that God's most holy Word contains something in it which is doubtful, or weak, or antiquated. It looks as though it needed to be defended by human wisdom. Brethren, the Word of the Lord can stand alone, without the propping which many are giving it. Those props come down, and then our adversaries think that the Book is down too. The Word of God can take care of itself, and will do so if we preach it, and cease defending it. See you that lion. They have caged him for his preservation; shut him up behind iron bars to secure him from his foes! See how a band of armed men have gathered together to protect the lion. What a clatter they make with their swords and spears! These mighty men are intent upon defending a lion. O fools, and slow of heart! Open that door! Let the lord of the forest come forth free. Who will dare to encounter him? What does he want with your guardian care? Let the pure gospel go forth in all its lion-like majesty, and it will soon clear its own way and ease itself of its adversaries. Yes, without attempting to apologize even for the severer truths of revelation, seven times a day do we praise the Lord for giving us his judgments, so righteous and so sure.

I have shown you now, dear friends, how this love lies deep in the heart, and how it includes much of honour and reverence; let me further remark that *this love is productive of many good things*. They that love God's Word will *meditate* on it, and make it the man of their right hand. What a companion the Bible is! It talks with us by the way, it communes with us upon our beds: it knows us altogether, and has a suitable word for every condition of life. Hence we cannot be long without listening to our Beloved's voice in this Book of books. I hope we realize the character described in the first Psalm: "His delight is in the law of the Lord; and in his law doth he meditate day and night. And he shall be like a tree planted by the rivers of water." Love to the Word of God creates great *courage* in the defence of it. It is wonderful how the most timid creatures will defend their young, how even a hen becomes a terrible bird when she has to take care of her chicks: even so, quiet men and women contend earnestly for the faith once delivered to the saints, and will not tamely submit to see the truth torn in pieces by the hounds of error and hypocrisy.

The love of the law of God breeds *penitence* for having sinned against it, and *perseverance* in obedience to it. It also begets *patience* under suffering; for it leads the man to submit himself to the will of God whom he loves so much. He saith, "It is the Lord. Let him do what seemeth him good." The Word of God begets and fosters *holiness*. Jesus said, "Sanctify them through thy truth; thy Word is truth." You cannot study the Scriptures diligently and love them heartily without having your thoughts and acts savoured and sweetened by them. A gentleness and kindness will be infused into your spirit by the very tone of the Word; a sacred delicacy and carefulness of conduct will surround your daily life in proportion as you steep your mind in Scripture. Let me commend to you, my beloved friends, that you live with the law of the Lord, till even men of the world perceive that you keep choice company. The trashy lives of most people are the fit outcome of the trash which they read. A life fed on fiction is a life of fiction; a life fed on divine fact will become a life of divine fact. I have not time in which to show you all the sweet uses of the law of the Lord: it doeth much every way for the formation of a perfect character. No moulding force is so much to be desired as that of the Word of the Lord in the love of it.

This much, however, I must add: if in any of us there is a love of the law of the Lord, *this is a work of the Holy Spirit*. Nature does not love God, and hence it does not love God's law. Human nature is in open and active rebellion to everything that is commanded or commended by the thrice-holy God. If, then, thou lovest God and his holy law, the Holy Ghost has been at work in thee; and by this new love it is proven that thou art a new creature. The old nature delights itself in everything which is of the earth earthy; it is only the new and heavenly life which can appreciate and love heavenly things. My brother, let thy love of the law be to thee a proof of thy regeneration; thou hast passed from darkness into marvellous light, for thou lovest light. Let this be to thee the evidence of thine election: thou hadst never loved God and his law if he had not loved thee first. What can thy love to God be but a reflection of his love to thee. Wherefore, hear him say, "I have loved thee with an everlasting love." See, also, in this love of God's law the prophecy of thine ultimate perfection. We do not keep the law as we would; but if we will to keep it, that which holds the will is the real law of our life. If there be in us a strong and passionate desire to accept and obey God's Word in everything, and to be conformed to it in thought and life, that desire will ultimately get the victory. Use well the sword of the Spirit, which is the Word of God, and by the force of thy love give sin sharp and heavy thrusts, and thou shalt conquer until every thought is brought into captivity to the law of Christ.

II. We have spent too long a time upon our first point, and shall have to be brief upon the other heads. Our second division is a very sweet part of the text; here is A SPECIAL POSSESSION, " great peace have they which love thy law." When Orientals meet each other their usual salutation is "Shalom"—" Peace be to thee." The word does not mean merely quiet and rest, but happiness or prosperity. Great peace means great prosperity. Those who love God's law have great blessedness in this life as well as in that which is to come. In loving the law of God we have intense enjoyment and real success in life.

Let us, however, take the text as we have it in our Bibles. By peace here is not meant that a man who loves God's law will have great peace with everybody, for that is not at all true. If David penned this sentence, he certainly was not an instance of great peace with men flowing out of his love to the Lord's law. He was a man of war from his youth. He had peace as a shepherd boy, but even then he had to kill lions and bears, and soon after he had to meet a giant in single combat. Neither in his family nor in Saul's court was he at peace. He was hunted like a partridge upon the mountains, and had to run for it from day to day. He had not much earthly peace; for when he had done with Saul, the Philistines invaded the land. If it be possible, we are to live peaceably with all men; but he who has put enmity between the serpent and the woman never meant that we should enjoy the friendship of the world. The great peace which they have who love God's law refers to a peace which can exist when strife rages all around us.

Does not it mean this—first, *great restfulness of the intellect?* If we love God's law in the sense in which we have explained it, so as to stand in awe of it, and rejoice over it, the result will be great peace of mind. Everybody must find infallibility somewhere. Some think it is with the Pope at Rome, others dream that it is in themselves: the second theory is no more true than the first. Others of us believe that infallibility lies in the Word of God: this Book is to us the final court of appeal. When God's Holy Spirit leads us into the truth which he has revealed in this Book, we feel a full assurance that we know the truth, and we speak from experience when we say that the loving belief of the Word brings us great intellectual repose. I care nothing what supposed philosophers may discover: they cannot discover anything true which is contrary to God's Word. I know that I am speaking that which is best for my fellow-men in the highest and best sense, when I am not venting a theory, but setting forth a revelation from heaven.

He who gave us the infallible Book has all the responsibility for its contents. If I believe what God tells me, and do what he bids me, the results are with him, and not with me. He is the ruler of the universe, and not I; and if there be any terrible mysteries, he must explain them, and not I, if they ought to be explained. I am like a servant who is sent to the door with a message; if I deliver the message which my master gives me as I receive it, you must not be angry with me, for I did not invent the message, I only repeated it to you. Be angry with my master, not with me. That is how I feel when I have done preaching. If I have honestly preached what I believe to be in God's Word, I am free from all responsibility for my ministry. My responsibility lies in endeavouring to interpret the Word as clearly as I can; I am not accountable for its teaching. I have not before me the unbearable burden of composing a gospel. I remember well a minister, whom I much respect, saying to me, "I wish I could feel as you do. You have certain fixed principles about which you are sure, and you have only to state them and enforce them; but I am in a formative state; I make my theology fresh every week." Dear me, I thought, what a hopeless state for progress and establishment! If the student of mathematics had no fixed law as to the value of numbers, but made a new multiplication table every week, he would not make many calculations. If a baker were to say to me, "Sir, I am always altering the ingredients of my bread: I make a different bread every week"; I should be afraid the fellow would poison me one of these days. I would rather go to a man whose bread I had found good and nourishing. I cannot afford to experiment in the bread of life. Beside, there is an intellectual unrest in all this kind of thing, which is escaped from when we come to love the Word of the Lord as we love our lives. Oh the rest of knowing within your very soul that the truth you rest upon is a sure foundation!

Those who love God's Word have also a great peace which comes of *a pacified conscience.* Conscience is as a terrible wild beast when aroused and irritated by a sense of sin. Nothing will quiet conscience effectually and properly but the great doctrine of the substitutionary sacrifice of Christ. When we see that God has laid on his only begotten Son all our iniquities, and that the chastisement of our peace was exacted of him, as our substitute, then conscience smiles upon us. If God is satisfied with regard to our sins, we are satisfied too. We see in the sacrifice of our Lord Jesus Christ that which must satisfy divine justice, and therefore our conscience receives a safe and holy quietus, and we have peace with God through our Lord Jesus Christ, by whom also we have received the atonement.

And the same conscience also brings great peace when it bears testimony to renewal of heart and life. When a man knows in his own soul that he seeks to do that which is right in the sight of God, and that he is aspiring after a pure, gracious, useful life, he has great peace even when others ridicule him. If you have taken your own way, and acted dishonestly for gain, peace will not visit your heart; but if you have loved God's law, and kept to the way of strict integrity, you will have within your own bosom an angel of peace to strengthen you in the hour of sorrow. "The testimony of a good conscience" is like the song of the angels to the shepherds at Bethlehem.

Beloved, what a peace the love of the Word brings to *the heart!* All hearts require an object of love. How many hearts have been broken because the thing beloved has disappointed them, and proved false to their hopes! But when you love God's Word, your love is not wasted upon an unworthy object. It introduces you to Christ, and you love him intensely, and however much you yield your heart to him, you are always safe. Jesus is never a Judas to his friends. Jesus cannot be loved too well, and hence the heart has great peace when it comes to him.

To love God's Word gives great peace as to *our desires.* You will not be grasping after wealth when the Word is better to you than the most fine gold. You will not be ambitious to shine among men when to you the Word of the Lord is a kingdom large enough. Your desires will be regulated by true wisdom when your heart is garrisoned by the Word of the Lord which dwells in you richly. When Christ himself is our all in all, we are harboured in the haven of peace. When our desires find their pasturage around the Great Shepherd's feet, our ambitions cease to roam, and we abide at home in peace. Content with a dinner of herbs in our Lord's company, we no longer pine for the stalled ox of the wicked who prospers in his way. To love the law is to cease from covetousness, and to cease from covetousness is great peace.

When we love God's law also, we reach forward to the peace of *resignation* to God, acquiescence in his will, and conformity to it. It is of no use to quarrel with God; let me say more, it is disgraceful, ungrateful, and wicked for a child of God to do so. When we perfectly yield to God, our heart's sorrow is at an end. The sting of affliction lies in the tail of our rebellion against the divine will. When we love God's Word intensely, we take pleasure in persecutions, tribulations, and infirmities, since they instruct us in the divine promises, and open up to us the hidden meanings of the Spirit. Our mind is so near to God, and so pleased with all that pleases him, that we do not desire to suffer less, or to be less weak, or less tried, than the will of God ordains. To love the law and the Lawgiver goes a great way towards loving all that he appoints and decrees; and this is a garden of peace to all who know it.

Besides, the love of the Word breeds *a happy confidence in God* as to all things in the past, the present, and the future. Whatsoever the Lord does or permits must be right, or work right. "We know that all things work together for good to them that love God, to them that are the called according to his purpose." This is a very peace-breathing belief. When we love God's Word, we see God at the beginning of everything, God at the end of everything, and God in the middle of everything; and as we see him present whom we love, we cease from anxious thought. "My soul is even as a weaned child." Of such a man is it written, "His soul shall dwell at ease." The Lord whom he takes to be his Shepherd makes him to lie down in green pastures, and he asks no more.

III. I am cramped by want of time; I must, therefore, in a very few words sum up what deserves to be spoken at length upon the third point. Here is A SINGULAR PRESERVATION: "Nothing shall offend them." There shall be no stumbling-block in their way.

Intellectual stumbling-blocks are gone. One asks me, "Do you mean to say that you read the Bible and do not find difficulties in it?" I regard the Word of God as being infallibly inspired, and therefore if I find difficulties in it, which I must do from the very nature of things, I accept what God says about those difficulties, and pass on. The Word of God does not profess to explain all mysteries: it leaves them mysteries, and my faith accepts them as such. When out in a yacht in the Clyde we came opposite the great rock called the Cock of Arran. Our captain did not steam right ahead, and rush at the rock; no, he did what was much wiser: he cast anchor for the night in the bay at the foot of it, so that we were sheltered from the wind by the vast headland. I remember looking up through the darkness of the night, and admiring its great sheltering wing. A difficulty was it. It became a shelter. Every now and then in Scripture you come before a vast truth. Will you steam against it, and wreck your soul? Will you not, with truer wisdom, cast anchor under the lee of it? Do we need to understand everything? Are we to be all brain, and no heart? What should we be the better if we did understand all mysteries? I believe God. I bow before his Word. Is not this better for us than the conceit of knowing and understanding? We are as yet mere children. We know in part. Of course, we are blessed, in this enlightened age, with some wonderfully great men, who understand more than the ancients, and either know the unknowable, or think they do. In a sentence I will give you the result of my observation upon men and things: "No man knows everything except a fool, and he knows nothing." I have not yet met with any exception to this rule; no, not even among the superior persons who prefer culture to Scripture. If thou lovest the Word of God, thou wilt see no difficulties which will in the least cause thee to stumble. Love to the Word is the abolition of difficulties. Things hard to be understood become stepping-stones on which to rise, and not stumbling-blocks over which to fall.

"Nothing shall offend them." Does not this also mean that *no moral duty shall be a cross to them* which shall cause them to turn aside? They will not turn away from Jesus because a sin has to be abandoned, a lust denied, or a pleasure given up. The man who has counted the cost will not be offended by his Lord's requirements. Does Jesus say, "Do this?" He does it without demur. Does Jesus say, "Cease from that?" He withdraws his hand at the instant. When a man once loves the law of God, albeit it involves self-denial, humiliation, loss, he shrinks not at the cost. Self-denial ceases to be self-denial when love commands it. The cross of Christ is an easy yoke, and soon ceases to be a burden. A duty which for a little season is irksome, becomes pleasurable before long to a lover of the law of the Lord.

Moreover, the man who loves God's law is *not offended if he has to stand alone*. To some persons it is impossible to traverse a lonesome way, but he that truly loves God's law resolves that if all men forsake him he will cleave to the Lord and his truth. Can you not stand alone? Does solitude offend you? As for me, I am resolved not to follow a multitude to do evil. I will keep to the old faith, and the old way, if I never find a comrade between here and the celestial gates. I do not think a man loves God's Word thoroughly till it breeds in him a self-contained peace, so that he is satisfied from himself, and drinks water out of the cistern of his own experience. Paul was not offended, though at his first answer no man stood by him. What have we to do with other men as supporters of our faith? To their own master they stand or fall. As for our Master in heaven, let us follow him through life, and unto death; for to whom else could we go? He only hath the words of eternal life.

Neither will such persons ever be so offended as to despair of God's great cause. The night grows darker and darker, but the man who loves the divine law expects the sun to rise at his appointed hour. Oh that the Lord would hasten it in his own time! If he delay, we will not therefore doubt. Grace has produced, in past ages, men who were confident as to the triumph of truth when others feared for it. Look at the dauntless courage of Luther, who, when everybody else despaired of the gospel, trusted his God and cheered his people, and would not hear of drawing back. He could not pronounce the word "despair." "Luther, canst thou shake Rome? The harlot sits enthroned upon her seven hills, canst thou hope to dislodge her, or loose the captive nations from her bonds? Canst thou do this?" "No," said Luther, "but God can." Luther brought his God into the quarrel, and yo know which way the conflict turned. Not to-day, nor to-morrow, no in twenty years, may God's truth win; but the Lord can afford t wait. His lifetime is eternity. O struggler for the truth, make tho sure that thou art with God and with the truth, and then be sure that God is with thee in truth, and will deliver thee. "Nothing shall offend them."

It is wonderful, if you love God's Word, how things which are stumbling-blocks to others cease to be injurious to you. Suppose you enjoy prosperity: if you love God's law, you will not be puffed up by deceitful riches or honours. You will be humble, when all men admire you, and all comforts flow in upon you. The Lord's Word in your heart will be as a salt to your estate, so that it breeds in thee neither worldliness, nor forgetfulness of God, nor pride. Your goods shall be your good, if you learn to use them for God's glory.

The same will be true of adversity. He that can stand on the hill-top can stand in the valley. If you love God's law, you are the man to be poor, to be sickly, to be slandered; for you can bear it all, because you have meat to eat that the world knows not of. Your love to God's law will furnish you with a ceaseless stream of consolation. Nothing will damp the flame of your spirit, because the Lord feeds it secretly with a golden oil. O servants of God, let us be glad together in this day of rebuke! The thunder is heard, but it is mere noise. The sea roars, but it is only roaring. Let us laugh at those who would silence faithful testimony; for the Lord God omnipotent reigneth, and great is the peace which he gives to the lovers of his law.

As for you who love not God's law, who know nothing of Jesus, because you have never submitted to the law of faith—there is no "great peace" for you. There may be the deceptive cry of, "Peace, peace, when there is no peace"; but may the Lord save you from it! Soul, there is no hope for thee, thou canst not rest till thou art at one with God. As surely as God made thee, thou must yield to thy Maker, and accept thy Redeemer, and be renewed by his Holy Spirit, or thou art lost for ever. I pray God the Holy Ghost lead thee to accept what God has revealed, and bow thyself to the supreme majesty of his Word, especially to the power and grace of the Incarnate Word, the Lord Christ Jesus; then wilt thou have great peace for this world and the next. God bless you, beloved, for Christ's sake. Amen.

11 Peace: How Gained, How Broken

"**I will** hear what God the Lord will speak: for he will speak peace unto his people, and to his saints: but let them not turn again to folly."—Psalm lxxxv. 8.

"I WILL hear what God the Lord will speak." There were voices and voices. There were voices of the past concerning God's wondrous mercy to his people: "Thou hast been favourable unto thy land; thou hast brought back the captivity of Jacob." But mingled with these were the sad voices of the present. He heard the wailing and the pleading of those who said, "Wilt thou be angry with us for ever? Wilt thou draw out thine anger to all generations?" From this mingling of singing and sighing, the Psalmist turned away, and cried, "I will hear what God the Lord will speak; I will get me into the secret place of the tabernacles of the Most High; I will hear that voice from between the cherubim which speaketh peace to the soul." Beloved, herein is wisdom. Resort to the sanctuary of God. When you cannot find harmony in the voices of the street, or the voices of the church, turn to the melody of that one voice which "will speak peace unto his people."

Again, the Psalmist had been praying. At the mercy-seat he had spread out this petition, "Wilt thou not revive us again: that thy people may rejoice in thee? Show us thy mercy, O Lord, and grant us thy salvation." When he had spoken, he desired an answer. He watched and waited till the Lord God should give him a reply. A friend, kindly wishing to spare me, puts at the end of his letter, "No answer expected." This is too often a foot-note to men's prayers. David did not pray in that fashion: he did expect an answer from the mouth of the Lord. He said within himself, "I have spoken: but now I will speak no more, but hear what God the Lord will speak." Always follow up prayer with holy expectancy. Prayers which expect no answer are guilty of taking the name of God in vain; they are a misuse of the holy ordinance of supplication; and they are a question put upon the divine existence, inasmuch as they reduce the Godhead to an idol, like to those images of the heathen which have ears, but they hear not, neither speak they through their throats. Prayers without faith are an insult to the attributes of God, and do dishonour to his sacred name. If thou prayest aright, in the name of Jesus, expect the Lord to hear thee, even as thou wouldst hear thy child, if he asked bread of thee.

In addition to this, it should be the daily resolve of every Christian man—"I will hear what God the Lord will speak." Not only when I am dazed and confused with other voices, nor only when I have expressed my heart in prayer, but at all times and seasons, I will hear what God the Lord shall speak. There are many doctrines and controversies; but "I will hear what God the Lord will speak." His voice, by his prophets and apostles, shall be the umpire of every dispute with me. I will also turn to the Word of God for the rule of my daily life, as well as for the instruction of my mind in doctrine. I will have regard to the precepts as well as to the promises. "Thy word is a lamp unto my feet, and a light unto my path." When I would know my duty, "I will hear what God the Lord will speak"; and, hearing his word of command, I will need neither whip nor spur, but will make haste in the way of his commands. I will listen to *his* Word, whatever I may do with the precepts of men. Has he spoken? Did the primeval darkness hear it? Shall not the light which he has given me be attentive to it? Even the dead shall hear that voice, and they that hear shall live. Shall not I, who have been quickened by his Spirit, joyfully say, "I will never forget thy precepts: for with them thou hast quickened me"?

Our Saviour speaks of some who enter into life halt and maimed, and having one eye; but he does not speak of anybody entering into life without ears. We must hear the voice of God, for it is written, "Hear, and your soul shall live." Faith cometh by hearing, and hearing by the word of God. By ear-gate the Prince Emmanuel enters the town of Mansoul. Men are saved, not by what they touch, or see, or taste, or smell; but by what they hear. Oh, that we all heard the voice of Christ with solemn attention! Our Lord saith, "He that hath ears to hear, let him hear." Be this our resolve: "I will hear what God the Lord will speak." Like young Samuel, let each one say, "Speak, Lord; for thy servant heareth."

There is one special reason given by the Psalmist why the people of God should be most willing and eager to hear what God the Lord shall speak, and that is because "He will speak peace unto his people, and to his saints." You, beloved, will hear nothing from the Lord but that which will calm your fears, and cheer your hearts. The Lord speaks no thunders against you. His tones are tenderness, his words are mercy, his spirit is love, his message is peace. I will hear what God the Lord will speak: for he will speak peace, and nothing else but peace, unto his own people. That is the subject for us to consider this morning. The Lord Jehovah gives peace to his holy ones.

First, *what we know the Lord will speak;* and, secondly, *what we fear may hinder our enjoying the blessing which he speaks to us:* "Let them not turn again to folly"—a notable word of warning, to which we shall do well to give heed.

I. First, let us consider WHAT WE KNOW THE LORD WILL SPEAK.

"I will hear what God the Lord will speak; for he will speak peace."

The first point is, *He speaks peace to a certain company*—"to his people, and to his saints." Let us, then, ask ourselves, Has the Lord ever spoken peace to us, or will he do so? He will certainly do so if we have an ear to hear his voice; for God will not speak sweet words to those who turn to him a deaf ear. He that will not hear the gospel of peace, shall never know the peace of the gospel. If you will not hear the Holy Spirit when he warns you of your sin, neither shall you hear him revealing peace through pardon. If you will not hear the Lord when he proposes to you reconciliation through the sacrifice of his dear Son, if you will not hear him when he bids you repent and believe, and be washed in the blood of the Lamb, then he will never speak peace to your soul. There is no peace out of Christ, who is our peace. There is one Ambassador, and one Mediator, and only one. There is one atonement by blood, and only one. There is one covenant of peace, and there can never be another. Reconciliation comes to men by Jesus Christ, but by no other gate; and if you will not hear the Lord when he speaks concerning his dear Son, who is the propitiation for sins, he will never speak peace to your heart. Oh, for the ear which is opened to hear the Lord, for this is the sure mark of grace! Does not Jesus say, "My sheep hear my voice"?

Those to whom the Lord speaks peace are his people, and they acknowledge him to be their God. Many men have no God. They would not like to be called atheists, but it practically comes to that. God is not in their thoughts, their plans, their actions, their business, their life. But there is peace to that man to whom God is the greatest fact of his existence. Happy is he who has God first, and last, and midst in all that he does. Look him through and through, and you will perceive that as the colour tinges the stained glass, so does faith in God colour all his life. God is with him in his loneliness, and among the multitude: God is above him to govern him, beneath him to uphold him, within him to quicken him. The man has a God to worship, a God to trust, a God to delight in. If God is everything to you, you are among his people, and he will speak peace unto you. That peace is, however, always connected with holiness, for it is added, "and to his saints." His people and his saints are the same persons. Those who have a God know him to be a holy God, and therefore they strive to be holy themselves. He that hath no saintship about him will have no peace about him. If thou livest a blundering, careless, godless life, thou wilt have much tossing to and fro, and many questionings of heart. "There is no peace," saith my God, "unto the wicked"; but to his people, his saintly ones, his sanctified ones, the people who follow after righteousness—to these the Lord himself will secure peace by his own word of mouth.

Do I hear anyone saying, "Alas! I could not venture to be classed with saints"? Listen one minute: these people, though they are now God's people, and though they are now made saintly by his grace, were once given over to folly. How do I know this? Because the text says, "Let them not turn again to folly;" which shows that once they did follow after folly. Once they followed sin with all their hearts; they knew not God, neither served him; but they have been turned away from folly, sin, and shame: a change, a conversion has taken place in them, by the grace of God. Therefore, dear hearer, let not thy past foolishness dismay thee, if thou wouldst now come to God. Fool as thou mayest have been, the Lord is turning thee from folly; and if he brings thee to be numbered among his people and his holy ones, he will speak peace to thee.

I think I hear one say, "I have turned away from folly, but I feel that there is in my heart a tendency to return to it!" I know it. I, too, have felt the old Adam pulling at my sleeve, to draw me back to the old way, if possible. So it was with these people, or else the Lord would not have needed to say, "Let them not turn again to folly." They were his people, they were his saints, too: and he spoke peace to them; but the old nature lurked within, and made the heart in danger of turning again to folly. If thou findest the old leaven working within thee, fermenting unto evil, and making thee feel sick at heart to think that thou shouldst be so base, then bow low at thy Saviour's feet, and cry to him in the language of the publican, "God be merciful to me a sinner." Yet remember, even if it be so with thee, yet nevertheless thou mayest be numbered with the Lord's people, of whom he has said that he will speak peace unto them. But if you have no horror of sin; if you have no conflict with evil; if you have no longing for righteousness, and no ear for the voice of the Lord, then God will not speak peace to you; but one of these days he will speak thunderbolts, and accent his words with flames of fire, and this shall be the tenor of his speech: "Depart, ye cursed, into everlasting fire, prepared for the devil and his angels." May you never hear that voice of wrath; but may peace be spoken into your soul!

But now, dear friends, I notice here that the peace which is to be desired is peace which God speaks, and *all other peace is evil.* The question is sometimes put—"We see bad men enjoy peace, and we see good men who have but little peace." That is one of the mysteries of life; but it is not a very difficult one as to its first part. Why do bad men enjoy a kind of peace? I answer: sometimes their peace arises from sheer carelessness. They will not think, reflect, or consider. They do not intend to look about them, or before them; for "they count it one of the wisest things to drive dull care away." They go through the world like blind men. They are on the verge of a precipice, and they do not know their danger, or wish to know it. They will go over the edge of the cliff, and be broken to pieces; but they have hardened their neck, and if you warn them they will hate you for it. These are your men that fill high the bowl, and chase the flying hours with glowing feet. They live right merrily, like the men of the old world, they marry and are given in marriage, they drink and are drunken, till the flood comes, and there is no escape.

Many are quiet in conscience because of worldliness. They are too much occupied to give fair attention to the affairs of their souls. They are taken up with business; at it from morning to night; shutters up and shutters down; they can find time for nothing but counting their money, or shifting their stock. Adam was lost in the garden of Eden; but these men are lost in their shops, lost in their warehouses, lost in their ships, lost in their farms, lost in the market. They give no thought to the world to come, because this world engrosses them. From this kind of peace may we be delivered!

Some have a brawny conscience—I mean a conscience hard, callous, horny; you cannot make it feel. A healthy conscience is tender as a raw wound, which fears a touch; but some men's consciences are covered with a thick skin, and are devoid of feeling. Certain sinners have a conscience seared as with a hot iron, and this brings with it that horrible peace which is the preface of eternal damnation.

Around us are persons who have a peace which Satan preserves. "When a strong man armed keepeth his house, his goods are in peace." When Satan is in full possession of a man, then no disturbing thoughts come in, and the sinful heart is well content. "They are not in trouble as other men; neither are they plagued like other men;" they may even die at peace, for the Psalmist complains, "there are no bands in their death: but their strength is firm." Satan has filled them with "a strong delusion to believe a lie," and so in peace they perish; they go willingly to destruction, like sheep to the slaughter.

And some have a peace of sullenness; an awful peace of despair, in which the man steels himself against that which he calls his fate. A man says, "I know I am to be lost; I have sinned myself beyond all hope of mercy; and why should I trouble myself further?" Like a condemned criminal, who hears the hammers fitting up the scaffold, and gives himself up to silent despair, he feels, "I am doomed: it is all over with me." O my friend, it is not so; this is a lie of Satan's own invention. Whilst thou livest, there is hope. Whilst thou art yet in the land where Christ is preached, thou mayest come to him and live. But deadness, sullenness, and obstinacy, are thy worst enemies. Waters of enmity to God often run silently because they are so deep. The man has a settled enmity against God, and this makes him set his teeth, and defy the Almighty in grim determination to perish. God save you from this! May you be driven out of every peace except that peace which comes from God! To that I now come.

God alone can speak true peace to the soul. When once a soul begins to feel its sinfulness, and to tremble at the wrath to come, none but God can speak peace to it. Ministers cannot. I have often failed when I have desired to bring comfort to troubled hearts. Books cannot do it, not even the most wise and gracious of them. The Bible itself cannot do it, apart from the Spirit of God. The ordinances of God's house, whether they be baptism, or the Lord's Supper, or prayer, or preaching—none of these can bring peace to a heart apart from the still small voice of the Lord. I pray that none of you may rest in anything short of a divine assurance of salvation. See how the waves are tossing themselves on high! Hark to the howling of the wind! Rise, Peter, and bid the waves be quiet! Awake, John, and pour oil upon the waves! Ah, sirs! the apostles will themselves sink, unless a greater than they shall interpose. Only he who lay asleep near the tiller could say, "Peace, be still!" May he say that to everyone here who is troubled about his sin! The voice of the blood of Jesus speaks "the peace of God, which passeth all understanding." We read that on the storm-tossed lake "there was a great calm." How great is the quiet of a soul which has seen and felt the power of the atoning sacrifice!

I have told you that only God can speak this peace; let me remind you that *he can give you that peace by speaking it.* One word from the Lord is the quietus of all trouble. No deed is needed, only a word. Peace has *not* now to be made : the making of peace was finished more than eighteen hundred years ago on yonder cross. The Lord Jesus, who was our peace, went up to the tree bearing our iniquities, and thus removing the dread cause of the great warfare between God and man. There he ended the quarrel of the covenant. Hearken to these words, "The chastisement of our peace was upon him." He made peace by the blood of his cross. Through his death, being justified by faith, we have peace with God. "It is finished." Righteousness and peace have kissed each other. Now is the way paved for man to come back to God by reconciliation through sacrifice. There is no more blood to be shed, nor sacrifice to be offered : peace is fully made, and it only remains for the Lord God to speak it to the conscience and heart by the Holy Ghost. Yet think not that for God to speak is a little thing. His voice is omnipotence in motion. He spake the universe out of nothing : he spake light out of darkness. Where the word of our King is, there is power. He speaks, and it is done. If he speaks peace, who can cause trouble? In Jesus Christ there is divine peace for the guilty soul. "Come unto me," saith he, "all ye that labour and are heavy laden, and I will give you rest." From a tempest of distress to perfect peace a word from the God of peace can lift us in an instant.

Sooner or later the Lord will speak peace to his own. How blessed are the *shalls* and *wills* of the Lord God!—"He will speak peace unto his people." Doubt it not. He will. He will. Some of you have lost your peace for a while; yet, if you are believers, "He will speak peace unto his people." You have come to Christ, and are trusting him, but you do not enjoy such peace as you desire. Yet "He will speak peace unto his people." There may be a time of battling and of struggling, the noise of war may disturb the camp for months: but in the end "He will speak peace unto his people." I have seen some of the Lord's true people terribly harassed year after year. One for a very long time was in the dark—wrecked on a barbarous coast, and neither sun nor moon appearing. I do not excuse him for some of his despondency; there was a fault, undoubtedly, and there may also have been weakness of the brain; but he was a true child of God, and at length he came out into the light, and wrote a book which has cheered many. If peace comes not before, yet "Mark the perfect man, and behold the upright: for the end of that man is peace." The Lord will not put his child to bed in the dark: he will light his candle ere he sleeps the sleep of death. Sickness of body, and weakness of mind, or some other cause, may be a terrible kill-joy; but in the end "The Lord will speak peace unto his people." He cannot finally leave a soul that trusts in him. No believer shall die of despair. You may sink very low: but underneath are the everlasting arms, and these will bring you up again. Many women of a sorrowful spirit have a hard time of it, but yet the Lord has set a day in which he will give beauty for ashes. O captive daughter, thy chains last not for ever! Hold you on to your hope: the night is very dark, but the morning will surely come; for as God is light, so shall his children be.

Beloved, when the Lord does speak peace to his people, *what a peace it is!* It is sound and safe. You may have as much of it as you will, and suffer no harm. The peace of God is never presumptuous. It is a holy peace; and the more you have of it, the more you will strive to be like your Lord and Master, Jesus Christ. It is a peace which rules the heart and mind, and not merely the face and the tongue. It is a peace that will rise superior to circumstances. You may be very poor; but you shall find an inward wealth of contentment. You may be lonely; but communion with God will bring you company. You may be very sick in body; but peace of soul enables a man to bear pain without complaining. There may even be a measure of depression of spirit about you, and yet an inward peace will enable you to reason with yourself, and say, " Why art thou cast down, O my soul? and why art thou disquieted in me?" If God gives you peace, the devil cannot take it away. If God breathes peace into your soul, the roughest winds of earth or hell cannot blow that peace from you. They that have ever enjoyed this peace will tell you that it is the dawn of heaven. They that walk in the light of God's countenance, at this moment, are as the courtiers of a king, and for them there is a Paradise Restored. Perfect peace brings a joy of which no tongue can fully tell. There is no war above; Father, Son, and Holy Ghost are all reconciled to us. There is no war within: conscience is cleansed, and the heart relieved. There is no fear even of the arch-enemy below; he may grind his teeth at us, but he cannot destroy us. Even the world of nature is at peace with us. "For thou shalt be in league with the stones of the field: and the beasts of the field shall be at peace with thee." "All things work together for good to them that love God, to them who are the called according to his purpose." A deep peace, a high peace, a broad peace, an endless peace is ours. "Who shall lay anything to the charge of God's elect? It is God that justifieth. Who is he that condemneth? It is Christ that died, yea rather, that is risen again, who is even at the right hand of God, who also maketh intercession for us." "Therefore being justified by faith, we have," in the most emphatic and unlimited sense, "peace with God through our Lord Jesus Christ." Beloved friends, do not be satisfied without the constant possession of unbroken peace. You may have it; you ought to have it. It will make you greater than princes, and richer than misers. This peace will shoe your feet for ways of obedience or suffering. "May the peace of God keep your hearts and minds through Christ Jesus!"

II. Now we must come down from our elevation, to talk about a more humbling theme, WHAT WE FEAR MAY MAR THIS BLESSING OF PEACE. "He will speak peace unto his people, and to his saints: *but let them not turn again to folly.*"

The grounds of a believer's peace are always the same, but a believer's enjoyment of that peace varies very greatly. I always have a right to the divine inheritance, but I do not always enjoy the fruits of that inheritance. Peace may be broken with the Christian, through great trouble, if his faith is not very strong. It need not be so; for some of those who have had the greatest fight of affliction have had the sweetest peace in Christ Jesus. Peace may be broken through some forms of disease, which prey upon the mind as well as the body; and when the mind grows weak and depressed from what are rather physical causes than spiritual ones, the infirmity of the flesh is apt to crush spiritual peace. Yet it is not always so; for sometimes, when heart and flesh have failed, yet God has been the strength of our heart, as he is our portion for ever. Inward conflict, too, may disturb our enjoyment of peace. When a man is struggling hard against a sin, when some old habit has to be hanged up before the Lord, when corruption grows exceedingly strong and vigorous, as at seasons it may do, the believer may not enjoy peace as he would wish. And yet I have known warring times when the fight within has not diminished my peace. "How so?" you may say. I have found peace in the very fact that I was fighting! I have seen clearly that if I were not a child of God, I should not struggle against sin. The very fact that I contend against sin, as against my deadliest foe, proves that I am not under the dominion of sin; and that fact brings to my soul a measure of peace. Satan, too—oh, it is hard to have peace under his attacks! He has a way of beating his hell-drum at a rate which will let no believer rest. He can inject the most profane thoughts; he can flutter us and worry us, by making us think that we are the authors of the thoughts which he fathers upon us—which are his, and not ours. It is a very glorious thing, then, to be able to say, "Rejoice not over me, O mine enemy; though I fall, yet shall I rise again."

When the Lord hides his face, as he may do as the result of grave offence that we have given him, ah! then we cannot have peace. Peace runs out to a very low ebb when we are under withdrawals; and then we cry, "Oh, that I knew where I might find him, that I might come even to his feet!" We can never rest till we again behold the smilings of his face, and take our place among the children.

But, after all, the chief reason why a Christian loses his peace, is because he "turns again to folly." What kind of folly? Folly is sin and error, and everything contrary to divine wisdom. I will briefly show you a few of the different shapes of this folly.

There is the folly of *hasty judgment*. Have you never judged without knowing and considering all the surroundings of the case? Have you not come to a wrong conclusion, when you have ventured to judge the dealings of God with you? You have said, "This cannot be wise, this cannot be right; at any rate, this cannot be a fruit of love;" but you have found out afterwards that you were quite mistaken, that your severest trial was sent in very faithfulness. Your rash judgment was most evidently folly; and if you turn again to such folly in your next season of sorrow, you will certainly lose your peace. What! will you measure the infinite wisdom of God by the foot-rule of your short-sighted policy? Are eternal purposes to be judged of according to the tickings of the clock? There can be no peace when we assume the judgment-throne, and dare accuse our Sovereign of unkindness or mistake.

> "Judge not the Lord by feeble sense,
> But trust him for his grace."

Consider things in the long run when you would estimate the ways of God. Behold, he dwells in eternity, and his measures are only to be seen in the light of the endless future. Oh, that we could either judge the Lord's ways upon eternal principles, or leave off judging altogether! My soul, be thou as a little child before the Lord, and thou wilt find peace!

Another kind of folly is of like order: it is *repining, and quarrelling with the Most High*. Some are never pleased with God; how can he be pleased with them? There can be no use in contending with our Maker; for what are we as compared with him? Let the grass contend with the scythe, or the tow fight with the flame; but let not man contend with God. Besides, who are you? "Who art thou, O man, that repliest against God?" It is true you may be, like Job, terribly smitten, and brought very low, and you cannot understand the why and the wherefore of it; but I pray you bow your head in sweet submission, for your heavenly Father must be doing the best possible thing for you. Kick not against the pricks. When the ox, newly yoked to the plough, kicks against the goad, what is the result? It drives the goad into its own flank. It would not have been so hurt had it not defied the driver. "It is hard for thee to kick against the pricks." No man, by quarrelling with God, can gain any advantage, for the right is on God's side, and eternal principles establish his government. When the barque wars with the rock, we know which will suffer. Yield thee, O my brother, yield thee to the Lord of love! Thine hope can only climb on bended knee; thy peace can only return with bowed head; for to proud rebellion there is no peace, since it is folly of the grossest kind.

Another kind of folly to which men often turn is that of *doubt and distrust*. What peace you have had has come by faith; and when faith departs, peace goes also. To doubt the Lord is folly; even the least degree of it is folly of the worst order. When you said, "God is true, and I will trust him," then your peace was like a river. One who lay dying was in such joy that his friends said to him, "You used to be much tempted; how is it that you are so happy?" He replied, "This is the reason: it is written, 'Thou wilt keep him in perfect peace, whose mind is stayed on thee: because he trusteth in thee.'" For the very reason that he trusts God, the Lord will keep him in perfect peace. Be satisfied with God, and you shall be satisfied in God. Go not back to your old doubts and fears, for they are as a thicket of thorns. It seems to me that some of you were born doubting, and have hardly left off ever since. Some professors never seem to be happy unless they are miserable. I hardly know whether to call some of you doubters or believers. Yes, I thank God that I hope you are really believers; but you are terrible old doubters still. I am persuaded you will get to heaven, but you will not have much of heaven on the road unless you shake off this pernicious habit of distrust.

Who ever gained anything by doubting the Lord, questioning his promises, or distrusting his providence? He abideth faithful: he will never deny himself. Believe in him, and so shall you be established. He will speak peace unto his people; but let them not turn again unto this inexcusable folly of doubting the word of him who cannot lie.

Some turn to the old folly of *looking for life upon legal principles*. You remember how Paul seemed astonished at this perversity. He exclaimed, "O foolish Galatians, who hath bewitched you, that ye should not obey the truth?" He demanded of them, "Having begun in the Spirit, are ye now made perfect by the flesh?" When you try to draw your comfort from what you are, and what you do, you are foolish. Self is at best a dry well. To seek consolation from your own consecration or sanctification is risky work. You must not turn your sanctification into an antichrist by putting it in the place of Christ. "Be ye holy," saith he, "for I am holy;" but he never bade you trust in your holiness. However sanctified you may become, even if you could attain to perfection, it would be wise to say with Job, "Though I were perfect, yet would I not know my soul." Your wisdom is to stand upon the finished work of Christ. If you get off from that ground, you have placed yourself upon the ice; and if it does not melt from under you, you will yourself slip down upon it. Mix anything of man with the work of the Lord, and you have turned again to folly. It brought you into great bondage years ago, and it will do so again, if you return to it. Hope in Christ, and in nothing else but Christ. When your expectation is in the Lord alone, then will your peace be like a river.

Some lose their peace by turning again to the folly of *intellectual speculation*. Some of our friends, who once walked in the light, as God is in the light, and were as happy as all the birds of the air, have now lost their joy, because they have read a pernicious book, which started for them a whole host of difficulties, of which they never dreamed before. Would you like me to answer those difficulties? Suppose I took the trouble to do so, and succeeded, what would happen? You would read another book to-morrow, and come to me with another set of doubts; and if we were to slay all these, you would simply invite another band of invaders to land on the shores of your mind. Therefore I decline to begin the endless task. At Mentone, the trouble of some of our friends is to catch the mosquitoes, which worry them. But there is little or no use in it; for if you catch a dozen of these little pests, twenty-four will come to the funeral. It is just the same with these intellectual difficulties; you may, by overcoming some of them, make room for more of a worse kind. No fact, however certain, is beyond a critic's questioning. I have done with the whole band of quibblers. People say, "Have you seen the new book? It is terribly unsettling." It will not unsettle me: first, because I know what I know; and secondly, because I do not care one atom what the unbeliever has to say. I care, indeed, so little that I am not curious even to know what his craze may happen to be. "I know whom I have believed." I am going no further than that which the Holy Spirit has taught me through the infallible Word. What is more, I am not going to waste my time by reading what every doubter may please to write. I have had enough of these poisonous drugs, and will have no more. Does anyone say, "We ought to read everything"? Nay, nay, if I go out to dinner, and there should happen to come to table a joint that is far gone, I let it alone. When the knife goes into it, the perfume betrays it, and I do not pass up my plate. Others may carve slices from the carrion of unbelief; but having long eaten sweet gospel food, I cannot bring my soul to feed on that which is unholy, and only fit for dogs. That which denies Scripture, and dishonours the blood of the Lord Jesus, is fitter for burning than reading. If you have once been staggered by modern thought, do not turn again to that folly. Be not like silly people, who seem to fall down in the mud for the sake of being brushed. Why desire to be befogged and bewildered for the sake of getting set in the right way after long straying? Stick to the Scriptures. When you have read so much of your Bibles that there is nothing more in them, then you may devote your time and study to some other book; but for the present keep to the book whose author is the All-wise Jehovah. Between the covers of this book you shall find all wisdom, and I pray you turn not again to the folly which opposes the infallible, and censures the perfect. God grant us grace to maintain our peace by never turning again to the folly of human wisdom!

But the worst form of folly is *sin*. Scripture continually calls sinners fools; and so they are. What a touching pleading there is about this use of language! " God will speak peace unto his people; but let them not turn again to folly;" as much as to say, "to turn aside will not only grieve me, but it will harm *you*. Sin is not only fault, but folly. It will be to your own injury as well as to my displeasure." Dear child of God, are you out in the storm just now? Have you no rest? Let me whisper in your ear. Is there not a cause? Somebody on board your vessel has brought this storm upon you. Where is he? He is not among the regular sailors that work the ship; he is neither captain nor mate; but he is a stranger. Down under the hatches is a man named Jonah; is he the cause of the tempest? " No," you say, "he is a good fellow, for he paid his fare." This makes me feel all the more suspicious. He is the cause of the mischief. You will never get peace until the Jonah of sin is overboard. Cast him into the sea, and it will be calm unto you. Many a child of God harbours a traitor, and hardly knows that he is doing so; and the Lord is at war with him because of the harboured rebel. When Joab pursued Sheba, the son of Bichri, he came to the city of Abel, where Sheba had taken shelter. A wise woman came to him out of the city, and pleaded for the people. Joab explained to her that he warred not with the city, but with the rebel; and he added, "Deliver him only, and I will depart from the city." Then they cut off the head of Sheba, and cast it out to Joab, and he blew a trumpet, and they retired from the city, every man to his tent. God is besieging you with trials and distresses, turning his batteries against your walls; and there is no chance of any peace until the traitorous sin shall be given up to vengeance. I do not know what particular sin it may be, but the head of it must be thrown over the wall: and then the warriors of the Lord will go their way. Bring forth the Achan, and the accursed thing, and let all Israel stone him with stones. Search and see! Arrest the hidden foe! "Are the consolations of God small with thee? is there any secret thing with thee?" God help us to institute a solemn search this morning, and may we discover the intruder, and destroy him!

Beloved, I pray that no one of us may go back to folly. If we have ever tasted the peace of God, and communion with God, can we leave it for earthly joys? Can we quit the banquets of infinite love for the coarse pleasures of sin? God forbid! Remember all the sorrow which sin has cost you already. Take not this viper a second time to your bosom. We were drowned in tears, and sunken in distress when we found ourselves guilty of sin. Further and further from it may we fly; but never, never may we turn back! Remember what it cost your Lord to make you free from the consequences of former folly; never return to it. He must needs die to save us from our folly; shall we count his death as nothing? Bethink you what tugs the Spirit of God has had with us to bring us so far on our journey towards heaven; are we now willing to turn our backs on God and holiness? Consider also what lieth just beyond. Look a little way before you. Think of the street of gold, the river which never dries, the trees which bear eternal fruit, the harps of ceaseless melody. Beloved, we cannot turn again to folly! O God, do not permit us to do so! Grant us thy peace, that by it we may be kept, both in heart and mind, loyal to thee! Peace spoken to the soul by the Holy Spirit is the sure preventive of turning again to folly. Be sure that, if it passeth all understanding, it also conquereth all folly. With minds at perfect peace with God, we set our face like a flint, and press on towards the haven where peace will never end. Glory be to God, who will bring us safely there! Amen.

12 A Gracious Dismissal

"And he said to the woman, Thy faith hath saved thee; go in peace."—Luke vii. 50.

THE main part of my subject will be—that gracious dismissal, "Go in peace." To her who had been so lately blest, the word "*Go*" sounded mournfully; for she would fain have remained through life with her pardoning Lord; but the added words "*in peace*" turned the wormwood into honey—there was now peace for her who had been so long hunted and harried by her sins. Rising from the feet she had washed with tears, she went forth to keep her future footsteps such as those of a believing, and therefore saved, woman ought to be.

We like a motto to begin the year with, and it has been useful to some spirits to choose a motto with which to enter on a new course of life. We climb the hill of enterprise, or dare the wave of trial, with an inspiring word upon our lip. To certain young men a word has come in life's early morning, wet with the dew of heaven, and that word of their day-dawn has kept with them. The echoes of that life-evoking word have followed them long after it was spoken; amid strange scenes it has come to them like a voice from the unseen. It has whispered to them within the curtains of their dying bed : it has murmured consolation amid Jordan's swelling waves. That first word of joy and peace from Jesus with which they began the new life came to them over again just as they were melting away into the invisible land : so they began the service of the Redeemer, and so he declared that their work was finished. Perhaps that love-note will be their welcome at the very gates of heaven.

Our Lord, in the instance before us, sent a penitent away from the chill atmosphere of self-righteous cavilling, and thus relieved her of a controversy for which she was not fitted ; but I see more than that in this benediction. It looks to me as if our divine Master, when he found this poor sinner so full of love to him that she washed his feet with tears, and wiped them with the hairs of her head, having by a parable explained to the Pharisee the reason for the greatness of her love, then said to her, "Go in peace,"—meaning that word not only to be cheering for the necessary purpose of the moment, but to go with her, and to attend her all the rest of her life, until, when she came into the dark valley, she should fear no evil, for she would still hear that sweet voice saying, "Go in peace." What music to have heard! What music still to hear!

Now, I would to God that the word which I shall speak at this time might be honoured of the Lord to serve that sacred purpose to some here present. May it be a life-word to certain of you! May it be to others of us who have long known the Saviour a revival of our rest, and may we get such a draught of peace from Jesus that we may never thirst again! The lips of our divine Lord are a well-spring of delight; each word is a chalice brimmed with sweetness. Imbibing this, we shall go our way henceforth even to our journey's end, after the manner of the hymn which we sang just now:—

> "Calm in the hour of buoyant health,
> Calm in my hour of pain;
> Calm in my poverty or wealth,
> Calm in my loss or gain;
>
> "Calm me, my God, and keep me calm,
> Soft resting on thy breast;
> Soothe me with holy hymn and psalm,
> And bid my spirit rest."

Oh, that our life may be as a sea of glass! May the sacred circle of our fellowship be within the golden line of the peace of God! Thou who didst bid us come to thee and rest, now bid us "go in peace."

I am going to say a little in my opening upon *a delightful assurance* which constituted the reason why the woman went in peace: "Thy faith hath saved thee;" or, as in the forty-eighth verse, "Thy sins are forgiven thee." Upon the strength of the assurance that she was saved, she might safely go in peace. When we have talked a little upon that subject, we will then come to *a considerate precept:* the Saviour directed her, in the moment of trial, to "go in peace." There was an assurance for her comfort, and a precept for her guidance.

I. First, then, consider A DELIGHTFUL ASSURANCE. The ground upon which the penitent woman might go in peace was that she had been saved. The Saviour assured her: "Thy faith hath saved thee."

She was not saved otherwise than we are saved; but she received the common salvation by like precious faith. The way of salvation to her was faith in Christ: there is the same way for us, but she had what some of you, no doubt, would greatly like to have: she had *an assurance that she was saved, from the Lord's own mouth.* I think I hear some saying, "I should go in peace, I am sure, if the Lord Jesus would but appear to me, and speak, and say with his own lips, 'Thy faith hath saved thee.'" It is natural that you should think so; it must have been rapture to receive a benediction from the mouth of our King, our Saviour. Yet, dear friends, we must not hang our confidence upon a mere circumstance. For a mere circumstance it is, whether Christ shall literally stand before you in the flesh, and say, "Thy faith hath saved thee," or whether he shall say it to you by the infallible record of his own Word. It does not make much difference as to my faith in what my father says to me, whether I meet the venerable man in the morning in my garden, and there hear his voice, or whether I get a letter by post in his handwriting, and he says to me upon that paper just what he would have said if I had met him face to face. I do not require him always to come up the hill to my house to tell me everything that he has to say: I should think myself an idiot if I did. If I were to say, "My dear father, you have assured me of your love by letter; but somehow, I cannot credit it unless you come and look me in the face, and take my hand, and assure me of your good will," surely, he would say to me, "My dear son, what ails you? You must be out of your mind. I never knew you to be so childish before: my handwriting has always been enough. I can hardly think you mean it when you say that you cannot credit me unless I stand manifest before your eyes, and with your ears you hear me speak." Now, what I would not do to my earthly father, I certainly would not do to my heavenly Saviour. I am perfectly satisfied myself to believe what he writes to me; and if it be so written in his Book, it seems to me to be quite as true and sure as if he had actually come from heaven, and had talked with me, or had appeared to me in the visions of the night. Is not this the reasoning of commonsense? Do you not at once agree with me?

"Well," say you, "we go with you there, dear sir; but, then, *he spoke that word to her personally*. We should never have any more doubts, but should go in peace, if he said that word of assurance to us. You see, it is not merely that Jesus himself spoke, and said, 'Thy faith hath made *thee* whole,' but he looked that way; he turned towards her, and she knew that he referred to her. There was no mistaking to whom the assurance was given. There were other people in the room, but he did not say it to Simon; he did not say it to Peter; he did not say it to James and John. She knew by the look of him that he meant it for her, and for her alone, for she was the only person to go, and consequently the only one to 'go in peace.' Our Lord put it in the singular number, and said, '*Thy* faith hath saved *thee*.' I want it to come home just so to me." Yes, but I think that this is a little unreasonable, too; is it not? Because if my father (to carry on my figure) were to speak to me, and to my brothers, and to my sisters, and were to say, "Dear children, I have loving thoughts concerning you, and I have laid up in store for your needs," I do not think that I should say to him by-and-by, "Now, father, do you know that I did not believe you, or derive any pleasure from what you said, because you spoke to others beside myself? I did not think your statement of love could be true, because you included my brothers and my sisters. You did not use the singular, but you put it in the plural; and you spoke to all my brothers and sisters, as well as to myself; and therefore I felt that I could not take any comfort out of your tender assurances." I should be a most unreasonable kind of body if I were to talk in that way; and my father would begin to think that his son was qualifying for a lunatic asylum. If he did not attribute it to unkindness of heart, he certainly would ascribe it to imbecility of head. Why, surely, surely, if my father says the same to each one of his children as he says to me, his words are all the more likely to be true, instead of being less worthy of belief; and therefore I derive comfort from his promises of love being put in the plural rather than in the singular. Surely, it should not be less easy to believe that God would deal graciously with me in company with thousands of others than that he should pursue a solitary plan with me as the lone object of his love. Is it not so?

"Ah, yes!" says one, "but you have not hit on it yet. I want to know that I am one that is in that plural, and I want to know that I really am one of those to whom Jesus speaks in his Word." My anxious friend, you may know it; and you may know it most certainly. It is written, "He that believeth on him hath everlasting life." It need never be a question whether you believe in him or not; if you trust him, that is the gist of the matter. You can readily ascertain whether you do really trust him, or do not trust him. If you do trust him, you are his, and every promise of his covenant is made to you. You have faith, and when the Lord lays it down as a general statement that faith saves—the statement is applicable to all the world, in every place, and in all time, until the present age shall end, and men shall have passed into the fixed state of retribution, where no gospel of faith is preached. "Thy faith hath saved thee:" if thou hast faith at all—if thou believest that Jesus is the Christ—thou art born of God. If thou canst say to the Lord Jesus,

> "All my trust on thee is stayed,
> All my help from thee I bring,"

that is faith, and Jesus testifies, "Thy faith hath saved thee." **Now,** because the infallible Witness says this of all who have faith, I do not think you ought to doubt it. It is true you do not hear his voice, because he says it rather by the written Word than by word of mouth; but surely this does not affect your faith. We believe a true man whether he writes or speaks: indeed, if there be any choice, we prefer that which he has deliberately put upon paper; for this remains when the sound of the voice is clean gone. It is most profitable for us that we should read our Lord's declaration over and over again, and put it in all sorts of shapes, and see how it remains evermore faithful and true. It is more assuring to you to find it in the volume of the Book than it would be if the Saviour met you to-night, and said to you, "Thy sins are forgiven thee. Thy faith hath saved thee." The record excels the voice. "No," say you, "I cannot see that." Well now, Peter was with Christ on the Mount of Transfiguration, and nothing could shake Peter's conviction that he had been there in the midst of that heavenly glory; and yet, for all that, Peter says, concerning the inspired Word, "We have a more sure Word of testimony." He felt that even the memory of that vision, which he had assuredly seen, did not always yield to him so much assurance as did the abidingly inspired Word of God. You ought to feel the same. If I were conscious to-night that, at some period of my life, I had seen the Lord, and that he had spoken to me, the very spot of ground on which it occurred would be exceedingly dear and sacred to my spirit; but I am certain that when I grew depressed, when darkness rushed over my soul, as it does sometimes, I should be sure to say to myself, "You never saw anything of the kind. It was a delusion, a figment of imagination, a delirium, and nothing more." But, beloved, when I get to this Book, and see before me the sacred lines, I know that I am not deluded. There it stands, "God so loved the world, that he gave his Only-begotten Son, that whosoever believeth in him should not perish, but have everlasting life." I am sure about that, and I am sure that I believe, and therefore I am sure that I am saved. I like to put my finger right down on the passage, and then say, "Lord, I know thou canst not lie. I have never had a question about this being thy Book. Whatever other doubts have plagued me, this has not. Thou hast so spoken it home to my soul, that I am as assured that this is thy Book as I am assured of my own existence; and, hence, thou hast done better for the removal of my doubts, and for the assurance of my soul's eternal salvation, by putting thy promise in thy Book, than if thou hadst thyself personally appeared to me, and spoken with thine own voice." O my hearer, the written Word is most sure! If thou believest, thou art saved, as surely as thou art alive. If thou believest, heaven and earth may pass away, but the Word of the Lord shall stand fast for thee. "He that believeth in him hath everlasting life." He has eternal life in present possession. Our Lord has put it thus: "He that believeth and is baptized shall be saved." "He that with his heart believeth, and with his mouth maketh confession of him, shall be saved." There are no "ifs" or "buts" about these words of promise. Salvation is put as a present thing, and as an abiding thing, but in every case as a certain thing; and why should we be worried and worn about the matter? It is so, and let us take the comfort of the fact. We must either throw away this Book by beginning to talk about "degrees of inspiration" and all that foul rubbish, or else we are logically bound to be sure of our hope, and to rejoice in it. I warrant thee, O my hearer, that as long as thou standest fast by the belief that this is a sure Word of testimony, thou wilt know that thou art saved! If this Book be true, every believer in Jesus is as safe as Jesus himself. To say, "I believe, but I am afraid I am not saved," is to say, only in a roundabout way, that you do not believe at all; for, if you believe, then you believe that God speaks the truth; and this is the testimony, that "God hath given us eternal life, and that life is in his Son." This is the testimony of the great Father, and the testimony of the eternal Spirit; and we must not dare to doubt it. You may doubt whether you believe or not; but given that you do really and unfeignedly put your trust in the Lord Jesus, then, as effect follows cause, it is certain that the cause of faith will be followed by its sure effect—salvation. "Thy faith hath saved thee: go in peace." Do not worry any longer: go in peace. Have done with questioning; end debate; go in peace. Go about your business, for the work of salvation is done. You are a saved soul: go and rejoice in finished salvation, and ask no more questions. "Wherefore criest thou unto me?" said God to Moses, "Speak unto the children of Israel, that they go forward." Wherefore do you question and doubt any longer? Go forward to enjoy what God has prepared for you; and as you are saved and justified in Christ, now seek sanctification, and all the other blessings of the covenant of grace which lie before you in Christ Jesus your Lord. The promise is sure; be sure that it is so, and in perfect rest of soul enjoy the good which God provides you.

I think I have thus brought out as clearly as I can that delightful assurance which is the ground of the command, "Go in peace."

II. We come, secondly, to hearken to A CONSIDERATE PRECEPT. Our Lord, with wise tenderness, dismissed the beloved object of his pardoning love, and bade her "Go *in peace*." May the Holy Spirit bless this to us!

This precept divides itself into two parts. There is, first, "Go," and then there is "Go in peace."

There is "*go*." Now, in "go" there are two things: to go *from* and to go *to*. *Where was she to go from?* First, she was *to go from these quibblers.* Simon and the Pharisees are as full of objections as a swarm of bees is full of stings. They say in their hearts one to another, "Who is this that forgiveth sins also?" They have even dared to question the character of the perfect One, and have hinted a suspicion of his purity for allowing such a woman to come so near him, and to wash his feet with her tears. Therefore the Saviour says to her, "Go." This was not a happy place for a childlike love to linger in. Her soul would have been among lions. Jesus seems to say, "Do not stay to be tormented by these cavillers. Thy faith hath saved thee; go. You have gained a great blessing; go home with it. Let these people argue with each other; you have a rich prize, take it out of the reach of these pirates."

Oftentimes I believe that the child of God would find it to be his greatest wisdom, whenever he is in company that begins to assail his Lord, or to denounce his faith, just to go about his business, and let the scoffers have their scoffing to themselves. Some of us have thought it our miserable duty to read certain books that have been brought out against the truth, that we might be able to answer them; but it is a perilous calling. The Lord have mercy upon us when we have to go down into these sewers; for the process is not healthy!

"Oh," says a man, "but you must prove all things!" Yes, so I will; but if one should set a joint of meat on his table, and it smelt rather high, I would cut a slice, and if I put one bit of it in my mouth, and found it far gone, I should not feel it necessary to eat the whole round of beef to test its sweetness. Some people seem to think that they must read a bad book through; and they must go and hear a bad preacher often before they can be sure of his quality. Why, you can judge many teachings in five minutes! You say to yourself, "No, sir, no, no, no! this is good meat—for dogs. Let them have it, but it is not good meat for me, and I do not intend to poison myself with it." The Saviour does not tell the woman, "Stop, now, and hear what Simon has got to say. Dear good woman, you have been washing my feet with tears, and here is a highly intelligent gentleman, a Pharisee, who has a very learned prelection to deliver; give him a fair hearing. You have to prove all things; therefore, stop and hear him. And here are more gentlemen who object to my pardoning your sins; and their objections are fetched from deep veins of thought. Listen to them, and then I will meet their questions, and quiet your mind." No; the Saviour says, "Go, go, go in peace. You have peace: do not stop till you lose it. You have your comfort and joy: refuse to be robbed of them." Why, if you were in a room, and you saw a certain number of gentlemen of a suspicious character, and you had your watch with you, you would not feel it necessary to stop and see whether they were able to extract your watch from you, but you would say to yourself, "No; I am best out of this company." We are safest out of the society of those whose great object it is to rob us of our faith. "Thy faith hath saved thee. Go home. Leave them. Go in peace."

I think that he meant, besides going away from the men, "*Go away from the publicity into which you have unwillingly stepped.*" If our Saviour had been like some excellent people of the present day, he would have said, "Stand before all these men, and tell your experience. I shall require you to be at half-a-dozen meetings this week, and you must speak at every one of them." A splendid woman, was she not, who washed the Saviour's feet with tears, and wiped them with the hairs of her head? She might have exhibited her eyes and her hair, and told their gracious story. Who can tell but several would have been impressed by the narrative? The Saviour said to the woman—so excitable, for she was all that, as well as grateful—"Thy faith hath saved thee: go in peace." As much as to say, "There are certain of your own sex that you can speak to. You will find some poor fallen woman to whom you can quietly tell of my pardoning grace. But yours is a case in which the very beauty of your character will lie in the quietude of your future life. 'Thy faith hath saved thee.' That is enough for thee. Thou hast come upon the stage of action by that splendid act of thy love; but do not acquire the habit of winning publicity. Do not aspire to display thyself in a bold and heroic attitude, but go in peace." He almost seems to say, "Subside now into thy family. Take thy place with the rest of thy sisters. Adorn by thy future purity my doctrine, and let all men see what a change has been wrought in thee; for, mayhap, that very weakness of thine, which made thee what thou wast as a sinner, may put thee in danger even as a saint. Therefore I do not ask thee to tarry here, and join my disciples, and follow me publicly through the streets, but thy faith hath saved thee: go in peace."

I think that the Master taught a great deal of wisdom here, which some of those who are leaders in the church of God would do well to copy. Yea, I think that I shall go a little further, and say, that I think *the Saviour there and then dismissed her from that high ministry which, for once in her life, she had carried out.* She washed his feet with tears, and wiped them with the hairs of her head. It was the action of a love which had risen to a passion. It was an action such as shall be told for a memorial of her everywhere; and we may well imitate her penitence, and her heroic courage, as well as her love to Christ. But, at the same time, we cannot always be doing heroic actions: life is mainly made up of common deeds. It would not be possible to be always washing feet with tears, nor to be always unbraiding tresses to use them as a towel. The difficulty with some people is that they are always wanting to practise the sublime. Alas!

they often fail by just one step, and become ridiculous. They are always straining after effect; and, hearing of what has been done once, by one choice person, they must do it themselves, and they must keep on doing it. O my sister! there may come a time when you will have to speak for Christ, and speak openly before many; but to-morrow you had better go home, and see to the children, and make home happy for your husband. You will glorify Christ by darning stockings, and mending the socks of the little ones, quite as surely as by washing his feet with tears. You make a great mistake if you have not a piety which will take you into domestic life—which will help you to make the common drudgery of life a divine service. We want men that can serve God with the axe and plane, or behind a counter, or by driving a quill. These are the men we want; but there are many that crave to vault at once into a conspicuous place, and perform an astounding deed. Having done it once, they become unsettled all the rest of their lives; and do not seem as if they ever could take to plainly keeping the ten commandments, and walking in the steps of Jesus. I wish that those who must flash and blaze would hear the Lord Jesus say to them, "Go in peace." I mean any of you who really did distinguish yourselves on one occasion, and deserved much praise from your Christian friends. I fear lest you should pine for unusual and even undesirable forms of service, and become useless in the ordinary course of life. Now, do not be spoiled for life by having been allowed in one unusual deed, but hear the Master say, "Thy faith hath saved thee: go in peace. Serve me in the daily avocations of life, and bring glory to my name at home. Go from the strain of publicity to the gentler pressures of family duty."

Do you not think that he even meant that she was now to cease *from that singular fellowship with him that she had enjoyed?* She had been very close to him; but she was, perhaps, never to be quite so near to him again. In spirit she should be; but certainly not physically. It happens that those who take to the contemplative life—and there is no life higher than that—are apt to think that they must forget the practical life. But it must not be so. We must do that which the Master bids us do, as well as sit at his feet. I am tempted to tell a story which most of you must know concerning the famous man of God, who, in his cell, thought he saw the Lord Jesus, and under that persuasion he worshipped with rapt delight. But just then the bell at the convent-gate rang, and it was his turn to stand at the door, and deal out bread to the hungry. There was a little battle in his mind as to which he should do—tarry with his Lord, or go to hand out bread to the poor mendicants. At last, he felt that he must do his duty even at the cost of the highest spiritual bliss. He went and distributed the bread, and when he came back, to his great delight, the vision was still there, and a voice said to him, "If thou hadst stayed, I would have gone; but as thou hast gone, I have therefore stayed still to commune with thee." The path of duty must be followed, and no spiritual enjoyment can excuse us from it. Never offer one duty to God stained with the blood of another. Balance your duties, and let not one press out another. "Thy faith hath saved thee: go in peace." Do not think that thou needest to be all day long at thy

Bible, or all the evening at thy prayer. There is a time for everything. Let every holy work have its place, that thy life may be a fair mosaic of brilliant colours, all set according to the divine pattern, to make up a perfect character. "Thy faith hath saved thee. Go in peace, and do the next thing, and the next, without weariness."

That leads me to speak of *what she was to go to*. It seems to me that the Saviour said, " Now *go home*. You have been a fallen woman: home is the place for you. Go home to your mother and father, or other relatives. Seek a home. Be domesticated. *Attend to your own work*. Whatever your place is, go to it. Leaving daily duty was the source of your temptation; return to walks of usefulness, and habits of order, and this will be your safety. You will be less likely to be led away if you have work to occupy head, and heart, and hands."

Did he not mean, " *Go now to your ordinary life-trial* " ? Do you think yourself a very peculiar person—a sort of saint, that has to float in the air, or live upon roses? Do not fancy such a thing. I have heard of the Chinese, that they sell shoes with which you can walk on the clouds; and I believe that some people must have bought a pair of these remarkable articles; for their lives are spent in cloudland, walking as in a dream, upon high stilts of fond imaginations. Do not think great things of yourself. You are but a commonplace man or woman. Do such duty as your fellow-Christians do, and do not think yourself a superior person. The worst people in the world to work with are superior people. Those are of no importance who think they are of great importance. Poor creature! it is not the grace of God which turns your brain, but your own silly conceit.

Go forth to your further service : " Go in peace. There are some to whom you can tell of my love. Oh, how you will tell it! You that have washed my feet with your tears, go and shower those tears over fallen ones like yourself. Go, use those eyes, that you may look my love right into their hearts as you are speaking to them. Go all your life in peace, and do for me all that I shall put in your way to do for me." That is what I think our Lord meant. Brethren, do not think of sitting here to enjoy yourselves; but go off, and glorify your Redeemer's name. Go!

But then here is the point of it: he said, " *Go in peace*." O my brethren, I desire that all of us who love the Lord may go henceforth all the rest of our life journey in peace. May pardoning love put us at peace concerning all our sins! O pardoned one, thou lovest much, for thou hast had much forgiven; let thy thoughts all run to love, and none to fear. Fret not about the past—the dark, dishonourable past. The hand that was pierced has blotted it all out. The great Lord has frankly forgiven thee all thy debt. Let not that disturb thee any longer. Go in peace. What a rest it is to be rid of the burden of sin, and to know of a certainty, from the teaching of God's own Word, that your sins are forgiven you! This is peace which passeth all understanding.

Our Lord meant, next, " *Go in peace* " *in reference to all the criticisms of all these people who have looked at you.* Do not mind them. Do not trouble about them. What have they to do with you? It is enough for a servant if his master accepts him: he need not mind what others have to say about his service. Thy faith hath saved thee. Forget all the unkind things they have said, and do not trouble thy heart about the cruel speeches they may yet make. Go in peace, and be under no alarm as to upbraiding tongues.

And then I think he meant, "*Go in peace about what thou hast done.*" I know the need of a word like that. I have preached the gospel : I have thrown my whole soul into it; and after it is all over, I have felt bound to chide myself that I did not do much better as to style, or spirit, or length, or some other matter. Oh, but if the Master accepts it, one may go in peace about it ! This woman had done a very extraordinary thing in washing Christ's feet with tears, and wiping them with the hairs of her head; and when she got away, she might have said to herself, "I wonder that I was so bold. Was I not immodestly conspicuous? How could I have done it? How must I have looked when I was bathing his feet? For me, too—such a sinner as I am—for me to have done it to the blessed and holy One! I fear he must have felt vexed at my rudeness!" Have you not sometimes done a brave thing for Christ, and then afterwards felt just like that. "I was a bold minx," say you, "after all, to push myself so forward." The good young man, who has just preached for the first time, says, "Well, I got through it this time, but I will never attempt it again, for I am sure that I am not fit for such holy work." So the Master says to this woman, " Go in peace. I have accepted thee and thy loving service. Do not trouble about what thou hast done. It is all sweet to me, and has a rich perfume of thy great love. Never fret about what you have done. You have done the right thing. Thy faith hath saved thee. Go in peace." I want us to have just that kind of peace—peace about what we have done for our Lord, even as we have peace about sin forgiven, and peace about human criticisms.

"Go in peace." Oh, to possess, from this time forth, a holy quiet! We are so apt to grow fretful. I know some good brethren who have a swollen vein of suspicion about them, that bleeds every now and then, and pains them greatly, and alarms other people. I know some sisters: they are very good, but unreasonably fearful. They say that they are "nervous." Perhaps that is the fact; and so I will say no more. But, oh, that we could get them cured of this disease of the nerves! I would they could be quieted! I admire the members of the Society of Friends for this virtue beyond almost any other which they exhibit : they seem to be so steady, self-contained, and equable. They are a little slow, perhaps; but then they are very sure, and firm, and steadfast, and calm. We are some of us too much in a hurry to go fast. If we were a little slower, we should be quicker. If we left our affairs more entirely with God, our peace might be like a river.

Yes, I would to God, dear friends, that we might feel henceforth a constant joy. Why not? Nothing ought to trouble us, for we know that all things work together for good. If we live by faith, nothing can trouble us; for between here and heaven we shall keep company with thee, thou Blessed One! And if the way thou takest be rough, the fact of thy being with us shall make it smooth to us. We will travel merrily with this as our march-music—" Thy faith hath saved thee ; go in peace."

Still, to come back to where I began, I dare say that the good woman thought that she would like to speak a word for the Lord. When they said that he could not forgive sin, would not she have liked to say, "But he did forgive my sin, and he changed my nature. How dare you speak thus"? But the Saviour said, "Go." She was not called to contend. Thank God every child of God is not called to fight with the adversary: those of us who are men of war from our youth up take no pleasure in strife. We wish that, like this holy woman, we could be exempt from this warfare. She might well rejoice in her escape from the sacred conscription. Many a cuff and blow she thus avoided; and as her Captain sent her off the field, she might go home right happily.

She might have lost the blessed frame of mind in which she then was, and this would have been a real injury to her. She was sweetly wrapped up in love, and there her Lord would have her abide. He seems to say, "You are too precious to be battered and bruised in battle. Go—go in peace. Dear soul, you are so full of love to me that I do not want you to be worried with fighting, and contending, and controverting. Go in peace." She would have done no good, I dare say, if she had ventured into a fray for which she was so unfitted. If she had spoken, she would have said something which the cruel Pharisees would have turned into a jest. So he said to her, "Go in peace." Why should her feebleness give them an occasion for unholy triumph? All true hearts are not fit for fight. Besides, she had her Lord to be her Advocate, and there was no need for her to speak. Therefore he said, "I can manage them without your presence. Go in peace." When we may believingly leave a difficulty with our Lord, it is faith's duty to go home quietly. No doubt, by going in peace, she would be doing greater service than she would by using her tongue upon these ungodly men. A quiet, happy life is often the noblest witness that we can bear for Christ. Therefore I say to everyone who loves the Lord, there are times when he will say to us, "Do not enter into any of this conflict, and turmoil, and muddle. Thy faith hath saved thee. Go in peace."

The last word I have to say is this. There are many poor souls who talk about coming to Christ, who are not yet saved, and they are always hearing about faith, and thinking of it, and yet they never do, in very truth, believe. Now, do not hear nor debate any more about faith, but *believe.* Trust Jesus Christ, and think no more about your own trusting. Thou shalt think of it as a thing done, I mean, but not as a thing to be done. God help thee now to believe in Jesus, and so pass over the bridge of belief to the golden shore of Jesus himself!

Well, but I notice some say that they believe, but it is not believing, because if it were believing, they would "go in peace." A person comes to the bank with a cheque. He believes it to be honestly his, and the signature to be correct. He puts it down on the counter, and the clerk puts out the money. But see! The man does not take it! He stands and loafs about; and the clerk looks at him, and wonders what he is at. At last, when the person has been there long enough to wear the good man's patience out, the clerk says, "Did you bring that cheque to have the money?" "Yes, I handed it in." "Well, then, why do you not take the money, and go about your business?" If he is a sensible man, he delays no longer; nay, he would not have delayed so long. He takes the money, and departs in peace. Now, dear soul, if thou hast a promise from God—" He that believeth is not condemned," or "he that believeth hath everlasting life"—dost thou believe? Then take the blessing, and go about thy business. Do not keep on saying, "Perhaps it is so," and "Perhaps it is not so." Do you believe that God speaks the truth? If so, then take the promised blessing: and enjoy it; for thou art a saved man. "But I have been going to a place of worship for years, and I have been believing in a sort of a way; but I have never dared to say that I was saved." Then you are acting the part of an unbeliever. If you do not know that you are saved, how dare you go to sleep to-night? How should a man dare to eat his meals, and go about his business, and yet say, "I do not know whether I am saved or not"? Thou mayest know it, and thou oughtest to know it. If you believe, you are saved: if you doubt that fact, you are rather an unbeliever than a believer. Take up your money, and go home. "O thou of little faith, wherefore didst thou doubt?" Trust Jesus! Thy faith has saved thee. Go in peace.

The Lord help you truly to believe, for Jesus' sake! Amen.